# ARAFAT AND ABBAS

MENACHEM KLEIN

# Arafat and Abbas

## Portraits of Leadership in a State Postponed

HURST & COMPANY, LONDON

First published in the United Kingdom in 2019 by

C. Hurst & Co. (Publishers) Ltd.,

41 Great Russell Street, London, WC1B 3PL

© Menachem Klein, 2019

Printed in India

A Cataloguing-in-Publication data record for this book
is available from the British Library.

ISBN: 9781787381438

This book is printed using paper from registered sustainable
and managed sources.

www.hurstpublishers.com

# CONTENTS

# PROLOGUE

On a hot August day in 1993, I was in my Jerusalem home, unpacking my luggage after a fellowship year at St. Antony's College, Oxford, when the phone rang. On the other end of the line was the Voice of Israel correspondent for Palestinian affairs. He wanted to interview me on the breaking news: Israel and the PLO had agreed on mutual recognition through the Oslo Accords. As a junior researcher at the Hebrew University, I had followed Palestinian affairs since 1990. However, my main field of study was Egypt's society and culture, on which I submitted my PhD in 1992. When I heard the news, I sharply switched my academic focus. I was later to become involved in formal and unofficial Israeli–Palestinian peace talks. The portraits of Arafat and Abbas this book offers, based on twenty-five years of following their lives closely, are the outcome of that phone call.

Like many others in the region and beyond, in 1993 I considered the Oslo agreement to be the precursor to a forthcoming peace treaty. It turned out to be much less, merely an interim agreement on establishing Palestinian autonomy, postponing for seven years the decision on its final status. I did not know that both Rabin and Peres opposed any solution that involved an independent Palestine.[1] Indeed, the road ahead looked open in those optimistic years. The Oslo Accords arrived in the era of the fall of the Berlin Wall, the liberation of Eastern Europe, the expansion of the European Union and globalisation. Twenty-five years later, it is clear that I was wrong to assume that the Oslo process was unstoppable or irreversible. Israeli–Palestinian peace, bringing this interim stage to an end, does not seem to be on the horizon. An ethnocentric–religious government rules Israel, and the Palestinian Authority is far from democratic. International media reports regularly on Israeli–Palestinian clashes, between stories on natural disasters. The young twenty-first century resembles the first decades of the twentieth century, rather than its end. Populist and authoritarian regimes have been elected in central Europe, American President Donald Trump is isolating the US from its western European allies and the European Union faces cracks in its foundations, not least with Brexit. The glory of the twentieth century's anti-colonial struggles is over. Along with the playing upon fear of jihadist terror, populists have warned that immigration from the Middle East and Africa will lead to western Europe societies losing their national identity and social cohesion. Wracked by civil wars and unrest, the Middle East seems in a hopeless situation.

However, as this book suggests, a close examination of Palestinian social dynamics shows that beneath the present state of affairs, the potential for change lurks. An occupation that today seems permanent could be pushed away tomorrow by a nation determined to achieve liberation and self-determination.

This book is a portrait of two political leaders, each at the head of a twenty-five year old political entity. The components of each portrait do not fit together perfectly, nor depict a photo-realistic view of the subject. In addition, as with any portrait, the depictions of Arafat and Abbas include my interpretation of the facts of history. The first chapter describes the two personalities and their roads to power. The second concerns their foreign policy, in particular the relations with Israel and the US. In the third chapter, I deal with domestic policy, with special attention to democratic institution-building and state logistics. This chapter also deals with Hamas, the political rival that grew to challenge Arafat and Abbas. The final chapter describes the struggle to succeed Abbas, already underway. Through the book, I compare the two leaders. The dual portrait of these two presidents is more than a description of iconic individuals. It is a political profile of the whole Oslo Agreements generation.

1

# ARAFAT, THE ICON AS PRESIDENT, AND HIS ANTIHERO SUCCESSOR

*The Iconic Personality*

Yasser Arafat, the first president of the Palestinian Authority (PA), left behind big shoes to fill. This was not because Arafat built well-functioning state-like institutions—quite the contrary. They were big due to what Arafat had already symbolised before his election as PA president in 1996, along with the mysterious illness and circumstances surrounding his death in 2004.

Already at an early stage of his public life, Yasser Arafat became an icon. This was a reason he survived politically, despite his personal limitations. It started with the Battle of Karameh, in March 1968, in which Israeli forces suffered heavy casualties in the first major engagement since their glorious victory in the Six Day War eight months earlier. The Jordanian army caused most of the Israeli Defence Force (IDF)'s losses—twenty-eight dead and ninety wounded—but Fatah benefited most by shrewdly claiming responsibility for the Israeli casualties. Styled as Fatah's leader and spokesperson, Arafat was interviewed and photo-

1

graphed in the Arab press, providing the media with an identifiable public figure. In his first public appearance, Arafat embodied the (successful) Palestinian armed struggle around which Fatah built a mythology.[1] He was not necessarily the most talented of the Palestinian activists at the end of the 1960s, nor a natural leader. His colleagues all knew his deficiencies, which Arafat did not try to hide. Nor did he gain leadership of Fatah due to his family ties with the Grand Mufti Haj Amin al-Husseini, the leader of the national movement during the first half of the twentieth century. In fact, Arafat omitted 'al-Husseini' from his family name. After the defeat of 1948, identifying with the failed Palestinian leader was a political burden, not a shortcut to the top.

But following a frequently trodden path within revolutionary groups, he was the only one among his Fatah comrades in the late 1950s and early 60s who agreed to devote all of his time to the new organisation. Unlike him, Arafat's colleagues were refugees obliged to support their families and secure their future by developing professional careers. Founded in 1959 in Kuwait, Fatah rejected Egyptian President Nasser's strategy for liberating Palestine through a well-prepared concerted attack by the surrounding Arab states. Instead of placing their trust in their neighbours, Fatah called on the Palestinians to rely upon themselves and launch a guerrilla war against Israel. Fatah was at that time a small organisation, founded by a dozen young activists, and until 1968 it had only about 500 members. The Palestinian public supported Nasser, and most of them had never heard of Fatah, let alone its counter-strategy. The young refugees who established Fatah looked elsewhere to secure their and their families' futures. Arafat, who was not a refugee, opted differently.

His comrades in Fatah and the Palestine Liberation Organisation (PLO) were aware of his periodic lack of credibility, and his occasional tendency toward public gaffes that did manage to earn him attention. The Palestinian public was not always inspired by his speeches, which were delivered in an Egyptian dialect (he was born in Cairo in 1929 after his parents had left Gaza city for economic reasons)[2] that he could not get rid of. Despite all this, no one in Fatah or the PLO could challenge his image as a national symbol. His symbolic standing was built upon his image as a struggler, a warrior and a survivor. His image was that of a fighter: the fatigues with military decorations he would wear; the pistol always at hand for when he felt his life was in danger; his speeches that stressed the motifs of jihad, self-sacrifice and martyrdom. The Palestinian public perceived Arafat as someone who was sacrificing his life for the revolution, who fought on the frontlines and survived several assassination attempts. Until he wed Suha in 1990, at the age of 61, Arafat had claimed to be married to the revolution. Very few knew anything of his former romantic relationships. Indeed, until his mother in law exposed the news, his marriage was kept a secret in order not to harm his image as a person that has no private life, and also because of Yasser and Suha's different social origins. Arafat came from a lower-middle class Muslim family, like most of his comrades in Fatah. Suha, however, who worked in his office in Tunis and was thirty years younger at the time they married, came from a wealthy Christian family from Nablus. Their daughter Zahwa was born in 1995. In 2001, while her husband was again locked in struggle with Israel during the second intifada, Suha left Ramallah and moved to Paris.

Even his leadership deficiencies became national property and were justified as a necessary survival method of a wanted freedom fighter. He frequently manoeuvred between past and present positions, and manipulated his partners at the top of the PLO. Arafat used divide-and-rule tactics to preserve his authority within Fatah and the PLO, alternately promoting one to his side then rejecting him from his inner circle. By allocating similar powers or mandates to competing agencies and several senior officers, Arafat presided over a system of patronage, dispensing power, jobs, income and arbitration. Together with delays in decision making, hesitation, a preference for improvisation and taking advantage of tactical opportunities rather than relying on strategic planning, these methods created a disorganised decision-making process in a situation with no state agencies to balance the power of the chairman. Arafat's use of fallacious reasoning and empty slogans, and his tendency to tell the listener what they wanted to hear, or use double and ambiguous meanings, were perceived by the public as a means of survival in a hostile environment, considering that alternate leadership styles had failed to prevent the 1948 Nakba (the 'catastrophe': the Arabic word for the establishment of the State of Israel and the expulsion of Palestinians from their homeland). In meetings with international leaders, Arafat projected a lack of credibility: offering answers that said yes and no at the same time. Consequently, an Arabic word was coined, *la'am*, which combines the two, to describe Arafat's speech. His awkward speechmaking, including his tendency to repeat key sentences over and over to compensate for his oratory weaknesses and poor style, his tendency to appear like a helpless *ingénu* who doesn't understand why he is being asked for something beyond his abilities—expressed, in the eyes of his people, the situation of the Palestinian nation after the 1948 defeat. Alongside these phenomena, he was also marked by tendencies toward forcefulness, aggressiveness, and a readiness for extended struggle that spoke to the Palestinians' determination to correct the historic aberration of 1948.

The construction of this symbolism provided the national movement what it had lacked: the perception of armed might and thus, power. It was aided by the fact that Arafat was frequently expelled from the Arab countries that hosted him: following the clash with Jordan in 1970, dubbed Black September, he and the PLO headquarters moved to Beirut, from where

Israel's incursion in 1982 forced them to move again to Tunis. Arafat even survived a number of assassination attempts by Israel in the 1980s and an airplane accident in 1992. If Arafat had not become a national icon, his invented biography, which said he was born in Jerusalem rather than Cairo, would instead have been comical.

## Arafat's Unique Leadership Style

Arafat's leadership was not the result of an extraordinary personality, the powers of tradition or religious authority, or membership of a prominent family or tribe. The defeat of 1948 and the population's expulsion shattered Palestinian society and destroyed its failed clan-based national movement elite. This conservative leadership had seized key political positions, ruled religious institutions and enjoyed the benefits of land ownership and financial resources.[3] The aftermath of 1948 paved the way for the educated middle class of the newly created diaspora, who were mostly refugees, to enter politics. Highly motivated and energetic, they were determined to change their personal and national fate as well as to retaliate for the loss they had suffered.

Arafat was not the type of person who could develop an ideology upon which to base his leadership. Fatah's political ideology was mainly developed by Khaled al-Hassan (1928–94). Within the PLO, George Habash (1926–2008), the founder and head of the Popular Front for the Liberation of Palestine (PFLP), and Nayef Hawatmeh (1938–), the founder and head of the Democratic Front for the Liberation of Palestine (DFLP), exercised great influence on the movement's collective thinking. Mahmoud Darwish (1941–2008), who left Israel in 1970 and joined the PLO in 1973, wrote the Palestinian experience into poetry.[4] Arafat, a single-minded politician, frequently manoeuvred between them, ever wary of losing his leadership position. Arafat the icon remained unburdened by intellectual exertion.

For an icon, Arafat was hardly the charismatic personality typical to the genre. He was not attractive like Che Guevara, and did not symbolise the romance of the Palestinian revolution. Physically unremarkable, short, unshaved and not particularly slim, he was no sex symbol. On the contrary, his image projected asexuality. The romance of the Palestinian cause came from the abstract, idealistic messages of the revolution—justice, freedom, self-determination, a struggle against Israeli occupation, colonialism and Western imperialism, and the correction of an historical injustice. In the 1960s and 1970s, these messages resonated with many in the West, in particular in the context of anti-Vietnam War mass demonstrations and the rise of the New Left, but what drew them in was not the physical image of the PLO's leader.

Arafat was not a leader who caused all in his presence to melt, keep their distance or be paralysed with fear. On the contrary, the leadership were always arguing among themselves and with Arafat. PLO and Fatah leadership meetings rarely stuck to the agenda nor would participants respect the order of business. Among his colleagues in the leadership, alongside his nom de guerre Abu Ammar, he was also known as al-Khit'yar (the old man) and al-Waled (the father). These names referred to the fact that he was about five years older than his fellow founding fathers in Fatah, including Abbas, in addition to his iconic seniority as the one who gave birth to the Palestinian revolution. In essence, among his colleagues he was considered the first among equals. As such, Arafat would build coalitions, and converted his dependence upon coalitions and the agreement of his colleagues into symbolic value. Thus, the arguments in the organisation were another form of struggle, alongside the fact that they served as a means for building a national consensus around the leader. From a symbolic point of view, Arafat was not seen as someone who forced his will upon the movement, but as someone who expressed the national consensus on its behalf.

While simultaneously building intra-PLO coalitions from 1968, when Fatah took over the organisation Ahmad Shukeiri had established in 1964, Arafat built Arab consensus around the PLO. Ten years after its establishment and six years since Arafat became its chairperson, the 1974 Arab League summit in Rabat, Morocco, recognised the PLO as the sole legitimate representative of the Palestinian people, denying Jordan's claim to represent her West Bank citizens. Jordan annexed the West Bank in 1951 and since 1964 had argued that the PLO represented all Palestinians except those with Jordanian citizenship. The new Arab consensus gradually brought the West Bankers, who after 1967 lived under Israeli occupation, to endorse the PLO. In the 1976 municipal elections, young PLO candidates in major West Bank cities won against the pro-Jordanian mayors of the older generation.

Coalition and consensus building were how Arafat survived politically, and were sources for borrowing symbolic capital. Moreover, consensus was the Fatah and PLO method to prevent imperialist powers and their Arab allies using the 'divide and rule' tactics that, they concluded, had caused the 1948 defeat. Lacking a solid territorial base and never having been elected by the public to chair the PLO, acting as a bridge between different views, including from the PLO itself and the Palestinian diaspora, was Arafat's modus operandi to preserve his leading status, prior to the Oslo agreements. Sometimes he provoked disagreement in order to initiate the consensus-building process and reemphasise his centrality. His inconsistent personality and leadership style were the subject of Israeli demonisation, and by this extended to the movement that he represented. His ability to overcome endless challenges symbolically identified Arafat with the national struggle to survive.

Arafat's watch always showed the same time: five minutes to midnight—a time symbolising emergency (that called for a closing of the ranks against external threats), a permanent state of alarm or the verge of a great opportunity or breakthrough. To justify this and to create a reality that justified his symbolic status, Arafat created a sense of disquiet; of bureaucratic chaos and tactical manoeuvring. A constant dispersal and reassignment of authority generated an ongoing sense of instability, the fear of losing status and a multiplication of competitors that reinforced his position as the one at the top. These tactics provoked internal criticism and unrest, but they also confirmed his status as a symbol. His leadership style also upset many, who protested against his one-man rule, and the personal element—in the decision-making processes and because his policy periodically strayed from the consensus. Arafat was not a team player, nor a dictator, but rather both the captain and the coach.

Arafat was never above tough criticism. Abd al-Aziz (known as Abu Ali) Shahin, one of Fatah's founding fathers that Israel deported from Gaza in 1985, published a critical pamphlet in the early 1990s in which he dubbed Arafat with thirty-two titles, accusing Arafat of being a megalomaniac, dictator, Pharaoh and financially corrupted. His criticism neither harmed Arafat's status nor prevented Arafat from including Abu Ali in his Palestinian Authority cabinet up to 2003.

The icon of total dedication to the national liberation struggle was based on blurring the lines between the personal and the national. This was epitomised by Arafat's dress, his place of residence, his lifestyle and his work habits. In each, the personal and the national were one. The formal position became personalised, and the specific person underwent a process of symbolisation. The same was true of his personal space, which became public space. His home served as a public meeting place, as both a reception centre and an office where Arafat and the Fatah leadership worked. He did not keep an ordinary meetings schedule, nor stick to a timetable. Partly for security reasons and partly in accordance with his revolutionary image, Arafat used to work late into the night, often changing pre-arranged meeting places and times. Arafat's burial in the courtyard of his Ramallah house-cum-office-cum-prison was in keeping with this persona, that of a consummate fighter who struggled until the end. As an icon, Arafat even continues to struggle from the grave, having asked that after Palestinian liberation, his remains be transferred to the Temple Mount/Haram al-Sharif. In other words, until one of the highest goals of the national movement is achieved Arafat, the leader, will not have his final resting place.

For Europeans, Americans, Israelis and some members of the Palestinian elite, Arafat's work pattern seemed problematic. His patronage, lack of delegation of authority, difficulties in managing systematic work procedures with institutions that were open to external regulation, all stemmed from the identification of the personal with the national, and they converted his image from a burden into an advantage. As external criticism of his work patterns and pressure to change them increased with the foundation of the Palestinian Authority in 1994—in particular with regard to covering up his allies' financial corruption and his own fiscal mismanagement—so did his symbolic image as a fighter struggling against external forces. However, the development of this symbol was not the only dimension of Arafat's public image. During his final years, criticism from Palestinian civil society of his flaws as a leader also increased. Abbas was among those who criticised Arafat before and during the former's short term as PA Prime Minister (March–September 2003), but he never seriously challenged Arafat's leadership. Paradoxically, the more he became a target of Israeli and American pressure during the second intifada, the more his image as a national symbol grew. However, his image as an effective leader at the head of a system providing services to the Palestinian public and bringing it closer to a realisation of its national goals decreased.

Before the establishment of the PA, Arafat preferred to use his underground name, Abu Ammar. His *nom de guerre* was layered with symbolic meaning. In the seventh century, Abu Ammar was a Muslim warrior in the Prophet Muhammad's army. As such, choosing the name Abu Ammar evoked both the image of fighter and Muslim true believer. Religion, however, was not just an instrumental choice for Arafat, a religious man whose rudimentary knowledge of the Qur'an he had gained during his childhood in Cairo. Drawing on his basic religious education and his deep religiosity he would insert passages from the Qur'an into his speeches, mobilising religion to serve Palestinian nationalism, which served to give further legitimisation to the icon. After the PA was established, the title *ra'is* (president) replaced his *nom de guerre*. The title expressed not only his symbolic standing but was also a product of the struggle for national self-determination. At the time that the Oslo Accords were being formulated, Israel refused to refer to the head of the PA as 'president' due to the term's political significance. It was felt that it pre-supposed notions of statehood and sovereignty, which the Oslo Agreements had postponed until final status negotiations. The compromise was the use of the Arabic term *ra'is*, which also means 'chairman.' The PA insistence on the use of the title 'president' in all languages was part of the symbolisation of the role and the man.

As long as Arafat was outside the Palestinian territories, he was careful to maintain his people's financial dependence on him, as well as written and verbal contact, mainly by telephone and short letters. He also received and approved applications for financial support. This helped him overcome the physical distance from the territory and the public living in it. It also reinforced the symbolisation of Arafat as the personification of the collective. He was perceived as a consultative and approachable leader who loved to be among his people. His approach was to foster a sense of equality without any patronising or formal manner toward his aides, his guests (whom he would be sure to treat for lunch or dinner) and his bodyguards. His folksiness blended in with the chaos and disorder of his work patterns and the organisation of his bureau. Many surrounded him: dozens of advisers, extended family members and visitors. Telephone calls frequently interrupted any conversation. Rarely did he accept one-on-one meetings. Almost every meeting with him became a symposium within which many things would be occurring simultaneously. Many people came and went with their different requests, demands, complaints and suggestions.

This flawed functioning of the Palestinian establishment and Arafat's eccentric work patterns were converted into symbolic capital. They were perceived as representing popular leadership, without any elitism, that was thus responsive to the hardship the movement faced. The dysfunctional, chaotic and informal leadership style helped him maintain his image as a humble leader who listened to and took care of his people's troubles. Although his bureau was inefficient, corrupt and politically biased, Palestinians meeting him experienced something extremely unlike that in their Arab hosting countries or under Israeli occupation, characterised by hierarchy, layers of guards and assistants to go through, and leaders living in expensive palaces. But this system, which worked so well for the PLO chairman, was less suitable for the new PA *ra'is*.

*Cracks in the Icon*

The creation of the PA as a ruling establishment significantly decreased Arafat's time spent in the public eye, and his contact with the people was no longer as direct as it had been in the past. In the early days, Arafat would travel through the districts under his authority, but he soon gave this up. Methods befitting him as the exiled head of a liberation movement were insufficient for running the daily affairs of a few million people. The PA's failure to bring about the end of the Israeli occupation and expansion of settlements led to increased criticism by elected Legislative Council members, Fatah members included. The national project of institution building, so it seemed, had stalled. The national symbol cracked. Alongside the national symbol, the sense arose that the branches of the establishment were suffering from increased corruption, and that governance was growing intolerably inefficient. Arafat, the symbol, could not be separated from these phenomena.

The siege that Israel placed on him in his Ramallah headquarters during the second intifada and the destruction of the Palestinian governing mechanisms by Israeli forces in 2002 cut the thin physical threads that tied him to his people. However, the re-occupation of the West Bank in 2002 shattered the PA but re-established Arafat's symbolic status. The Israeli assault cut the link between Arafat's iconic stature and his performance and responsibilities as the head of the executive branch.

What remained was the symbol, which burst forth at Arafat's funeral. The contrast between the hundreds who came to bid him farewell when he left for medical treatment in Paris, and the hundreds of thousands of mourners who burst into the Muqata'a (Arafat's Ramallah compound) area two weeks later, on 11 November 2004, to touch the coffin and disrupt the funeral arrangements gave powerful expression to this. The masses wanted to physically touch the symbol to whom they were so attached.

The funeral released the symbol from the constraints of the establishment, and turned Arafat into a *shahid* (martyr), someone who sacrificed his life for the nation, who continued to struggle from his gravesite. A widespread public belief is that he did not die naturally but was poisoned by the Israelis. This notion is based not only on Ariel Sharon's obsessive attempts to assassinate Arafat in the early 1980s and during 2001–4, along with those of

Shimon Peres in 1985,[5] each believing that the leader's disappearance would end the Palestinian national movement. Nor is it simply another Palestinian and Arab popular conspiracy theory, based on a perception of Israel as an omnipotent demon. It is also an inseparable part of his rejuvenated iconic myth. The icon does not die, melt or evaporate. It fights on. The belief that he was poisoned revives his symbol within Palestinian popular consciousness and discourse.

His graveyard in the presidential compound became a national memorial site, if temporary, until the Palestinians liberate the Temple Mount and bring him to his final resting place.

*Arafat in the Eyes of the Israelis*

The formulation of the reports on Arafat's death in the Israeli mass media and the graphics in the tabloid press expressed deep-felt wishes rather than hard facts. 'Finished' shouted one tabloid paper. A few days later, it declared with a sigh of relief: 'Buried.' The reports were not based on medical bulletins, but rather on a mixture of suppositions, leaks, expectations and emotional positions. As Arafat's medical condition worsened, Israel declared he had died. It was a prolonged death, many waiting with bated breath as if for confirmation of the kill. And, as expected, those in the Palestinian establishment who found it difficult to digest the very fact of Arafat's hospitalisation because of his difficult and unclear illness, announced from Paris that Arafat had been revived, and was joking with his doctors. This was a war between two opposing symbols and a struggle between two emotional and cultural systems of reference over Arafat the symbol. Upon the renewed outbreak of violence that marked the second intifada in 2000, Arafat became once again a demonic icon within Israeli political culture. At both its elite and popular levels, he was perceived as the mastermind of evil orchestrating the second intifada.

The same characteristics that made Arafat a national symbol in the eyes of Palestinians rendered him a demon for the majority of Israelis. His Muslim beliefs and frequent use of the term 'jihad' served as proof of the link between the ultimate national goals of his movement and those of Hamas and Islamic Jihad.[6] This demonising daubed a sneaky and cruel hue upon Arafat the symbol and the movement he led. His mannerisms, his military fatigues, the pistol he wore, and his talk of struggle, threats and steadfastness, combined with his unusual operating style, formed a potent adversary in the Israeli popular imagination. His political manoeuvring, double talk (though this is typical of many politicians), chaotic management style and aspirations to keep all authority within his grasp—all this was the proof that he was an ever-dangerous revolutionary.

As the symbol of Palestinian nationalism, Arafat was perceived as someone who, via guile and terror, aspired to wipe Israel from the map by means of the return of 1948's refugees to their homes, or even simply via the demand to recognise the principle of their right of return. In Israeli eyes, Arafat wished to undermine Israel's moral foundations by demanding acknowledgment that it was founded upon the crime of the 1948 deportation, denying any Arab responsibility for rejecting the UN partition plan of November 1947 and initiating the subsequent war. In Israeli popular consciousness, the Palestinians continue to reject the partition plan and hence Israel continues to struggle for its very existence, rather than over a borderline. Israelis tend to forget that in 1988 Arafat led the PLO to accept the 1947 United Nations Partition Plan, known also as United Nations General Assembly Resolution 181, on establishing a Jewish state next to an Arab one.

Arafat's unwillingness to accept Israel's demand for sovereignty over the Temple Mount and his outright rejection (during the Camp David summit in 2000) of any historic Jewish connection with the place, gave Israeli politicians and spin-doctors a justification to market him as a demonic Palestinian icon. They declared that the Palestinian side seeks the moral and political defeat of Israel, given that it does not recognise the national existence of the Jewish people. The Palestinian insistence on sovereignty over the Temple Mount during 2000's Camp David negotiations, and the way that Arafat and his colleagues expressed their position, reflected the fact that Israel remained immersed in a confrontation with a fundamentalist national-religious culture.

## No Demonisation Without Alienation

There is no demonisation without alienation. Arafat's work habits were perceived by Israelis as marked by a non-Western and non-modern essence—the lack of readiness to adjust to Western cultural norms of truth telling, delegation of authority and acceptance of public criticism, democratisation and transparency. Based on Arafat symbolising the national movement, Israelis quickly moved from demonising Arafat to perceiving the entire Palestinian nation negatively. 'The Palestinians would have to become Finns' before this demonic label could be removed and it could become possible to achieve a political settlement with them, stated Dov Weisglass, the chef de cabinet of Prime Minister Sharon and his special political envoy.[7] At the least, it would be necessary to wait one or two generations, until the passing of the generation for whom the experience of 1948 shaped their personal experience and collective memory, concluded many in the Israeli establishment.

Estrangement is a means in the struggle against evil forces. The demon has to be marked, isolated and removed, its passing must be yearned for and its death, expulsion or disappearance from the arena will remove the problem and protect the afflicted.

The ministers' conclusion at the end of 2001 that Arafat had concluded his historical role,[8] and the decision by Ariel Sharon's government that Arafat was no longer relevant, should be viewed as the creation of a charm to expel the demon. Nevertheless, in actuality the demon-figure continued to preoccupy Israel. To this day, both the Israeli public and the security establishment remember Arafat as the mastermind and conductor of the bloody second intifada. This version of history records that Arafat totally controlled it, turning its flame high or low according to his political preferences. Arafat coordinated with Hamas its suicide attacks and funded the perpetrators of terror. He did not have to express a command, but merely intimate. His followers immediately understood him. He could simultaneously conduct this battle in a manner clear and easy for Palestinians surrounding him to understand, while ensuring his role was unclear to the rest of the world. Arafat misled Israel and the entire international community; he was never sincere in any peace talks.[9] The reality on the ground was different. The second intifada increased the chaos that characterised the PA prior to it. Worse, under heavy Israeli pressure, the Authority as an overarching central establishment, providing law and order through its legal and security systems, disintegrated. Local armed militias without coherent and disciplined organisational structures, or a unified command to lead them, challenged what remained of the official security forces. In this fragmenting society, customary law and conciliation committees replaced the collapsed legal system, and clan structures provided social protection.[10]

*Sometimes Individual, and Sometimes Collective*

This practice of demonisation operated at both the individual and collective level. The movement between the negative symbolisation of Arafat and that of the entire Palestinian leadership or generation was rapid and simple. Right-wingers alone did not shape this caricature of Arafat after the summer of 2000, as they had throughout the Oslo period, but it was rather the entire establishment: prime ministers, ministers, heads of the army and intelligence, shapers of public opinion, senior officials and even academics—each took part in the framing and promotion of Arafat as a demonic icon. Arafat was a terrorist and a revolutionary, who refused to part from the original means and goals of the revolution. He misled Israel and the world, pretended to be moderate and fraudulently received a Nobel Peace Prize, until his mask was removed. In the narrative put forward by Ehud Barak, he was the one who courageously, at great personal risk, revealed Arafat's true face, with his generous peace offer that Arafat could not evade.[11] The bloody intifada was the answer that came from the depths of Arafat's being, and from the authentic realms of the national movement. According to Barak, the mask was not an instrumental tool for the Palestinians, but rather the expression of a society in which lying and falsehood are the norm. This was another facet of demonisation, with the mask serving both as a means of camouflage and as an authentic expression. These were demonic qualities, rather than flaws in the logic of the speaker. As such, Barak felt he should be praised because he was able to understand this, while others were blind to it. Not only did Barak reveal Arafat's demonic face, he served his people in doing so. He awakened Israelis from their illusions and forced them to understand that their national home is a villa in a jungle, and not an apartment in a building in which all of the tenants have agreed to behave toward each other in a reasonable manner, as the innocent, naïve, mistaken and misleading leftist architects of Oslo believed.

In the 1950s and the 1960s Israel demonised Egyptian President Gamal Abd al-Nasser. Ben Gurion used to compare him to Hitler, and together with Britain and France initiated the

1956 Suez War to get rid of him. Egypt's defeat in the 1967 War undermined Nasser's malevolently powerful aura and his death in 1970 deleted him from Israel's collective memory. Then Israel found Arafat.

During the years of cheap and 'enlightened occupation,' 1967–73, the Israeli narrative totally denied the existence of the Palestinian 'Other.' Arafat and the PLO were outside Palestine, struggling to build bases in the occupied territories. The majority of the West Bank and Gaza Strip residents were unfamiliar with them. The pro-Jordanians among them even saw the PLO as a dangerous destabilising factor. The change came when Israeli self-confidence began to waver following the Egyptian-Syrian surprise attack in 1973, and continued with Arafat's first appearance before the UN General Assembly in 1975. Palestinian terrorist actions knocked repeatedly on the door of Israeli consciousness. Israel furthermore found it difficult to ignore the strengthening of support for the PLO in the Occupied Territories and among the Arab states. The disappearing occupation became the present occupation. Menachem Begin and Ariel Sharon reinforced Arafat's presence in the Israeli national consciousness during the year that they prepared public opinion for the 1982 war, with its original far-reaching goals of destroying the PLO and remaking Jordan as the state of Palestine. Begin called him 'the man with the hair on his face,' and 'Hitler sitting in his Beirut bunker,' thus granting him a demonic visage in all its glory. The failure of the war to lock the demon in his basement was a turning point. Geographically Arafat was exiled to Tunis, but his reach now extended to the Occupied Territories. The first intifada in 1987, that broke out in the form of mass demonstrations against the Israeli occupation, and in support of the PLO and independence, forged his icon at the fore of the Israeli imagination.

A demon can be dealt with by reduction; by describing it in all its ugliness, weakness and absurdity. Reduction of the demonic icon neutralises its potency and converts it into something controllable. Israelis used this method in the years following Oslo. The desire to pacify the demon and to domesticate it was behind the Arafat puppet on the 'Chartzufim' satirical puppet show—depicted as an old, sick and naïve man, whose bite wasn't so bad. Humour was used as a weapon to neutralise the bête noire. This should not be mistaken, however, as a move towards the humanisation of Arafat. The failure of the Camp David summit in 2000, continual government propaganda and the psychological pressure of Palestinian terror converted the farcical puppet image into a mask beneath which hid the previous demon. For a brief period, the image of the old, sick, harmless man from the Oslo period returned when Arafat was filmed in pyjamas and a woollen hat being taken by helicopter from the Muqata'a to hospital in Paris. Arafat's hospitalisation inspired more jokes on popular satirical TV shows. The deterioration in his health turned that strategy into a very brief, passing episode that was replaced by the hope that the icon would disappear. But it would not.

Almost two decades later the demon still rules the Israeli mind. The Israeli mainstream endorses the establishment's view of Arafat the cheater, forgetting that in September 1993's Oslo Agreements he recognised the state of Israel without receiving in exchange any mutual recognition, or even that of the Palestinian right of self-determination. Palestinian popular opinion holds, however, that Israel has been the misleading side, having trapped Arafat through the Oslo Agreements. For his defenders, Arafat truly wanted peace and naïvely believed in Israel's good intentions. Arafat's critics perceived him as a seeker of political status. He gave up his national principles in exchange for enjoying the benefits of being chairperson of a statelet with limited autonomy.

*Demonisation Purifies Israel*

Israel's struggle with the Palestinian demon is conducted not only externally, but also with the dark, repressed side of Israel's self-perception and experience. The attitude toward the Other is part of a counter-discourse with the collective self. The demonised Other is created by the collective self so as to destroy it over and over again and purify the Israeli psyche.

Israel is not a canvas free of blemishes upon which it is possible to paint such a sharp image. It is another expression of the symbiotic connection with the Palestinian Other that has existed since the beginning of modern Zionism. 'Israelis walk and with them walk their shadow, the Palestinian people,' wrote the historian Meron Benvenisti. 'They beat the shadow with a big stick but it does not leave them alone.'[12] Zionism tried to cope with the Palestinian side of its identity, expressed in the struggle between the Palestinian native competing with the Zionist immigrant who wants to become a native, in a number of ways. At times Zionism assumed the role of educator with a *mission civilisatrice* to accomplish with the Arab Palestinian (and the Oriental Sephardi Jew), and at times the movement wished instead to supplant the original Palestinian native and erase their presence both upon the land and in the Zionist/Israeli mind. Zionism also converted the Palestinian Other into an object of imitation, as it drew upon elements of its spoken language and popular culture, food or architecture. Sometimes it even saw it as a well preserved, ideal model for the ancient Hebrews. In each of these instances, Zionism created an antithesis to the actual Palestinian Other, and built a hierarchal relationship with it. Yet the Zionist perspective of the Other Palestinian was multi-dimensional. It included positive aspects that the Zionist/Israeli self-perception endorsed. Even when it drew from it culturally, Israeli Zionism placed itself on a higher moral plane. Empowerment, imitation and borrowing are strategies that contain elements of identification, alongside elements of envy, mockery, admiration and anger. However, this constructed utter foreignness shows the difficulty of trying to become liberated from the Other within ourselves. The mental wall that Israeli society has built between itself and the Palestinian Other since 2000, and its current expression in a physical fence/wall, are expressions of an attempt to resolve the dilemma of the self via an act of redemption.

*The Anti-Icon Sisyphean President: From the Margins to Power*

Mahmoud Abbas was the foremost candidate to succeed Yasser Arafat in 2004 and his road to the Muqata'a was straightforward. Many hopes were pinned on Abbas after his election. For Israel and the international community, he was the perfect option—in the right post at the right moment not because he had proved his extraordinary management skills in his previous posts in Fatah and the PLO, but because he had shown that he was different from Arafat.

Abbas was born in 1935 in the small city of Safed, in the north of Palestine, where he spent his childhood. A few months after his twelfth birthday he became a refugee. As a Palestinian native, he did not have to invent his birthplace for symbolic value as Arafat did. When Fatah's founders began their armed struggle in 1965, Abbas remained in Qatar where, besides running his private business, he collected donations for the young movement. He arrived in Qatar in 1957, first working as a teacher. He later moved to the growing oil industry that offered him a much higher income. Abbas returned to Damascus in 1970 and threw himself into political activity with Fatah and the PLO. In the late 1970s and early 1980s, when the PLO confronted Israel from Lebanon, he was a PhD student in Moscow, helping to advocate for the Palestinian case. Between 1970–82, when the PLO's headquarters were in Beirut's Faqahani neighbourhood (which PLO members dubbed the Faqahani Republic), Abbas preferred to remain in Damascus, where he and his family had fled in 1948. Damascus was a parochial city, whereas Beirut in the early 1970s was famously the 'Paris of the Middle East.' The Lebanese civil war of 1975 and the Israeli invasion in 1982 were to make it the focal point of conflicting armed groups and regular armies. These two faces of Beirut did not attract Abbas. As such, he did not experience the Israeli siege on the PLO headquarters in the 1982 war. He joined his PLO comrades in September 1982 when they moved to the quiet city of Tunis.

Unlike most Fatah and PLO senior members, Abbas did not make his living from the Revolution, nor did he have a key position in Fatah or the PLO. He played a minor role in maintaining PLO relations with Arab leaders, taking care of what PLO Chairman Arafat and Farouk Kaddoumi, the head of the PLO Political Department, both at centre stage, had left for him. He also chose to keep distance on the field in which he considered himself the PLO's foremost expert: Zionism and Israel. Before 1993, he knew Israelis only from a distance and had never argued in favour of reaching a compromise with them. Issam Sartawi (1935–83, the PLO representative to the Socialist International) represented the PLO in meetings with the Israeli Council for Israeli-Palestinian Peace from 1975 until his assassination in 1983. Said Hammami (born in 1941, the PLO representative in London from 1973 until his murder in 1978) publicly promoted a two-state solution in the second half of the 1970s and Abu Eyad (Salah Khalaf, 1933–91, number two in the PLO and Fatah) argued for it in the 1980s and 1990.[13] Interestingly, at no point did Abbas' interest in Zionism lead him to any involvement with the PLO Research Centre, which studied Israel and Zionism, nor the use of its library and archive. Abbas' name is absent from the Centre director's memoirs. Arafat did show interest in the Centre's work, if limited. Arafat would typically demand to approve every nominee, and imposed his view without consulting the director or studying the issue at stake. As elsewhere, he wanted to impose his control over the Centre and receive political loyalty from its staff.[14]

On the margins, somewhat of an outsider, wealthy and financially independent, Abbas was free to differ with Arafat. Abbas did not like Arafat's one-man-show management style and preference for political loyalty over qualifications and performance when appointing senior positions. Abbas was also against the militarisation of the second intifada that Arafat, according to Abbas, could have prevented. In addition, based upon his PhD on Zionism, he considered that he understood Israeli society much better than his leader. Indeed the disrespect was mutual. Arafat thought that Abbas' view on Israel was simplistic, that he was too soft with Israelis and that therefore, he should not be allowed to negotiate with them by himself.

Abbas remained on the sidelines for many years, which was exactly where the Oslo talks began—as a private initiative of two Israeli peace activists, Ron Pundak and Yair Hirschfeld, and PLO representatives Abu Alaa [Ahmad Qurie] and Hanan Ashrawi. Once the Oslo initiative broke into the mainstream in summer 1993, Abbas found himself in the spotlight. However, he was once again relegated to the margins. His Israeli counterpart, Shimon Peres, won the Nobel Peace Prize along with Yitzhak Rabin and Arafat, while Abbas never received credit for his contribution to the deal. Between 1994–5, he continued to remain on the sidelines. Immediately after the signing of the 1993 Oslo agreement, Abbas called for a move from revolutionary governance to state-building, which requires professional manpower, functioning institutions, and performance patterns that could provide the Palestinian population with adequate services.[15]

Accordingly, in 1994 Abbas came to an agreement with Yossi Beilin, who worked under Peres in the Foreign Ministry, on the principles for a long-term peace deal. Rabin's murder drove a stake through those plans. Regretfully, Peres rejected both the plan and the very idea of making the principles a central component of his campaign to succeed Rabin. He neither wanted to move forward what had already been agreed, nor then did he support the establishment of an independent Palestine.

The Oslo process led Abbas to maintain close contact with Shimon Peres. In 2010, when Peres was Israeli president, they secretly met five times to discuss the establishment of a Palestinian state on territory 'similar' to the West Bank. Netanyahu let Peres talk but did not approve the Israeli president's proposal. The talks ended in July 2010 when Netanyahu ordered Peres, who was already on his way to Amman, to return home.[16] In September 2016 Abbas agreed to Peres' family request to participate in the funeral of the former President in Mount Herzl, Jerusalem, alongside US presidents Obama and Clinton, the King of Spain, the French president and the Prince of Wales. Despite facing heavy criticism within Fatah and the wider public, he travelled to Jerusalem and shook hands with Netanyahu. Palestinian members of the Knesset boycotted the ceremony, but Jewish Israelis warmly received Abbas' respect for his peace partner. As was typical, Abbas did not confront his critics or tell his people why he decided to participate in Peres' funeral. His spokespersons, trying to control the damage, argued that it was a diplomatic achievement. The PA President arrived despite Likud ministers' opposition, was treated like a head of state and spoke with international leaders on the need to resume the peace process. The Palestinian public remained unconvinced.

Arafat established in the PA a chaotic system like that which characterised the PLO in Beirut and Tunis. This chaos flourished as a result of lack of coordination between PA branches and its senior members. By duplicating authorities, the president sought to promote competition between his ministers as well as between the different police and security service units, in order to solidify absolute control. As will be discussed in Chapter Three, Abbas worked in a different fashion toward the same goal. However, neither Arafat nor Abbas were successful in this endeavour.

The absence of systematic planning units in administrative departments, and the personification of the political process under Arafat, whereby he would insist upon his personal participation in any high-level forums, compounded the chaos he had established. The political and administrative systems suffered from a high degree of de-institutionalisation. Decisions were made on an *ad hominem* basis instead of on the merits of the issue or proposal at hand. The personification of the political and ruling systems was centred upon a patron-client structure operating from the top down.[17] Abbas did not abolish Arafat's system but, unlike his predecessor, has kept ordinary working hours, is generally consistent, and maintains a sharp distinction between his home and office. Abbas' wife is not in the public spotlight, and the president excludes his personal life from the duties of his office.

In early 2003 Western leaders and Egypt forced Arafat to create the position of prime minister within the Palestinian Authority, which until then had been a purely presidential system. He appointed Abbas in March and transferred to him some presidential powers, including parts of the security remit. The president, as could be expected, undermined his prime minister's authority, limiting his executive power and causing his resignation after just five months in office. Similar power struggles developed under Arafat, with his executive branch on the one hand and the Legislative Council on the other (see Chapter Three).[18] Leaving office after such a brief tenure was not considered a result of Abbas' weakness and incapability of withstanding pressure. The international community charged Arafat. Ironically, Abbas was to prove a good student. Later, he did the same to Salam Fayyad, another prime minister the international community had heavily favoured. Moreover, as shown in Chapter Three, Abbas endorsed many of Arafat's centralist methods.

From 2000 and until his death, international leaders grew increasingly tired of Arafat, while Abbas earned praise from Israel and the international community. The reasons for this were clear: unlike Arafat, Abbas was not theatrical but business-minded. Arafat did not hesitate to promise things far beyond his capacity to accomplish, although he would often say 'we are not asking for the moon.' Like an accountant, Abbas was cautious. Insofar as leaders are players on the diplomatic and political stage, and they are, Arafat was a player, though on more than a few occasions he was unconvincing and melodramatic. Abbas has no skills in that regard; he does not play a heroic drama. His style is dry and straightforward. Indeed, all politicians mix fantasy and wishful thinking with reality, but differ in intensity. Arafat often played with facts and not infrequently even invented them. Abbas, on the other hand, creates an impression of trustworthiness—though unimpressive physically, his image is that he is consistent and his word can be counted upon. World leaders have warmly endorsed and helped to maintain the Oslo Accords of which he was one of the architects. Abbas openly opposed the violence and terrorism of the second intifada, which to his mind was catastrophic for the Palestinians and their state-building project.

The 2003 conflict between Prime Minister Abbas and President Arafat led to increased international appreciation for the former, whom the global community viewed as an ideal leader to succeed Arafat. It was hoped that through his leadership the Palestinians would undergo the same change that Abbas himself underwent. The man who began as a supporter of armed struggle and the establishment of a Palestinian state to replace Israel has, since the 1980s, supported negotiations and a smaller

Palestinian state alongside Israel. The Israeli peace camp was sure that the public that elected Abbas president would stand behind him when the time came for the Palestinians to approve a peace deal with Israel.

Abbas is not a political entrepreneur nor a manipulator. He actively dislikes this side of politics, which explains the distance he kept from Arafat and his poor relations with Muhammad Dahlan (see Chapter Three). He did not fight his way to the presidency through underhandedness or political intrigue, as it was instead given to him as the first choice (for the international community) and the default option (in the domestic realm).

In 2005, Abbas won the support of both the population and the Palestinian establishment. He is the last of Fatah's founding fathers still around today. Abu Eyad and Abu Jihad (full name Khalil al-Wazir, 1935–88, Fatah's number three), his superiors, were both murdered. A Palestinian opponent killed Abu Eyad and Israel assassinated Abu Jihad, while Farouk Kaddoumi (1931–, the head of the PLO Political Department) rejected Oslo, remained in Tunis and became irrelevant. Marwan Barghouti (born in the West Bank in 1959, the leader of Fatah's young guard) became more popular and militant than Abbas but he challenged the old guard that came from Tunis in 1994,[19] and never won international support. In 2002, Israel arrested Barghouti, convicting and sentencing him to five life sentences. Israel has never shown any intention of releasing him from prison. Abbas was, and remains, a more convenient rival.

However, it was not just his age and veteran status that worked in Abbas' favour. Thanks to international support, many Palestinians and the entire Israeli peace camp viewed him as the only person who could force Israel to end the occupation and win independence for his people. Conversely, based on Abbas' statement that he did not intend to return to live in his hometown of Safed,[20] many in the West Bank and Gaza were afraid that the president was willing to compromise too much and give up the 1948 refugees' right of return to what is now Israel. The hope that Abbas would gain them their freedom from occupation lessened the worry among Palestinians that his weak personality, when faced with strong Israeli objections, would induce him to give up on the dream of return. In actual fact, in his speeches and negotiations with Israel Abbas continues to insist upon Israeli acknowledgment of the right of return, though he is flexible on the form of its realisation.

## Avoiding the Public Eye

Since his election Abbas has frequently travelled abroad to promote Palestinian independence, though this has provoked criticism from his fellow Palestinians for removing himself from the everyday suffering of occupation. Abbas functions within a dissonant reality. On the one hand, he uses the head-of-state title, along with its symbols and ceremonies. For Abbas, the state of Palestine under his leadership is not illusory but rather gradually emerging from a national rights-based discourse into reality. On the other hand, he has to receive Israeli permission for each of his trips, and ask his people to remain steadfast in the face of an occupation that will one day end, and a time when full independence will be achieved.

As mentioned above, the PLO never operated a well-functioning political planning department, nor worked to systematically adjust goals to available means, resources and capacities. This would have contradicted its revolutionary ethos and Arafat's chaotic leadership methods. Strategic planning, translated into policy options for the short-, medium- and long-term, are still underdeveloped in Abbas' PA and PLO offices. In his case, it is not just due to the PLO's administrative culture but also his own background. He spent almost forty years in the PLO before entering the Muqata'a as Arafat's successor without establishing or managing any of its main departments. He is a closed-door dealmaker who prefers to meet heads of states and international politicians than tour Palestine and build institutions from the bottom up. Whereas from Beirut and Tunis Arafat maintained direct contact with his people through letters, public speeches and the media, and after 1994 enjoyed addressing mass rallies in the West Bank and Gaza, Abbas rarely meets Palestinians outside his headquarters. His visits to Palestinian cities and institutions are few and rarely does he address a crowd. Indeed, the lack of enthusiasm is mutual. When his office was opened for the public to welcome prisoners released by Israel, few showed up. The event was wooden, forcibly orchestrated as a spontaneous demonstration of support. Abbas' speeches are dry, factual and uninspiring. He reads them in a monotone, usually at the opening of a leadership meeting or an official reception in his office. When he is angry, he sets aside the text to express himself in colloquial language using, sometimes, a popular aggressive style. True, neither was Arafat an extraordinary orator, but he had a talent for standing on the podium in front of his people and making a performance of his speeches. Abbas is his opposite, and is no better in writing.

Arafat attracted young activists. He started his career in Cairo as an activist student in his twenties and became involved in Fatah in his thirties. Later, Arafat the symbol attracted the young generation despite lacking the special wisdom expected of an elder leader. Abbas has almost no connection with young Palestinians. Abbas, unlike Arafat, does not fascinate the young generation. He did not build direct contacts with them during his many years in the PLO, and was elected president in his seventies. For Abbas, age has been an obstacle rather than an advantage in building cross-generational support.

Over the years neither Arafat nor Abbas turned into a Western liberal or social democrat. Universal human rights or Western morality are not their points of departure nor the guidelines for their politics. If Abbas adopted some Western tendencies, they were the capitalistic ones he picked up in Qatar—but without any of the theory that stood behind them. Macro- or microeconomics and social or welfare state theories are not on his reading list. Abbas does not dialogue with intellectuals and is not interested in literature or history. In his free time, he prefers to stay with family members, unlike Arafat who had almost no family or private life. Abbas would smoke heavily (until a few years ago when his physician advised that he reduce his smoking due to his heart problems) and consume Arab popular culture. In particular, he likes popular Arabic music and films. Arafat, who never smoked, was also uninterested in, or rather incapable of, managing intellectual discourse or consuming elite culture. However, he liked elite society, as he enjoyed meeting international celebrities and receiving legitimacy through them. Only technocrats surround Abbas. Unlike Arafat, Abbas does not see himself as a great world leader, but rather a guardian serving the Palestinian nation. Still, no leader lacks for ego, high personal motivation, a self-commissioned mission and sufficient self-confidence. Abbas has each of these.

No less significant than the company is the symbolic attire. Arafat always covered his head with the black and white keffiyeh that had become a symbol of Palestinian nationalism during the 1936–9 revolution, and wore an army-style khaki uniform. Since the 1970s he even pushed forward his iconisation by claiming that he shapes the keffiyeh on his head to resemble Palestine's borders. On the rare occasions that Abbas wears a keffiyeh, he folds it on his shoulders as a shawl. Their different personalities are also reflected physically. Arafat's eyes would move restlessly, seeking approval or checking as to the impact his words had made. Moreover, he easily became emotional. Abbas, on the other hand, is usually restrained, looking directly forward and exuding self-control.

Gender wise, the PA remains a male-dominated elite under Abbas. Only one of the Fatah Central Committee's nineteen members is a woman, and ten out of eighty-one members in the Revolutionary Council.[21] The PLO's Executive Committee has only one woman, Hanan Ashrawi. In addition, there is slow generational mobility within the Palestinian elite. PA, Fatah and PLO elders aged between their mid-50s and late 60s enjoy high status, political power and financial resources.[22] They are older by far than the majority of West Bank and Gaza Strip Palestinians. According to the Palestinian Central Bureau of Statistics, in 2015 the median age in the territories was 19.8. Those under fifteen years of age amounted to 39.4 per cent of the population and only 2.8 per cent were above 65.[23] The young generation is underrepresented in leading institutions, nor does it have a voice in the decision-making process. Abbas and his colleagues expect them to respect the old guard's hierarchical status and abide by its decisions. Younger activists are forced to find an old guard patron if they wish to survive politically, otherwise they are considered subversives and face exclusion from the leadership's higher echelons. The old leadership controls Fatah's youth movement (the Shabibah) and its student associations. Actually, the PLO's patronage structure stems from its early days, and in the political systems prevailing in surrounding Arab countries. Without significant inter-generational promotion and representation, the young generation has begun to distance itself from existing political parties and criticise their undemocratic leaderships (see Chapter Three). Furthermore, in the 2010s a spate of young, angry and frustrated lone wolves occasionally attacked Israeli soldiers, border policemen, settlers or civilians, both in the West Bank and inside Israel. They used knives, stones and sometimes even homemade guns. These sporadic, unorganised, and desperate individuals' attacks are not just strikes against the occupation, but also a protest at the neglect faced by the younger generation.

Lacking experience in institution building and mass mobilisation, or doubting his party men's capabilities to stick to a plan, Abbas considers the Palestinians incapable of running an unarmed intifada. The Palestinian public, according to Abbas, lacks self-control and restraint. It will soon react violently to the expected Israeli provocations. Violent intifadas only serve Israel in letting her use military might and condemn the Palestinians to further repression. Abbas has consistently rejected Marwan Barghouti's request to establish a central apparatus to coordinate non-violent popular resistance. Based on Barghouti and his followers' experience in running mass demonstrations during the first intifada, they suggested establishing public education campaigns and non-violent enforcement teams that would assuage Abbas' understandable concerns (see Chapter Four). However, Abbas has either been unconvinced, or fears Barghouti's popularity. His security forces and Israeli army block weekly non-violent civil society demonstrations from spreading outside two or three villages in the central West Bank. These attract local and international activists unaffiliated with Barghouti's grouping within Fatah. Without expanding to main cities, settlement gates and IDF roadblocks, the demonstrations remain ineffective—an anti-occupation ritual and catharsis rather than a snowball gathering momentum. Abbas limits non-violent resistance to advocating for Palestinian rights internationally, increasing the number of states that recognise Palestine and joining as many international organisations as possible. According to Abbas, simply surviving on the ground is a non-violent form of resistance that complements his international diplomatic campaigns.

In order to cement his rule and confront the growing opposition, Abbas gradually appointed new heads of security branches at the rank of major general, and made sure to dominate Fatah's key institutions. In 2008 he put Munir al-Zuabi in charge of the Presidential Guard; in 2011 he appointed Nidal Abu Dukhan to the head of national security. Hazem Atallah was appointed in 2008 to head the civil police. The chief of military intelligence between 2005 and 2015 was Ibrahim al-Balawi, and since 2015 has been Zakaria Musleh. For the preventive security brief he nominated Ziad Hab al-Rih in 2007. Finally, at the top of the general intelligence directorate he put Majed Faraj, who is the most powerful among the above, in 2008. They all owe their nomination to Abbas' who was the man who promoted them, and each are Fatah Revolutionary Council members. Their professional commitment merges their political affiliation and personal loyalty. Unlike Arafat, who nominated as key security commanders persons that already enjoyed high prestige due to their role before and during the first intifada (Mohammed Dahlan and Jibril Rajoub were Arafat's heads of preventive security in the Gaza Strip and the West Bank, respectively), Abbas appointed professionals, trained by western European and US security experts. They lack their own political power base inside Fatah, are fully loyal to Abbas and enjoy direct access to the president. In addition, in 2009 and 2016 Abbas arranged for the election of his civilian loyalists to Fatah's Revolutionary Council and Central Committee, sidelining his competitor Barghouti and his camp, and excluding his rivals Abu Alaa and Mohammed Dahlan.[24]

As shown earlier, during his many years in the PLO Abbas kept a political and even physical distance from Arafat. Thus, when he succeeded Arafat, Abbas decided to forge his own image and style. However, Abbas has been unable to disconnect himself from his predecessor. Lacking any great leadership credentials, Abbas walks in the path that Arafat paved. Abbas has widened and improved Arafat's political way, but unlike the first PA president, he is not a pioneer, nor a leader that creates new opportunities. Abbas is a Sisyphean leader. He is destined to carry on a mission while his qualifications and international and domestic circumstances make this mission almost impossible to accomplish. The contemporary national movement, wrote Hussein Agha and Ahmad Samih Khalidi in August 2017,[25] is reaching its end. The movement is caught in the trap of Oslo. Its mission is incomplete and suspended. It is failing to liberate the nation, bring good governance or hasten peace. Fatah is divided along lines set by local West Bank interest groups, and is ever further disconnected from those who live outside the territories. Its spirit of activism and dynamism has moved aside. But a national movement requires genuine mass engagement in a political vision and a working project that cuts across boundaries of region, clan and class, along with a defined and acknowledged leadership with the legitimacy and representative standing that empowers it to act in its people's name. 'This no longer holds for Fatah, the Palestinian Authority, or the PLO,' Khalidi and Agha conclude. 'What used to be [under Arafat] a vibrant if fractious political debate, nourished, tolerated, and often exploited by the leadership,' has been turned by Abbas 'into a dull and dismal discourse, steered by political directives, and driven by fear of suppression and the loss of position inside an ever-swelling bureaucracy.'

Abbas' diminishing base of supporters praise him for insisting upon securing the little autonomy that remains in PA hands. In sharp contrast to the way Arafat is remembered, they do not describe him as a mythological hero who successfully opposes much stronger forces, or as a tragic hero that powerful Israeli and American forces will eventually crush. Their attitude corresponds with the post-heroic era that characterised Arafat's funeral. Alternatively, it may be remembered as a pre-heroic time—the break between the revolutionary Arafat and Abbas the successor.

2

# FOREIGN POLICY

## ABBAS, THE DESERTED PEACE SEEKER

*Restricted Foreign Relations*

The two-state solution was not the PLO's first choice. It accepted the Partition Plan in 1988, fifty-one years after the Zionist leadership accepted the Peel Commission plan to divide Palestine between the two struggling national movements, and forty-one years after the UN General Assembly accepted Resolution 181, to establish in Palestine a Jewish state next to an Arab one. The PLO was forced to accept the hard reality that it had neither the required power nor the international legitimacy to conquer Israel. At most, it could get a statelet within the 1967 territories. Israel, on the contrary, started expanding the boundaries of the possible after its mega-victory in the 1967 war. Against international consensus, Israel gradually expanded into the West Bank and Gaza Strip by annexing East Jerusalem and building settlements in the occupied areas. The Oslo Accords institutionalised the race over the occupied territories by creating a level of provisional Palestinian autonomy.

35

Unlike states, this type of autonomy had no power to run foreign relations. Moreover, outside actors would intervene in its domestic affairs. Thus, the PA continues to struggle for both the right to manage foreign relations and to prevent external intervention in its domestic affairs. In the talks on PA powers, from late 1993 to mid-1994, a PLO demand was to let the future PA run foreign relations, which Israel refused. Israel argued that only states enjoy this right, whereas in the Oslo framework accord of September 1993, the sides agreed to postpone Palestinian sovereignty to the permanent status negotiations stage. They compromised on the PA's right to manage foreign relations limited to issues around autonomy. Israel agreed to expand the degree of autonomy that could be exercised in exchange for the donor countries funding it. The Palestinian Authority seized the opportunity to feign statehood and endorsed a state-like structure by putting PLO delegations and embassies under the new PA Ministry of Foreign Affairs.

In his book on the Oslo negotiations Abbas defines sovereignty very broadly. Not only is an entity that enjoys exclusive legal rule and effective control over territory and violence sovereign, argues Abbas, but so also is the PA with its limited powers.[1] He expected, like many inside and outside Palestine, that the limited power the Oslo agreements granted the Palestinians would smoothly develop into full sovereignty. Seeing the future Palestinian independent state on the horizon, he concluded that the nucleus of sovereignty already existed. However, a huge gap exists between the reality on the ground and Abbas' 'as though' perspective and consequent policies.

Abbas surely did not imagine that thirteen years after he became president, and at over eighty-four years old, he would still be asking permission from the Israeli army to exit and enter Ramallah. He also did not imagine that twenty-five years after the signing of the Oslo agreements, of which he was one of the architects, Israelis and Palestinians would find themselves trapped between what is unachievable today—a two-state solution—and what is unrealistic to accomplish—a unitary non-ethnic democracy based on the principle of one-man one-vote. An egalitarian federal state with two ethnic components is also not on the horizon.

Abbas believed that his moderate positions would pay off. The US and western Europe would press Israel to accept a peace agreement along the principles outlined in the 2002 Arab Peace Initiative. This asks Israel to withdraw completely to the 4 June 1967 lines; suggests achieving a just solution to the problem of the Palestinian refugees based on 1948's UN General Assembly Resolution 194; and to accept the establishment of an independent and sovereign Palestinian state with East Jerusalem as its capital. The Arab states, in return, would sign peace agreements with Israel and establish normal relations with her. During his presidency, Abbas has learned that the path is longer than assumed and that the implementation of the Oslo agreements is not a process running on auto-pilot.

The comparison with Arafat's greatest achievements is not exactly flattering to Abbas. The legitimate criticism of Arafat's strategic concessions during Oslo and his naïve assumption that the Oslo interim agreements would inevitably lead to Palestinian independence[2] could not overshadow the success he and his colleagues brought to the national movement. Under Arafat's leadership, they pushed Fatah and the PLO from the margins of the Arab political system to the spotlight without enjoying a solid territorial base from where the PLO could uninterruptedly function. They accomplished this despite the diasporic structure of their society. Through the Oslo agreements, the Palestinian national movement entered from exile into the land it claims sovereignty over, and joined the people it represented. For a diasporic national movement hosted by indifferent, or sometimes hostile and manipulative regimes, this was a remarkable achievement.

Abbas' achievements are modest. He cannot move forward and accomplish liberation in his lifetime. When Abbas looks out of his car windows on his way abroad, he sees how settlements are expanding on the ruins of the Oslo agreements, and he is simply unable to stop it. Israel is working hard to prevent the establishment of a sustainable Palestinian state with territorial contiguity, while deepening the cantonisation of the West Bank that resulted from the Oslo Accords. At best, Abbas saves what can be preserved given the power imbalance with Israel, the changing international order and the chaos of the Arab world since 2011.

*No Israeli Partner*

Fatah was established in 1959 on three inter-related principles that since 1968 also became the PLO's guidelines: self-reliance, liberation and armed struggle. Self-reliance aimed to transform the Palestinian mindset from a mentality of defeat and passiveness to becoming agents of liberation and actors within the pages of history. Arab states were not going to fight for the Palestinians. Self-reliant armed struggle was perceived then as the only way to liberate both Palestine's mentality and its land. Since the mid-1970s, gradually, the political track became the primary or the only way to achieve independence. The outbreak of the first intifada in 1987, initiated by the Palestinian masses in the occupied territories, rendered the PLO's guerrilla and terror operations from neighbouring Arab countries irrelevant. Thus, when the PLO reaped the rewards of the first intifada, that forced Israel to negotiate with the national movement that for decades it had tried to shatter, and then during the peace process years, the PLO changed tactics. The PLO moved from guerrilla and terror operations—carried out in public to achieve maximum psychological impact—to discussing political deals behind closed doors. This strategy ended up, however, counterproductive as the peace process proved a failure, mostly under Abbas' watch. The PA and its president lost public support (see Chapter Three).

Israeli settlement expansion and armed operations inside PA areas since 2000 have stripped political negotiations of nearly any value and have returned the Israeli–Palestinian conflict to its original status—it is once again primarily an ethnic, rather than territorial, conflict. Indeed, the Abbas regime in the West Bank has tried to maintain the overarching framework of the Oslo period—that is, to keep the struggle a border conflict. Yet Israeli military superiority and the failure of any third party to intervene has brought the conflict back to its ethnic origins, albeit in a different form. Due to its demographic and territorial expansion, especially since 2000, and its heavy military response to the second intifada, Israel has already assumed *de facto* control of the entire area stretching from the Jordan River to the Mediterranean Sea. As of 2019, there are more than 600,000 settlers in the West Bank and East Jerusalem, controlling about 60 per cent of the territory (see Appendix 2).[3]

There is a need to distinguish between 'settlements,' defining Israeli Jewish locations beyond the June 1967 armistice lines, and 'settlers' as having material and non-material invested interest in sustaining the project. Not all settlers are 'hawks.' On the other hand, many Israeli Jews, perhaps the majority, are 'settlers' with respect to their nationalist views though they may live outside any settlement. Israel's territorial expansion project and control over the Palestinian population is the largest national project the country has ever carried out. Almost the entire state is invested in this endeavour. This does not refer only to ideological commitment and the transfer of sections of the population into the Palestinian territories, but also the provision of employment for hundreds of thousands, or even millions, of Israelis and the profit gained from the export of technological expertise and security products, which have been developed in order to maintain Israel's control over the Palestinian population and territory.[4] The cost of a peace deal along the lines of the 2002 Arab Peace Initiative would be very high, 'perhaps the greatest political upheaval in the country's history; [with] enormous demonstrations against— if not majority rejection of—Palestinian sovereignty in Jerusalem and over the Temple Mount/Noble Sanctuary; and violent rebellion by some Jewish settlers and their supporters.'[5] Rabin, it should be mentioned, was assassinated for much less than this. He did not evacuate a single settlement nor give up one inch of Jerusalem. For Israel, sustaining her present system of control is the less costly option. Israel has, since 2002, exerted effective control even over those territories that, under the Oslo agreements, were handed over to the exclusive control of the Palestinian Authority. While it does not rule these areas directly as it once did, it controls them by using the PA as a proxy.

The settlers 'import' Israeli law with them to the territories of the West Bank, and it applies to them in the broad legal jurisdictions of the local and regional councils. In addition to the settlers, military, police and intelligence forces are dispersed throughout the area, and their numbers are estimated in the tens of thousands. Israelis who live and serve in the West Bank enjoy a modern system of roads, some of which are for their exclusive use. Officially, 60 per cent of the West Bank (Area C) is administered as an occupied territory by the head of the army's Central Command, but in fact Israeli civil law and Israeli citizens constitute a strong presence there, and this has major significance. At the end of 2017 and the beginning of 2018, the Israeli government initiated measures that would link the settlements, all located in Area C, directly to the Israeli legal system, essentially bypassing the 'intermediate station' of the army Chief of Central Command. Accordingly, a new law moves the academic institutions in the settlements from the authority of the Council for Higher Education in Judea and Samaria that operates under the Chief of Central Command to the authority of the civilian Council for Higher Education.[6] A clear illustration of the new reality in the West Bank can be seen from the refusal of the Israeli cabinet in 2017 to allow the Qalqiliya Municipality to expand in Area C and through gradually building 14,000 new housing units. Qalqiliya is spread over just 4 square kilometres, within which 53,000 people live. The cabinet's refusal was determined by settler pressure, against army and security service recommendations.[7]

Just as Israelis move east of the Green Line, the 'West Bank' (a borrowed term) moves west. Palestinian citizens of Israel, mostly the young and educated, identify as Israeli Palestinians, and not as Israeli Arabs as the Israeli establishment calls them. No less significant, the clashes of the second intifada in 2000 spread to Israel's mixed Jewish–Arab cities, and groups of national-religious Jews, who in the past would have moved to the settlements, are now moving to these cities with the aim of 'Judaising' them.

Hence, the border that existed before the Arab–Israeli war of 1967 (known as the Green Line) exists only in international law textbooks. Israel has been able to gain suzerainty without formally annexing most of the Palestinian territories it gained in the 1967 war. The exception is East Jerusalem, which Israel unilaterally annexed *de jure* following the war, immediately setting out to change its urban fabric. Outside Jerusalem, it has *de facto* annexed Palestinian areas by expanding settlements and building the Separation Barrier inside the West Bank.

Israel's ethnic regime controls the Palestinians (in both Israel and the occupied territories) by implementing differential levels of state supervision, security control, bureaucratic rules, civil rights and citizen benefits. The most fundamental and visible division is the territorial/legal one that divides Palestinians into five groups, the first of which are the Israeli Palestinians, who are Israeli citizens, yet systematically discriminated against by the Jewish-majority regime. In July 2018 the Knesset passed the Jewish Nation State Basic Law that formalises the Jewish identity of the state without providing for equality to non-Jewish minorities. Moreover, it downgrades the status of Arabic from an official language, equal to Hebrew, to 'special' status.[8] Jerusalemite Palestinians, the second group, are permanent residents in Israel but do not have citizenship. Palestinians who reside between the Security Barrier and the Green Line under a special 'temporary permission' compose the third group. Palestinians in the rest of the West Bank, under PA direct rule and indirect Israeli control, are the fourth. The fifth are the Gaza Strip Palestinians whose territory Israel and Egypt, with brief exceptions, have completely closed since 2007.[9] Israel has created a sophisticated system of control to manage and supervise the Palestinian population. This subordinates the occupied territories' population and maintains its dependency on the regime's permission to move in and out of Palestinian cities, to work in Israel or in the settlements, and to import or export. Israel collects data on Palestinians' views, activities, social relations, and private and family life. The extreme dependency Palestinians have on this system of Israeli permissions pushes many to collaborate.[10]

However, not only individuals collaborate. Security cooperation has turned Abbas' regime into Israel's subcontractor. Israel remunerates him by taking care of Hamas—his political rival that won a majority in the 2006 parliamentary elections—in the West Bank. He also, however, receives in turn the continuous expansion of settlements and a lack of Israeli willingness to reach a permanent status agreement. Abbas never had great expectations of Israeli Likud governments; he had hoped the US would shoulder some of the effort by putting pressure on the government in Jerusalem. The US trained and funded the Palestinian security forces and declared that the Palestinians had made good on their side of the deal,[11] but the political assistance from Washington never came. Western and US leaders praise Abbas for keeping in line with their key interest: maintaining the status quo. They invest many financial resources in the PA for that purpose. It is the largest per capita recipient of international aid in the world, with development assistance per person exceeding that of the other top ten aid recipients combined. As the Palestinians' largest aid donor, the European Union alone has contributed 6 billion euros in bilateral cooperation assistance since 1993.[12] The sympathy Abbas enjoys in the West is more pity than an attempt at empowerment to uproot the status quo.

Under Abbas, cooperation with Israel has expanded from security to civil affairs. Beyond cooperation against car thefts, PA officers prefer not to confront the occupier on civil affairs but serve as an interim establishment that transmits Israeli refusals to West Bankers' requests for various permissions, or simply implements the occupation's regulations. Indeed, those PA officers are caught in a lose-lose situation. If they refuse to comply, Israel will cut services, civil society suffers further and the political status of the PA is damaged. Cooperation with the occupation leads to the same political loss.[13]

Mahmoud Abbas was unable to mobilise those within Israeli society to put pressure on various right-wing governments. Since winning the presidency, he has directly addressed Israelis and has said the right things based on his optimistic evaluation that more Israelis would prefer securing a solid Jewish majority than annexing Palestinian territories and creating a single state. Even after the collapse of US Secretary of State John Kerry's mission, Abbas said on Israeli TV that Netanyahu was a partner for peace, denounced violence and declared 'I want to see peace in my life-time... I believe that the people of Israel want peace and that the

Palestinian people want peace.'[14] Contrary to Arafat's style, Abbas believed that speaking clearly and rationally could help Israeli Jews overcome their primary fears, collective trauma and the continual propaganda of the right-wing parties. His reputation as Israel's security partner and a peace seeker would ease his way into Israeli hearts and minds. But instead, Israeli society has responded with scepticism and reelected right-wing governments.

Unlike Arafat, Abbas cannot be charged with using double-talk. He offers Israel peace deals without hiding his heavy criticism of its brutal occupation and military operations. In his speech at the UN General Assembly in September 2014, he vociferously denounced Israel and expressed his frustration at the international community's unwillingness or inability to stop the Israeli aggression against the Gaza Strip a few weeks earlier (codenamed Operation Protective Edge). He spoke 'full of grief, regret and bitterness, raising the same long-standing conclusions and questions after a new war, the third war waged by the racist occupying State in five years against Gaza.' Israel was charged with 'genocidal crime,' one among a series of such crimes. 'Israel refuses to end its occupation of the State of Palestine' and instead suggests to them 'isolated ghettos... under the subjugation of the racist settlers.' Israel had developed a 'culture of racism, incitement and hatred' toward the Palestinians. The Palestinians, on the contrary, want 'peace and building bridges of mutual cooperation with [their] neighbors.'[15] Abbas neither idealises Israel nor bases his peace policy on purifying Israel. He balances the Palestinian peace proposal against Israel's inhumane brutality, which he has even compared with Nazism. Indeed, in UN speeches of other years Abbas chose less aggressive expressions, blaming Israel for being a ruthless colonialist and implementing a policy of ethnic cleansing. The Palestinians are victims, but their peace proposal is not an offer of surrender. Rather, it is the fulfilment of their rights. Abbas has made clear that he is not an anti-Semite. 'Our problem is with the Israeli colonial occupation and not with Judaism as a religion,' he stated at the UN General Assembly in 2017.[16]

Nevertheless, the Israeli public is unable to accept Abbas' peace policy and his unforgiving attitude toward Israeli operations. Abbas' image in Israel's political imagination is more a reflection of that psyche than Abbas himself. The Israeli right views Abbas as a wolf in sheep's clothing,[17] while the centre views him as feeble and unable to subdue the radicals in his camp. His soft style has led the Zionist left to the mistaken conclusion that Abbas will give up on the right of return for Palestinian refugees. Abbas, the refugee from Safed, is unwilling to join the Israeli left in denying his family and his nation's tragedy, but is ready to settle the refugee issue within the solution that envisages two ethnic states. Interestingly, though he was not the first to do so, the centrist Israeli Prime Minister Ehud Olmert changed his mind about Abbas. While they negotiated, he described Abbas as a serious and honest partner. When Abbas did not endorse Olmert's peace deal diktat, the prime minister claimed that Abbas was 'not a big hero.'[18] Unfortunately, conservative Israeli politicians have convinced their constituencies that the Palestinians are incapable of building a peaceful democratic state, Hamas is preparing to take over the West Bank and the PA must accept fundamental Zionist principles in order to render it a legitimate peace partner. Abbas has won the support of the Israeli progressive camp, which, to his chagrin, is not in power or capable of changing the dominant public mindset. The Israelis he agrees with are essentially powerless and their constituency shrinking, while he remains at odds with those who do hold power.

*How to Mismanage Peace Talks*

The Camp David Summit of July 2000 stands as a model of how to make almost every possible mistake in building a peace partnership and still wonder why it then results in catastrophe. Or, in other words, it shows what happens when a gap between highly unrealistic expectations and lousy performance remains unacknowledged.[19] Each side presumed it could achieve its entire agenda in the negotiations. With such high expectations, it became politically untenable to make the required concessions. Each issue became a matter of principle, with symbolic, and not just practical, importance. A mediator that empathised with Israel invited the sides to Camp David too early, when their differences were too great. In addition, each of them played their cards unconstructively. Beside fundamental disagreements on all permanent status issues (borders, sovereignty, Jerusalem, refugees and settlements) gaps existed between the sides' capabilities and approaches.

The Palestinians' lack of organs of statehood precluded the adoption of working procedures typical of governments. The Israelis did not help their Palestinian counterparts, refusing to grant the Palestinians access to its databases, such as aerial photographs of settlements, for the purposes of the territorial negotiations. The lack of political planning, together with low levels of coordination between different PLO branches, encouraged competition between negotiators and office-holders, and kept institutionalisation and organisation at low levels—longstanding characteristics of the PLO's dysfunctional operation. The result was that decision-making was carried out on a personal rather than an institutional basis, allowing Arafat to intervene directly with those at the lower levels of the PLO bureaucracy.

The Palestinian leadership tended to remain passive during negotiations, and pursued no politically costly initiatives. The PLO hoped to bridge the gap between its high expectations and its limited ability to realise them via the 'international legitimacy' of UN decisions, along with their consent to a solution involving a Palestinian state in the 1967 territories—comprising only some

23 per cent of the area of mandatory Palestine—and through American mediation and involvement. Unlike Israel, the Palestinian leadership sought to begin the talks from these principles, and not from the details. This point was important substantively, but all the more so in light of the structural constraints of Palestinian working procedures. Yet, Israel and the US refused to make international law the framework for an agreement. Worse, Arafat did not know how to communicate properly with the Americans.

Like Israeli Prime Minister Ehud Barak, Arafat put together his negotiating team in consultation with a small number of close advisors. However, the lack of a state apparatus put the Palestinian side at a distinct disadvantage. Arafat's principal criteria were political loyalty and the patron-client relationship he had with the appointees. He placed much less weight on experience in previous negotiations and professional expertise. Attempts by the PLO's negotiations department to place their experts in the delegations either failed or were only partially successful. As Omar Dajani wrote from his own experience, the technical and professional assistance teams, led by lawyers from the PLO's negotiations department, were fumbling in the dark. In many cases, the technical staff did not know in advance what issue was to be discussed at a given session and what possibilities the leadership was prepared to entertain, approve, and mould into a formal position. Concessions and compromises were achieved without advance planning, solely in response to negotiating pressures. Sometimes PA and PLO agencies did not provide the teams with information, because conveying it was perceived as giving up prestige and bureaucratic power.

In addition, the Palestinian negotiating teams were large, with little coordination among their members. The teams did not hold preparatory sessions to establish their agenda, devise their priorities, discuss ideas, or establish negotiating tactics. When the leadership met to discuss the negotiations, they made speeches and issued political declarations, but conducted no operative discussion about strategic goals and the tactics for achieving them. No criteria were set for possible concessions. They did not define clear roles and authorities. The result was that every member of the Palestinian negotiating team was involved in the discussions on every issue.

Arafat involved himself in the details of the negotiations and did not give his representatives much freedom of action. He frequently reversed decisions made by the negotiators, or replaced the head of the team. Arafat's management style made the Palestinian negotiators passive—they sought Arafat's approval for every minute step. It also created suspicion and uncertainty among the negotiators, and the consequence was competition between the senior negotiator and those who were potential replacements, and between him and those who conducted parallel negotiations. Each of them wanted to be the one who would close the deal and enter the history books, but at the same time each feared being accused of being weak and of surrendering to Israeli diktats. Some Palestinian negotiators displayed considerable flexibility in private talks, where they sought to promote an agreement, but took a hard line in official sessions. In practice, the Israelis and Americans received contradictory messages that made them doubt whether the Palestinians were serious and sincere.

The Israeli team, however, included establishment figures and experienced negotiators. Israel's working procedures were, in contrast, efficient and professional—that is, characteristic of an established state. Invariably, the Israelis tabled proposals, thus setting the agenda. Their red lines, and the low price they were prepared to pay, became the starting points. The asymmetric power relations of the Oslo period were thus reproduced in the negotiations, instead of being replaced by an exchange between equals and joint decision-making. Israel's attitude put the

Palestinians on the defensive, so at Camp David they adopted a strategy of survival in the face of Israel and the US, and with consideration to their own public opinion at home.

Israeli positions were shaped by military personnel keeping key political and negotiating positions and maintaining military patterns of thinking. The Arabs, and most of all the Palestinians, were permanently suspect, and no third-party guarantees were to be trusted. Israel had to secure itself against every threat and could not take any significant risks. It needed to play tough in negotiations, and give preference to the short term over long-term goals. Israeli negotiators were blunt and condescending, impatient and unwilling to listen. The Palestinians felt humiliated. The military ethos makes the Israeli side goal-oriented, interested in practical details rather than abstract principles or legal and formal questions. Territory was conceived of in practical military terms, such as topography and what areas must be demilitarised, rather than in symbolic and emotional terms. The typical Israeli negotiator equips himself with maps, charts, quantitative data and presentations. He expresses himself with great self-confidence and eschews sentiment. Israel tends to solve diplomatic problems by military means, and prefers the defeat of a rival to compromise. If necessary, Israel will mislead its rivals, make large numbers of demands, and exert heavy and ongoing pressure. Israel's diplomats use ideas and proposals the way its army uses exploratory fire—to probe, expose and exploit the enemy's weaknesses. It uses divide-and-rule tactics to dominate the opposing negotiating team. The goal is to obtain the maximum gains in exchange for minimal concessions. Each concession is perceived as a sign of weakness and capitulation, rather than as a consensus-building act and a means of achieving mutual gain. For the Israelis, Palestinian weakness is an opportunity to be exploited, and a fact to be perpetuated in the agreement. This was diametrically opposed to Palestinian expectations. Israel's goal was to push the Palestinians into a corner so that they would make the concessions that Israel sought. Israel had suspicions about how serious Palestinian intentions were, about the professionalism of the Palestinian partner in negotiations, and about the Palestinian negotiators' ability to display flexibility and to stand behind the commitments they made. Israel had no hesitation about manoeuvring between the personal interests of the Palestinian negotiators and manipulating them in accordance with their rivalries, the organisations they represented, and the internal rifts that divided them.[20]

The Palestinian team's preparatory work improved after the failure of the Camp David talks and continued to improve under Abbas. Most of the improvement after Camp David came by virtue of the much greater involvement of professional experts in the negotiations, and the establishment of goals and red lines by the Palestinian leadership. Professional input became vital as the discussions became focused on more pragmatic issues.

The last three Israeli prime ministers have been very different from Abbas in both their personality and their political positions. They have been energetic, dominant, charismatic and manipulative. They are driven by political struggles, enjoy the company of their comrades and take care to maintain social contacts with followers and associates. Abbas, on the other hand, is drab, lacking all charisma, sense of humour or charm. His rare public speeches do not provoke high expectations, and the audience are not exactly electrified when he enters the hall. He is a lone wolf, has few friends and dislikes political or social intermingling. His approach is all business, and he avoids confrontation. Whereas these Israeli prime ministers constantly played with facts and tactically changed positions to the extent that it was hard to identify when the change was strategic, Abbas is different. He takes strategic decisions and sticks to them. He is stubborn, and unlike Arafat he does not forget or forgive those who betray him or lose his confidence. To this day Abbas remains ready to meet his Israeli counterparts or their envoys and try to convince them to change their minds. Unlike Arafat, who doubted his Israeli counterparts' intentions, Abbas, observed Ron Pundak, one of the Oslo Agreement's architects, is inclined to trust their good will.[21] Abbas met with Sharon, Netanyahu and Olmert. He achieved nothing from Sharon, secured prisoner releases from Netanyahu—though many of them were criminals rather than the freedom fighters Abbas had expected (see below)—and together with Olmert advanced negotiations and the makings of a peace deal.

Sharon insisted on unilaterally evacuating settlements from the Gaza Strip in 2005, strongly rejecting proposals to coordinate this with Abbas or let him enjoy any achievement from the Israeli disengagement. Sharon disparaged Abbas and called him a chick without any feathers. Hamas exploited this during its 2006 election campaign, claiming that one year of its armed struggle achieved more than Abbas could in all his years of negotiations. Abbas did not mislead himself and assume Sharon could be a partner of any peace deal. 'By rebuilding Palestinian institutions and the national movement, genuinely renouncing violence, rekindling international ties and clearly articulating basic and unalterable Palestinian requirements, he believes that the post-Sharon stage can be prepared for or even accelerated and that, meanwhile, his people will benefit from new and long-awaited tranquillity,' according to Robert Malley and Hussein Agha's assessment of Abbas' policy at that time.[22] However, the gap between pretending to run a state-like entity and the deepening occupation on the ground drained Abbas' policy of its meaning. The public, consequently, became cynical and alienated, critical, or desperate.[23]

Indeed, Abbas and Olmert, who succeeded Sharon, made serious progress in early 2008. But unlike the perception the two leaders created retrospectively, they were not within touching distance of a final status agreement. Their opinions remained divided on substantial issues (see Appendix 1). Olmert and Abbas managed intimate negotiations and succeeded in building mutual trust. Olmert strayed from his rightist origins but made his journey too late. In addition, Foreign Minister Tzipi Livni and Defence Minister Ehud Barak advised him to wait for them be re-elected with a fresh mandate. Without any political support from Livni and Barak and with Olmert's legitimacy deficit, he was simply unable to bridge the remaining fundamental gaps with Abbas. Olmert was on the verge of being removed due to corruption allegations, arriving on the heels of criticism from the Winograd Commission of inquiry on his decisions leading to and during the 2006 war in Lebanon. The talks ended when Olmert put on the table a unilateral 'take it or leave it' proposal. Although gaps on substance continued to exist between Olmert and Abbas, Olmert's proposal could have been the basis for the next stage of negotiations and brought the sides close to a possible agreement. However, trying to save his position and legacy, Olmert needed the deal done immediately whereas Abbas preferred to receive clarifications on key issues that Olmert kept vague. Abbas had learned the lesson of his talks with Netanyahu for the Wye River Memorandum in 1998, which included a clause on prisoner releases. Abbas did not pay close enough attention or naïvely assumed that Netanyahu, like him, intended to release Palestinian terrorists (for the Israelis) or prisoners of war (for the Palestinians). When, of the 250 released, 150 were simple criminals, Abbas faced serious criticism at home.[24]

Abbas took into consideration the division with Hamas when he negotiated with Israel. He was ready to consider signing a comprehensive agreement that would be first implemented in the West Bank with Fatah, and afterward expanded to Gaza where Hamas ruled. This tactical flexibility had two aims. First, it sought to not let Israel use the domestic split as an excuse to escape negotiations. Second, if successful in the West Bank it would pressure Hamas to accept Abbas' deal. Nevertheless, what he consistently rejected, even as tactical manoeuvres, were Oslo-style new interim agreements, a mini-Palestinian state in the West Bank with provisional borders (as the Quartet's road map suggested in 2002), a peace agreement that excluded a Palestinian capital in East Jerusalem, or ignoring the right of return.

According to Netanyahu, Abbas refuses to recognise the Jewish state within any borders, and thus proves that the Palestinians do not want to solve the conflict. By rejecting Trump's decision to recognise Jerusalem as the capital of Israel and transfer the American embassy from Tel Aviv to Jerusalem, 'he has revealed his true beliefs,' the Israeli Prime Minister said. 'He has torn off the mask and shown to the public the truth that I have been working to instil for many long years: The root of the conflict between us and the Palestinians is their steadfast refusal to recognise the Jewish state in any borders whatsoever.' Thus, 'without change in Abbas's professed stance there can be no peace.'[25] In other words, any peace-seeking position Abbas professes is a mask unless he fully accepts Netanyahu's demand. What Netanyahu expects from Abbas is surrender, not compromise. Naturally, Abbas' talks with Netanyahu have been empty and defined by their deep mutual mistrust. Abbas has entered them in the hopes of winning over the American envoys, first and foremost Secretary of State Kerry under President Obama, who unsuccessfully managed the shuttle diplomacy between the two leaders.

Abbas' negative image increased following his speech to the Palestinian National Council in April 2018, in which he concluded that the Jews were not massacred in the Holocaust because of their race, ethnicity or religion, but due to their preponderance in the moneylending profession. Thus, the European

Jews brought the Holocaust upon themselves by their social behaviour.[26] Ignoring the Nazi race doctrine, Abbas' statement was historically false (on Abbas' historical narrative, see below), and counterproductive politically. Netanyahu tweeted 'apparently a Holocaust-denier remains a Holocaust-denier,' who out of ignorance and audacity echoes 'the most contemptible anti-Semitic slogans.'[27] In addition to Israeli denouncements, the EU, the UN Special Coordinator for the Middle East Peace Process, and the governments of Germany and Sweden condemned Abbas. 'No doubt he feels embittered and besieged on all sides,' the *New York Times* editorial wrote, 'But by succumbing to such dark, corrosive instincts he showed that it is time for him to leave office.'[28] Abbas acknowledged his error. 'If people were offended by my statement, especially people of the Jewish faith, I apologize to them,' Abbas announced three days later, trying to conduct some damage control:

> I would like to assure everyone that it was not my intention to do so, and to reiterate my full respect for the Jewish faith, as well as other monotheistic faiths. I would also like to reiterate our long held condemnation of the Holocaust, as the most heinous crime in history, and express our sympathy with its victims. Likewise, we condemn anti-Semitism in all its forms, and confirm our commitment to the two-state solution, and to live side by side in peace and security.[29]

His apology had no impact. Abbas, in the eyes of Israelis and many outsiders, is ending his political career in the same fashion as his predecessor—isolated, though not physically, and illegitimate.

## *Abbas's Historical Narrative*

Given the topic of his dissertation, Abbas considers himself the PLO's expert on Jewish and Zionist history. In 1982 Abbas submitted his PhD thesis to Moscow's Patrice Lumumba University under the title 'The Secret Relationship between Nazism and Zionism.' In it, Abbas claimed that the Zionist movement enjoyed close ties with Germany's pre-World War II Nazi regime and cast doubt upon the number of six million Jews murdered in the Holocaust. In this, as in following articles published in the 1980s, his perception of Zionism was well within the Arab mainstream. Western imperialism, and first and foremost the British Empire, created Zionism as a means to take over the region. However, against the Arab consensus, Abbas drew a sharp distinction between Judaism and Zionism. The latter was a modern racist movement that differed from classical Judaism. Abbas wrote at length on Arab Jews arguing that they were, like the Palestinians, victims of Zionist racism. Without manipulating them into immigrating to Israel, the Zionist movement would have been unable to achieve its goal. Unlike many Arabs who rejected Israel's very existence and refused to study its history and politics, Abbas believed in knowing the country in order to learn how to confront it. He argued that Israel would not disappear overnight. Had Arab states taken back their Jews, and provided them with full citizenship, equality and compensation, he believed, Israel would have collapsed. Alternatively, in the 1980s, he suggested two avenues through which to implement the Palestinian national project: Palestinian armed struggle and a Soviet Union-led political struggle.[30] History showed that both failed. Consequently, Abbas changed his political conclusions but not his historical perspective.

In late 2017 and early 2018, following President Trump's decision to recognise Jerusalem as the capital of Israel and transfer the American embassy there (see below), a resolute Abbas confronted the Zionist and American narratives. In a series of speeches,[31] he updated his earlier historical arguments aiming to reshape the Palestinian collective mind.

Abbas reiterated the national myth that the first Palestinians were the Canaanites and the Jebusites, to prove that the

Palestinians were in Palestine long before the Jews. They were, in fact, the sole legitimate natives of that land which belongs only to them. Abbas turned history upside down by arguing that the Canaanites and Jebusites were not just proto-Palestinians, but also Arabs. The Arabs had not in fact conquered Palestine in the seventh century AD and brought Islam and Arabic; they were there from time immemorial.

Following Arthur Koestler's groundless theory, Abbas argued that the Ashkenazi Jews were descendants of the Khazars, a Turkic tribe from central Asia that moved to Europe after converting to Judaism. They differ from the Semitic Jews that Abbas sees as the original Jews. These—the Oriental, or Arab, Jews—had maintained good relations with their Arab neighbours, unlike the Ashkenazi Jews that served imperialist and colonial powers. Jewish nationalism is driven by a fictitious European identity that did not arise through a Jewish collective consciousness, but was manufactured by those powers.

Abbas believes, as do many Arabs, that the Palestinians do not struggle solely against the Zionists; they are victims of worldwide imperialist-colonialist collaboration. The Zionists are foreigners. The imperialist/colonialist West, and specifically Cromwellian Britain, invented Zionism in 1653 to serve its expansionist plans through sending Jews to settle in Palestine, but failed. Following his unsuccessful campaign to occupy Acer in 1799, Napoleon Bonaparte also utilised Zionism for the same purpose, and failed as well. Abbas wrongly refers to Theodor Herzl, the founder of the Jewish Zionist movement, as the person who coined the popular Zionist motto: a land without a people for a people without a land. Herzl designed the Zionist strategy of cooperating with colonial powers to take over Palestine from its people and change its identity. Zionist–imperialist cooperation produced the Balfour Declaration in 1917 in which Britain promised a land it did not own nor have any attachment to, to a people who did not belong there.

Supported by its First World War allies, Britain was the force behind the colonisation of Palestine by the Zionists, a part of its divide-and-rule strategy for the Arabs. However, until the Holocaust the number of Jews immigrating to Palestine remained low simply because it was not their land. Following the Holocaust and the 1948 war, Israel brought uprooted Oriental Jews to take the place of the Palestinian refugees, though the Israeli Ashkenazi elite also discriminated against these newcomers. Thus, they too are victims of Zionism like the Palestinians, and are potential political allies.

The shift came with the foundation of the PLO, which Abbas sees as the most significant moment in the history of the Palestinian people since 1948. The PLO turned the Palestinians from passive victims to active agents in their own liberation. The PLO's decision in 1988 to build a state on the territories Israel occupied in 1967 and to accept the 1947 UN partition plan, Abbas reminded his critics, enjoyed national consensus. 'I did not violate [these principles]... and we are committed to them up to this day.'[32] Palestine in its entirety is the Palestinians' homeland, Abbas stressed. They lost the territory they held in 1948 to much stronger enemies, but thanks to international law and the PLO's policy, they might yet regain that lost in 1967.

Trump's policy is rooted in American cooperation with European colonialism. Already by 1850, Abbas argues, the American Council in Jerusalem was in favour of establishing a Jewish state. Later the Americans supported, together with France and Italy, the Balfour Declaration and Britain's pro-Zionist policy. Nazi Germany, too, had a share in the anti-Palestinian conspiracy. In 1933, it concluded the Transfer Agreement with the Zionists, according to which German Jews were permitted to emigrate to Palestine with a limited portion of their possessions. After the war, US President Truman recognised Israel immediately when the British mandate forces left.

The Camp David summit of 2000 was an American conspiracy with Israel to offer the PLO less than 100 per cent of the territory occupied in 1967 and allow the Jews to establish a prayer space inside the al-Aqsa compound. Abbas' conspiracy theory was even to include the Arab Spring—an American attempt to redraw the Middle East's political map by inciting civil wars and dividing Arab states into ethnic and tribal mini-states. It is impossible to resolve the contradiction between this image of the US and Abbas' high expectations of President Obama's mediation efforts. No less peculiar is his cooperation with the Bush administration a few years prior. Abbas' politics, thus, do not necessarily follow his historical narrative.

Abbas, perspective on Jerusalem is the mirror image of Netanyahu's. He does not relate to Jerusalem merely as a city where people live, study and commute, nor as a historical or archaeological monument. Jerusalem symbolises over 5,000 years of continuous Palestinian civilisation. It is a locus of identity rather than a material reality; a spiritual entity that shapes Palestinian consciousness and lives, being the city where God gave Prophet Muhammad the eternal Holy Qur'an with its universal message. Achieving the liberation of Jerusalem is the key to worldwide peace and harmony. Based on its holiness to the three monotheistic religions, Jerusalem should be an open city where freedom of worship is guaranteed, under Palestinian sovereignty.

Following his writings in the 1980s, the PA president opposes the popular Arab view, and the Zionist and Israeli self-perception, where Zionism is the present national incarnation of Judaism. Abbas stresses that Zionism has nothing to do with Judaism. Palestinians oppose Zionism, but are not anti-Jewish. Moreover, he often reminds his people that Jerusalem is holy for Jews also, and that honourable Jews reject the Zionist argument that Muslims abandoned Jerusalem upon changing the direction of their prayer to Mecca, while Jews remained faithful to their holy city.

The fundamental mistakes that Abbas made in his narrative show that he is far from the professional historian he claims to be. In addition to ignoring the racist Nazi doctrine behind the Holocaust, Abbas did not follow the historical consensus in distinguishing between the hatred of Jews in medieval Europe (due to their high profile in tax collection and moneylending) and very different circumstances that characterised Nazi Germany. Moreover, he argued that Stalin was a Jew, and followed Arthur Koestler's unreliable theory. Most embarrassing for the PLO Chairman was his error regarding the National Council vote in 1988. In his PLO National Council speech of April 2018,[33] Abbas argued that in 1988 only 10 or 15 out of the 736 Council members opposed the PLO's new political platform. However, the Council then had 309 members, with 253 voting in favour, 46 against and 10 abstaining. No one around Abbas corrected him. Most probably, they also did not remember the numbers.

In conclusion, Abbas's narrative is actually the mirror image of the hegemonic Israeli narrative. However, unlike Netanyahu, who is consistent, his policies fundamentally contradict his historical perspective. 'We do not want to kill you [Israelis]. We call for coexistence,' Abbas stated in the PLO National Council. Abbas' contradictions catch him in a lose-lose position. Israeli right-wing governments judge Abbas based on his narrative, not his politics. At home, Abbas' narrative does not protect him politically. He faces heavy criticism for his policies, in particular on security cooperation with Israel and insisting upon continuing a futile political process.

*No Honest Broker*

Right-wing Israeli governments aim to de-politicise the Palestinians, whereas Abbas wishes to enhance their international political status. He believes rationality and moderation will pay off and lead the international community to support establishing an independent Palestinian state, in particular at times when the occupation intensifies. Answering Israeli brutality with Palestinian violence is counterproductive. This weakens the Palestinians internationally, provides justifications for tough Israeli reactions and unites Israeli society behind its right-wing leaders. Political pressure on Israel is Abbas' only hope for gaining independence, but he does not have the tools nor the ability to push the West to leverage this.

Abbas is at a disadvantage competing with Israel over the hearts and minds of American administrations and their publics. His interests and cultural background are entirely different from those that a Western audience consumes or appreciates. George W. Bush and Condoleezza Rice personally liked Ariel Sharon and Ehud Olmert, but not Abbas. The cold relationship between Obama and Netanyahu, and the sharp differences in their personalities, did not translate to closer relations between Abbas and the liberal president. The Israelis 'were never sincere in their commitment to peace,' Benjamin Rhodes, one of Obama's closest foreign policy advisers, told the *New Yorker*. 'They used us as cover, to make it look like they were in a peace process. They were running a play, killing time, waiting out the Administration.' Abbas, however, did not turn this mistrust to his favour.[34] Actually, it is hard to conclude whose failure is greater: Arafat in Camp David in 2000, when he destroyed his relationship with President Clinton, or Abbas during 2009–16, when he failed to exploit the deep divide between Obama and Netanyahu. Furthermore, pro-Israel and Christian fundamentalist lobbies have imported the Israeli–Palestinian conflict to become a domestic issue in American political life. Abbas' position in Washington DC's Congress and Senate is far inferior to that of Israel, which enjoys the services of a powerful pro-Israel lobby and the religiously motivated support of the Christian Zionists.

Abbas' attempts at speaking to the Americans and the Europeans were a default position, based on pragmatism. Until the end of the 1980s, he depended on the Soviet Union. His turn to the West came only after the collapse of the Soviet bloc, and his acknowledgment that considering its demography, political power and military might, Israel was not going to collapse. It would be better for the Palestinians to aim to live alongside Israel in their small independent state. To achieve this they would have to rely solely on political pressure. Abbas gave up on the romantic nationalism to which he was so committed during the 1960s and 1970s, coming to realise that the armed struggle, and in particular the terror of the second intifada, only harmed Palestinian interests.

So long as Israel slows down settlement expansion, and Palestinian popular protest is limited to no more than a few localised clashes, the international community is satisfied with an absent or illusory peace process. Both the US and Europe are not ready to face radical changes in the status quo, be this security and administrative chaos in the Palestinian territories in the context of another intifada, nor impose on Israel peace agreement parameters that it strongly rejects.

When Abbas shared his frustration with Israel's policy with American secretaries of state—Condoleezza Rice under George W. Bush, and Hillary Clinton and John Kerry under Barack Obama—and warned that he was considering compromising with Hamas, the US reacted (behind closed doors) with a big stick and a small carrot. Without mincing words, the US on several occasions threatened to cut all relations with the PA and cause his downfall. Israeli top security officials privately expressed a similar massage on behalf of their government. To soften this stick, the US promised Abbas that it would pressure Israel and play an active role in the peace process. Publicly, however, US representatives expressed their great admiration for Abbas' leadership.[35]

The Obama administration's primary goal was to prevent escalation. It put pressure on Netanyahu to freeze settlement expansion and when this failed, the US limited their condemnation of
settlement and annexation activity to that in Greater Jerusalem.
Instead, it asked Netanyahu to release Palestinian prisoners as a
confidence-building measure while Secretary Kerry tried to
resume the peace process. The US asked Abbas to maintain security coordination with Israel, not to apply for state membership
in international organisations and not to join the International
Criminal Court to pursue Israel. Abbas complied in the hope
that the US would side with him on most of the final status
issues, or at least would not blame him for causing the failure of
negotiations. Acknowledging the huge gap on core issues
between the sides, achieving a comprehensive peace agreement
was not the first priority of President Obama, nor his Secretary
of State Hillary Clinton. On the contrary, her successor John
Kerry tried hard to establish a foundation on which to enable the
resumption of talks toward a permanent agreement, but could
not work this out.

Kerry's failure was inevitable. He accepted Netanyahu's position as a point of departure, despite his administration's suspicion
that the Israeli prime minister was not sincere but playing for
time while settlements could expand. Only late into Obama's
second term did the president and Secretary Kerry's eyes open to
see the obvious, that was by this point well covered in the media,
discussed by civil society organisations and reported on by settlement watch lobbies. 'We knew this [the expansion of settle-
ments] all along,' said former senior State Department official
Frank Lowenstein. 'I just couldn't figure out how to explain it to
people until I saw those maps,' which illustrated to Kerry and
Obama the reality of Israeli entrenchment in the West Bank.[36]

Abbas, on the other side, had lost all faith in the administration's efforts. 'You've been telling me to wait, and telling me to

wait, and telling me to wait,' Abbas told the Americans. 'You can't deliver the Israelis.'[37] Abbas insisted on the internationally agreed 4 June 1967 borders and UN resolutions as his terms of reference. In addition, Abbas wanted to continue from where he and Olmert had ended, but both Kerry and Netanyahu disagreed.

After leaving office Secretary Kerry admitted that he felt 'genuinely passionate about Israel' and Zionism. Motivated by his care 'for the long-term ability of Israel to be able to be what it has dreamt of being and what the people of Israel, I believe, want it to be,' Kerry said, 'I have talked to Bibi Netanyahu more than 375 times… That's only the public recording, because I was in the habit of picking up the phone and calling him at home or calling him here and there and just getting him eating. I've talked to him in those public transactions more than 130 hours.' Kerry travelled to Israel 'over 40 times… I've met Bibi in Rome for eight hours at a time. I've met him in New York. I've met him in Israel, met him in Jerusalem, met him in Tel Aviv, met him everywhere—New York multiple times. And Bibi and I are friends.'[38] Kerry's honest presentation was an apology for debating with the Israeli prime minister while holding a fundamentally pro-Israel stance. He did not express similar empathy towards Palestinian nationalism, or use the 'tough love' strategy that, according to Aaron David Miller, former assistant to the US secretary of state, would be necessary to move Israel away from her hardline positions.[39]

As a result of Kerry's pressure in 2013, Abbas relaxed the conditions for entering negotiations with Israel, for example by replacing the demand for a settlement freeze as a confidence building measure with a prisoner release in three portions, according to a list that Israel would draw up. His main objective remained gaining US support for the final permanent status agreement. Abbas hoped that the US would respond positively to his security cooperation with Israel. Were moderation, rationalism and justice not the principles that guided US political discourse? He was to be disappointed. The document formulated by Kerry in early 2014 to form a basis for the Israeli–Palestinian talks was very different from that for which Abbas had hoped.

It is worth looking into this case in detail. Following the example of the secret Oslo channel that Abbas coordinated in Tunis, he believed that only secret talks could bear fruit. With American help, two special envoys thus entered into negotiations in 2013, far from the public eye. Attorney Yitzhak Molcho represented Netanyahu and Hussein Agha was Abbas' representative. Based on these talks Kerry and his team formulated a document that was presented to Abbas in the winter of 2014. It accepted Netanyahu's demand that the Palestinians recognise Israel as the nation-state of the Jewish people. To satisfy Abbas, who was afraid that such a recognition would give Israel a green light to continue discriminating against its Palestinian citizens, the document conditioned this with Israel preserving national and religious minorities' rights. Since Netanyahu refused to consider the 1967 Israeli–Jordanian Armistice line as the basis for the future Israeli–Palestinian border, the document was vague. It said that Palestine's territorial size would correspond with the area Jordan ruled until the 1967 war. Interestingly, the term 'correspondence,' used by Kerry in 2014, is close to the term 'similar' that—for a short period during 2010—Netanyahu allowed President Peres to deploy in his talks with Abbas (see Chapter One). However, Netanyahu invalidated his territorial concession by not agreeing to the principle that Palestine would have territorial contiguity nor to any land swaps between West Bank settlements (that Israel could annex) in exchange for Israeli sovereign territories. The American team rejected Netanyahu's reservations on these issues, but he did not give up. The main problem for Abbas in the American document were the parameters on Jerusalem. It did not include the principle that East Jerusalem would be the Palestinian capital. Instead, it stated that each of the two sides wished to achieve international recognition of Jerusalem as their capital. Abbas reacted angrily when Kerry presented this to him in Paris. He had other reservations as well. The document did not fix a deadline for an Israeli withdrawal from Palestinian territory, nor settle the 1948 refugee issue along the terms he had hoped. The American team, therefore, softened the document. The new version said that the Palestinian side would recognise Israel as the homeland of the Jewish people only after all core issues were solved. This document stated that East Jerusalem would be the capital of Palestine but that the status of the Old City, the Holy Sites and the Israeli settlements in Jerusalem would remain open for future negotiations. In other words, Kerry's document did not include the guiding principle, which featured in President Clinton's parameters, that Jewish areas would be under Israeli control and Arab areas, including in the Old City, under Palestinian control. In his meeting with Obama in March 2014 Abbas rejected the American document.[40]

In his farewell speech, in December 2016, Secretary Kerry presented the principles that guided his mission.[41] 'No changes by Israel to the 1967 lines will be recognized by the international community unless agreed to by both sides,' he stated. From Abbas' point of view, this was insufficient. Kerry omitted the removal of settlements, Palestine's contiguity and viability, and the limited 1:1 land swaps for settlements that Israel preferred to retain. Abbas could have agreed with Kerry's second principle that the PLO had already accepted in 1988: 'Fulfill the vision of the UN General Assembly Resolution 181 of two states for two peoples, one Jewish and one Arab, with mutual recognition and full equal rights for all their respective citizens.'

To some extent the third principle is in keeping with the March 2002 Arab Peace Initiative[42] that Abbas welcomed: 'Provide for a just, agreed, fair, and realistic solution to the

Palestinian refugee issue, with international assistance, that includes compensation, options and assistance in finding permanent homes, acknowledgment of suffering, and other measures necessary for a comprehensive resolution consistent with two states for two peoples.' Yet the Kerry Principles ignored the right of return and UN General Assembly Resolution 194, each of which were included in the Arab Peace Initiative. Both are essential ingredients for Abbas.

The fourth principle in Secretary Kerry's speech, on Jerusalem, remained vague, as it was when Kerry met Abbas: 'Provide an agreed resolution for Jerusalem as the internationally recognized capital of the two states, and protect and assure freedom of access to the holy sites consistent with the established status quo.' Thus, Kerry withdrew from President Clinton's parameters providing for the division of sovereignty in Jerusalem, including in the Old City and the Temple Mount.[43]

On previous occasions Abbas had already agreed to the fifth principle: 'Satisfy Israel's security needs and bring a full end, ultimately, to the occupation, while ensuring that Israel can defend itself effectively and that Palestine can provide security for its people in a sovereign and non-militarized state.' In his speech, Secretary Kerry revealed that American experts, in coordination with Israeli military leaders, had prepared a detailed proposal for implementing this principle.

The US was unwilling to impose these principles, said Kerry. 'We can only encourage them to take this path; we cannot walk down it for them.' Thus, the power imbalance between the sides remained intact. At most, Kerry tried to reach the Israeli public over the head of Netanyahu and his coalition. He hoped to convince the Israelis that his principles were in accordance with their long-term interests:

> The truth is that trends on the ground... are combining to destroy hopes for peace on both sides and increasingly cementing an irrevers-

ible one-state reality... So if there is only one state, you would have millions of Palestinians permanently living in segregated enclaves in the middle of the West Bank, with no real political rights, separate legal, education, and transportation systems, vast income disparities, under a permanent military occupation that deprives them of the most basic freedoms. Separate and unequal is what you would have. And nobody can explain how that works. Would an Israeli accept living that way? Would an American accept living that way? Will the world accept it?

Up until Kerry's speech, the Obama administration's response to settlement expansion was that it was jeopardising the two-state solution. In his assertion that the settlements were creating a racist regime, Kerry moved the public debate from the possible future to the present. The alternative to his principles, Kerry argued, was systematised Israeli racism, or apartheid. However, with the Trump administration protecting an ever-more right-wing Israel, and western Europe keeping a low profile (see below), his warning did not capture public attention beyond a few human rights activists.

It is unclear whether John Kerry naïvely assumed that many Israelis were willing to impose his principles on their government, or voluntarily give up the privileges born of occupation. In either case, he failed spectacularly. The Israeli public remained indifferent to the questions Kerry put on the table. Kerry also disappointed Abbas who became bitter and frustrated seeing the superpower unable or unwilling to impose its plan on a client state. Indeed, it was not the first time that the US disappointed him. 'In autumn 1999, in the aftermath of Ehud Barak's election as Israel's prime minister,' write Robert Malley and Hussein Agha, Abbas presented US officials with his final status principles:

a Palestinian state within the borders of 4 June 1967; East Jerusalem as its capital; and recognition of the principle of the refugees' right of return. Within those parameters, and consistent with international legality, he left room for discussion. There would be minor and equitable swaps of land to take account of some Israeli settlements; provisions to allow Jews unimpeded access to their holy sites; and the right of return would be implemented in a manner that would not threaten Israel's demographic interests.

Abbas suggested basing the Camp David talks in 2000 on these principles. 'The US and Israel ignored his suggestion. Negotiations followed a bazaar-like route of posturing and deal-making.'[44] He was therefore relieved to leave the Camp David summit for his son's wedding.

Abbas' line was bolstered in December 2016 when the UN Security Council accepted Resolution 2334. The resolution 'reaffirms that the establishment by Israel of settlements in the Palestinian territory occupied since 1967, including East Jerusalem, has no legal validity and constitutes a flagrant violation under international law and a major obstacle to the achievement of the two-state solution and a just, lasting and comprehensive peace.' The resolution also 'reiterates its demand that Israel immediately and completely cease all settlement activities in the occupied Palestinian territory, including East Jerusalem.' The Council 'underlines that it will not recognize any changes to the 4 June 1967 lines, including with regard to Jerusalem, other than those agreed by the parties through negotiations.' Unprecedentedly it 'calls upon all States, bearing in mind paragraph 1 of this resolution, to distinguish, in their relevant dealings, between the territory of the State of Israel and the territories occupied since 1967.'[45] Fourteen out of fifteen Security Council members supported the resolution while the US abstained. By not opposing, Obama allowed the resolution to pass. It was certainly an achievement for Abbas' diplomacy, but the US was less interested in benefitting Abbas than punishing Netanyahu for placing obstacles to John Kerry's mission, ignoring US warnings that settlement expansion was making the two state solution impossible, and for intervening in US domestic politics by explicitly lining up with the Republican Party against the Obama administration.[46]

Abbas' major accomplishment took place four years earlier, in 2012, when, despite US opposition, the UN General Assembly upgraded the status of Palestine to a non-member observer state. In December 2014, Abbas tried to go one step further and get the UN Security Council to support Palestine's full membership bid. The US deployed its veto and the resolution was rejected. Abbas' strategy of internationalising the conflict's resolution has failed not only due to the US. Pressing matters occupy the western Europeans' agenda: illegal immigration and refugees; growing Muslim domestic radicalism; the war on ISIS; Putin's foreign policy and the Ukraine crisis; the rise of conservative-authoritarian regimes in the heart of Europe; and Brexit and the future of the Eurozone (more on this below).

As an alternative, Abbas asked parliaments in western Europe for virtual recognition of a Palestinian state. Twelve parliaments acquiesced, mainly as a protest against Netanyahu's policies. Only one Western government, Sweden, recognised the PA as a state. Abbas also appealed to the International Criminal Court in the Hague, accusing Israel of committing war crimes. These tactics did not, and most probably will not, bring about Palestinian independence; they merely keep alive the desire for independence, which may be realised, hopefully, by the next leader.

Since the PA does not have the advantage of a state, Abbas could use Arab interstate political cooperation—so as long as it was functioning, meaning prior to the civil wars in Syria, Libya, Yemen and Iraq—to push the West to pressure Israel. Moreover, financially and politically the PA is entirely dependent on other countries and international organisations. Abbas needs the backing of Arab leaders to stand up to internal criticism by Hamas, while the parliament elected in 2006 is paralysed and there is no elected body to legitimise his actions. With the Arab League deeply divided he is left with limited options.

Mubarak's downfall in 2011 and the immobilised Arab League left Abbas without a political umbrella. He has cooperated with Egyptian President Sisi against Hamas in the Gaza Strip, and with King Abdullah in Jordan to block the Israeli national-religious government's initiatives to change the prayer arrangements on the Temple Mount.[47] As opposed to Arafat, who dislodged Jordan from the management of the site—and rendered meaningless the clause in the peace agreement between Israel and Jordan,[48] which gave the latter preferred status over the holy places in the city—in 2013 a weakened Abbas let Jordan be the guardian of Muslim holy sites in Jerusalem, first and foremost on the Temple Mount. In exchange, Jordan recognised Palestinian sovereignty over East Jerusalem, if and when it comes to pass.[49]

Abbas is in trouble. Unlike Arafat, he is not an adventurist or revolutionary leader. After a decade and a half in office, politics for him is the art of the possible, where all desirable outcomes are impossible. Israel and the US, and by default Europe, have prevented the realisation of the two-state solution, the scenario in which he deeply believes and with which he identifies. At the same time, he is unwilling to switch to pushing for a bi-national state or accepting Israeli rule. His speech to the UN General Assembly, in September 2015, reflected this dead end. He demanded Israel take full responsibility for its occupation given the unsustainable status quo. On the other hand, he did not opt to dissolve the PA and throw the key over the Separation Wall to Israel. On the contrary. Abbas stated that the Authority was a necessary mechanism for the Palestinians, lifting them from occupation toward independence. Moreover, he said, the Palestinian side could not commit unilaterally to Oslo agreements while Israel continued to violate them systematically. He did not elaborate, nor declare an end to security coordination with Israel, as PLO and Fatah elders had demanded.[50]

The aging and beleaguered Abbas increasingly faces problems in keeping both feet grounded in reality. In summer 2016, in his Arab Summit and the UN General Assembly speeches, Abbas appealed to Britain to apologise for penning the 1917 Balfour Declaration 'by which Britain gave, without any right, authority or consent from anyone, the land of Palestine to another people. This paved the road for the Nakba of the Palestinians and their dispossession and displacement from their land.' Abbas asked that Britain:

> bear its historic, legal, political, material and moral responsibilities for the consequences of this Declaration, including an apology to the Palestinian people for the catastrophes, miseries and injustices that it created, and to act to rectify this historic catastrophe and remedy its consequences, including by recognition of the State of Palestine.[51]

The head of a limited autonomy, that needs Britain's help to achieve independence, raising this demand regarding a hundred-year-old colonial policy appeared absurd. Privately, Western diplomats saw this curiosity as evidence for the growing gap between Abbas' insights and the real world.

## 'State Minus': Where Netanyahu and Trump Meet

In January 2017, Prime Minister Benjamin Netanyahu gave a slip of the tongue response, saying, 'What I'm willing to give to the Palestinians is not exactly a state with full authority, but rather a state-minus, which is why the Palestinians don't agree [to it].'[52] Such slips almost never happen with Netanyahu. He is calculated, in contrast to Defence Minister Avigdor Lieberman who once threatened to execute Hamas leader Ismail Haniyeh and destroy his movement.[53] In his public appearances, Netanyahu's statements are carefully worded. His mind operates mechanically, and it is for this reason that a slip of the tongue warranted attention. Twenty-two months later, in October 2018, it became his declared policy. 'A potential solution is one in which the Palestinians have all the powers to govern themselves but none of the powers to threaten us,' he said. 'West of the Jordan, Israel and Israel alone will be responsible for security... You can give it any name you want: state-minus, autonomy-plus, autonomy plus-plus.'[54]

Netanyahu's words need to be linked to his stance during the negotiations with Abbas, as part of the 2013–14 peace talks initiated by Secretary Kerry.[55] Netanyahu's position was that, even following an agreement, Israel would retain security control over the entire area between the Jordan River and the Mediterranean Sea over the coming decades. The best-case scenario for the Palestinians would have been a severely handicapped state. For them, it was hard to imagine a less ideal scenario.

This was not inconceivable, however, if we look at Netanyahu's support for the Formalising Law for settlement expansion, which retroactively legalises dozens of settlements; almost 4,000 housing units built on private Palestinian land. Netanyahu supported the law although Israel's Attorney General said that the legislation as it existed was unconstitutional and that he would not be able to defend it in the High Court.[56] In addition, since Donald Trump entered the White House at the end of 2016, Netanyahu has pushed forward settlement expansion. In 2017, Israel started building 2,783 new West Bank settlement houses, an increase of about 17 per cent on the annual average expansion since Netanyahu took office in 2009. In addition to this *de facto* annexation, between March 2015 and April 2019 the Knesset approved eight laws to allow settlements' *de jure* annexation.[57]

Netanyahu's ultimate principle is power. 'Power is the most important [component] of foreign policy. "Occupation" is baloney. There were huge countries that have occupied and transferred populations and no one talks about them... Power changes everything.'[58] This is the nail in the coffin of the 'temporary occupation' argument used by Israel since 1967 to stave off inter-national criticism. After more than fifty years of expansion, sixty per cent of the West Bank has *de facto* been annexed to Israel. Where Netanyahu differs from New Right head Naftali Bennett, his main opponent to the right, is not in the principle of annexation but on its pace. Bennett wants to advance from legal to practical annexation as soon as possible. Netanyahu is more cautious. He wants *de facto* annexation first, and to do this gradually and in accordance with circumstances dictated by his foreign policy. This would be followed by a self-evident *de jure* annexation, which would seem almost natural. Palestinians would be left with what they currently have: enclaves that are barely connected to one another. Israel would govern these ban-tustans externally and enter them at will. As far as Netanyahu is concerned, if the Palestinians want to call this kind of autonomy a state, that is their affair. This would also mark the definite end of the Oslo Accords; fully foreclosing the possibility that the Palestinian Authority would at any point be upgraded to a sover-eign state on the entirety of the 1967 territories.

Although Netanyahu is exploiting Abbas' weakness to practi-cally annex most of the West Bank and avoid the establishment of an independent Palestinian state, Abbas pays no attention to the voices calling on him to shutter the PA and hand over the keys to Israel, which would then have to bear full responsibility for its policies. He persists in security cooperation with Israel on the grounds that they share the same enemies: Hamas and the Islamic State cells in the West Bank. Abbas and the PA senior leadership also have an interest in keeping the VIP benefits that they receive as part of a ruling class sponsored by Israel.

The continued existence of a hobbled PA is also in Europe's interests. European countries donate heavily to keep the PA in its current incarnation, on the premise that it is a stable factor in fighting radical Islam and prevents the Israeli–Palestinian conflict from engulfing the continent's cities. Since the establishment of the PA international aid has totalled more than $30 billion, almost half of which has come from EU states. The EU and its individual states provided $4,360 billion from 2012 to 2016, and covered 40 per cent of the PA's budget in the years 2012–14.[59] Each intifada and Israeli operation in Gaza that killed many hundreds of civilians pushed western Europeans to the streets demanding their governments stop Israel. They are, however, unwilling to impose upon Israel peace deal parameters that she rejects. Confronting the Israeli government, European decision-makers admit behind closed doors, could end or significantly reduce their intelligence cooperation against radical Muslims. Such a confrontation, they claim, is within the US' purview since Israel depends on American military and political support. Actually, the Israeli government has also drawn encouragement from the various messages coming out of Europe that continued settlement building endangers the two-state solution. This is, after all, the aim. Western Europe may have an impact if it moves from a two-state discourse to discuss human rights violations by an Apartheid-like regime, and the implementation of UN Security Council Resolution 2334.

Trump's position on Israel-Palestine developed gradually. Due to his limited attention span that prevents him from getting into the details, Trump relies on his close White House advisers to build his administration's peace parameters: Jason Greenblatt, his son-in-law Jared Kushner, and David Freidman, the ambassador to Israel. The State Department was mostly excluded in Trump's first year in power, as was the CIA. The CIA mission then, while the White House drafted its initial plan, was to keep Abbas hoping he could achieve the best possible offer from a president promising the deal of the century. This was done through personal and professional relations between the two agencies' heads—Majed Faraj who heads the PA's General Intelligence, and his counterpart at the CIA, Mike Pompeo. In February 2017, Pompeo met Abbas in Ramallah and promised that the US would consult with the Palestinians on its deal if they remained patient. Pompeo even arranged a meeting with Trump for Abbas in the White House in May 2017.[60]

These and his meetings with Greenblatt left Abbas cautiously optimistic. The American envoy listened carefully, an act that made Abbas think that unlike his predecessors, Trump, the outsider dealmaker, was ready to impose on Israel what establishment politicians disliked. However, Abbas' optimism later transformed to outrage when Kushner, who followed Greenblatt in a separate visit to Ramallah, demanded that the PA stop paying compensation to families of prisoners and cease any kind of incitement to terrorism. Kushner, a senior Palestinian official said, 'sounded like Netanyahu's advisers and not like a fair arbiter.'[61] Not long after, Abbas learned that Trump and Netanyahu are even closer in their personalities and positions. Whereas the Obama administration's position corresponded with the Israeli centre and the state security establishment, Trump's administration uses the terms of reference of the Israeli hard right, in particular those of the settlers (see below). Like previous US administrations, Trump does not aim to change the power imbalance between Israel and the Palestinians but rather to exacerbate it. In reality, besides their shared values, the US has much to gain from its special relations with Israel. The poor Palestinians, however, have nothing to offer. They can only demand that the US respect human rights and the principles of international law.

'One of the biggest differences between the Obama and Trump Administrations on Middle East policy,' writes Entous,[62] 'was their approach to, and understanding of, the Palestinian question.' Kushner told aides that he thought Obama 'tried to beat up on Israel and give the Palestinians everything.' American and Israeli right wingers share this view. Trump's advisers, by contrast, want the Palestinians to think that their stock value is declining—a strategy advocated by Netanyahu and his US ambassador Ron Dermer. The goal is to get the Palestinian leadership to accept more 'realistic' proposals than had been offered to them by former Prime Minister Ehud Barak, in 2000, and by Ehud Olmert, in 2008. One senior Trump Administration official used stock prices as an analogy: 'Like in life—Oh, I wish I bought Google twenty years ago. Now I can't. I have to pay this amount of money. It's not that I'm being punished. I just missed the opportunity.'[63]

Netanyahu and Trump hold similar positions and personalities. They are unapologetically nationalist, strongly oppose progressive views and advocate for a neoliberal socio-economic order. They also are obsessed with holding power and securing media coverage of their activities. Trump rejected UN Security Council Resolution 2334, which reaffirmed the international understanding of the borders of 4 June 1967 as the future border between Israel and a sovereign Palestinian state, and condemned Obama's decision to let it pass.[64] Moreover, Trump denounced Kerry's end-of-mission speech in which he portrayed Israel's policy as an attitude of 'separate but unequal,' referring to the racist regime that formerly prevailed in the US.[65] According to Kerry, such a regime is in opposition to America's democratic principles, and therefore the US could not support it. Trump's tweets and executive orders, however, have shown that he has a different understanding of American democracy and minority rights.[66]

By supporting Netanyahu in implementing his state-minus goal, Trump is helping Israel to shift the occupation from being a global issue where international law matters, to a domestic policy in which foreign countries and international institutions need not intervene.

*Besieged Abbas Reclaims the Leadership*

Conferences around the Arab world in 2017 marking the centenary of British Foreign Secretary Lord Balfour's statement 'viewing with favour the establishment in Palestine of a national home for the Jewish People,' had just concluded before President Trump gave a mini Balfour statement of his own, handing occupied Jerusalem to Israel on a silver platter. Naturally, there are myriad political and social differences between today and 100 years ago: the US under Trump is not imperial Britain, and the young Zionist movement is a far cry from today's strong state of Israel. Nevertheless, what inflamed Palestinian and Arab political opinion was not the historical reality, but the image, context, and framing that connected Balfour's declaration to the present day. For the first time Abbas felt under siege. Whereas Arafat experienced physical sieges by the Israelis in Beirut (1982) and Ramallah (2002–4), the Syrians in Tripoli, Lebanon (1983), and the Jordanians in Amman (1970), and since the mid-1960s had escaped many Israeli assassination attempts, Abbas' siege is political. Like Arafat in his last years, a weakened Abbas is facing a similar experience.

Abbas senses that the United States has betrayed him and his nation. It did not matter how much he strove to maintain security coordination with Israel despite his falling public support (see Chapter Three), whether he tried to place obstacles to the reconciliation process with Hamas, or if he supported a peaceful two-state solution to the conflict. For Palestinians, as well as Arabs and Muslims worldwide, Trump recognising Jerusalem as the capital of Israel; his decision to move the American embassy from Tel Aviv to Jerusalem; and his declaration that Jerusalem had therefore been taken off the Israeli–Palestinian negotiation table, all signify that the US has sided unequivocally with Israel not only on the issue of Jerusalem, but also on maintaining the occupation of the 1967 territories. Trump emphasised that the US would support two states 'if agreed to by both sides,' thus giving Israel the right to veto any solution it deems unsuitable. Netanyahu, as mentioned above, is willing to grant the Palestinians a 'state minus,' and only in part of the West Bank. After eight years of debate between the Obama administration and Netanyahu, an American-Israeli consensus has now been created. This stands opposed to the Palestinian and Arab consensus, which continues to support the establishment of a Palestinian state in the West Bank and Gaza Strip, with its capital in East Jerusalem.

Indeed, in the past the US was always closer to Israel than to the Palestinians, but it had always been openly committed to the principles of a peace process based on international law and previous UN resolutions. This commitment allowed the Palestinians to accept the US as broker, despite its clear support for the Israel side, since it accepted a legal and international framework that also provided support for the Palestinian position. Trump has exempted the US and Israel from all commitments to international law and UN Security Council resolutions, which had established that annexing Jerusalem and the settlements were both illegitimate and unlawful acts. Abbas' inevitable conclusion was clear: the US had moved from acting as mediator to blind, open support for the Israeli right. Any opportunity to progress from interim agreement to comprehensive peace, since such an intention was ceremoniously signalled on the White House lawn in September 1993, was no more.

The rift between Abbas and the Trump administration widened when Trump worked to remove the issue of Palestinian refugees from the agenda by cutting financial support for the United Nations Relief and Work Agency for Palestine Refugees in the Middle East (UNRWA). In January 2018, Trump cut $60 million of the US' aid to UNRWA, an agency already operating with a deficit. 'It is important to have an honest and sincere effort to disrupt UNRWA,' Special Advisor Jared Kushner emailed on January 11 2018. 'This [agency] perpetuates a status quo, is corrupt, inefficient and doesn't help peace,' he wrote. Victoria Coates, a senior advisor to Jason Greenblatt, sent an email to the White House's national security staff indicating that 'UNRWA should come up with a plan to unwind itself and become part of the UNHCR [UN High Commissioner for Refugees] by the time its charter comes up again in 2019.'[67] Eight months later, following Netanyahu's request, Trump decided to cut US funding to the agency completely.[68] The assumption was that by weakening UNRWA, or even forcing it to close, the question of the Palestinian refugees would disappear. Responsibility for the Palestinian refugees could be transferred to the UN commission on refugees, which deals with an array of human tragedies around the globe. Refugees' living conditions in Syria, Iraq, and Myanmar (where the persecuted Rohingya Muslim minority live) are far worse than for the Palestinians, who would fall to the bottom of the list. Without an international agency to deal with them, Washington and Jerusalem assumed that the issue of the Palestinian refugees would disappear. So far, this scenario has not materialised. UNRWA has managed to survive by cutting jobs and receiving extra budgetary allowances from its other donors.[69]

The PA learned of further close coordination between Jerusalem and Washington regarding other final status issues to be included in Trump's deal, each contrasting with the Palestinian national interest.[70] There would be no territorial component in the plan. Trump's deal would not include the evacuation of settlements, nor mention the pre-1967 border as a term of reference for solving the territorial dispute. Similarly, the plan would not support establishing the Palestinian capital in East Jerusalem. At most, only four neighbourhoods outside the Old City: Jabel Mukabar, Isawiya, Shuafat refugee camp and Abu Dis, would form the capital.[71] The plan would not recognise any right of return for the refugees or suggest practical solutions for their plight. UNRWA would be dismantled, to be replaced by a new endowment for hosting countries to settle Palestinian refugees wherever they live. No constraints would be put on Israeli security operations or limits to army deployments, and as such the proposed security arrangements would severely compromise Palestinian sovereignty. Israeli forces would deploy along the Jordan River and on the hills looking over it, and enjoy overriding responsibilities and power over the limited Palestinian security forces. Israel would also control Palestine's water resources, border crossings, airspace and electromagnetic sphere. The Gaza Strip would have a separate local administration, without a territorial corridor to the West Bank. Unlike previous peace plans, including the Arab Peace Initiative of 2002, that allocated a secondary role to the Arab countries and started with a bilateral Israeli–Palestinian agreement, the Trump administration's plan involves only Egypt, Saudi Arabia and the Gulf states as sponsors and enforcers. Moreover, while in previous plans, and in PA political discourse, the Palestinians claim that they hold the key to overall Arab peace relations with Israel, the Trump administration and Israel think that the unresolved Palestinian issue has stood in the way of founding a strong anti-Iranian and pro-American regional front. The anti-Iran alliance is the key element, and therefore, the Trump administration has encouraged Arab leaders who prioritise the Iranian threat to pressure Abbas (see below). Abbas, for them, is part of the problem, not the solution.

The benefits that the Trump plan offers to the Palestinians are limited. They would not receive state sovereignty, independence, territorial continuity or an end to Israeli military operations. They would continue to live as an unwanted second-class ethnicity next to the powerful Jewish lords of the land. Instead,

Trump supposes he can offer them an improved life-style via some rather thin political make-up. Saudi Arabia and the United Arab Emirates have pledged to invest $10–20 billion to rebuild and develop the Palestinian territories if Abbas accepts Trump's deal. Much of it could go to the Gaza Strip if Hamas were to renounce terror. In addition, Trump may rhetorically recognise the scattered PA areas as a state, but it will not determine any changes on the ground, nor bring the American president to clarify within which borders his recognition is granted. Finally, Trump's deal will be a 'take it or leave it' offer, with no bargain on its components allowed. If Abbas rejects the deal, the Trump administration may punish him. The Israeli–American discourse on possible recriminations includes letting Israel unilaterally annex between 10 to 15 per cent of the West Bank settlement areas.

Indeed, Trump started to punish Abbas prior to the official publication of his plan. Following Abbas' decisive rejection of what he had heard of its components, the campaign he initiated to undermine the plan's forthcoming publication (see below), and his boycotting of US representatives, Jared Kushner, Trump's son-in-law and special advisor on the peace process, stated in June 2018: 'I do question how much President Abbas has the ability to, or is willing to, lean into finishing a deal. He has his talking points which have not changed in the last 25 years. There has been no peace deal achieved in that time. To make a deal both sides will have to take a leap and meet somewhere between their stated positions. I am not sure President Abbas has the ability to do that.' Pretending to speak on behalf of the international community, he added: 'The global community is getting frustrated with the Palestinian leadership and is not seeing many constructive actions towards achieving peace.'[72]

Since Abbas burned his bridges with the Trump administration, in September 2018 Trump ordered the closure of the PLO diplomatic mission office in Washington, DC.[73] In October, the state department decided to downgrade the status of its diplomatic mission to the Palestinians by placing it under the authority of the US Embassy to Israel. The Jerusalem consulate had for years served as a de facto embassy to the Palestinians. The Palestinian Affairs Unit of the embassy to Israel opened in March 2019.[74]

In addition, the Trump administration has cut off all funding to the Palestinians, including that from the US Agency for International Development (USAID), which in 2017 transferred $268 million to Palestinian civil society. The US also financed the Palestinian security forces to the tune of $60 million every year for training and equipment. The cuts in funding started in June 2018, when the US administration freezed its aid budget of $1.3 trillion following the Taylor-Force Act. The Act orders that no funds are disbursed unless the Secretary of State certifies that the Palestinian Authority has met four conditions: terminating payments to terrorists' families (see below), revoking laws authorising this compensation, taking 'credible steps' to end Palestinian terrorism, and 'publicly condemning' and investigating such acts of violence.[75] The American aid stopped completely when the Anti-Terrorism Clarification Act (ATCA) went into effect in February 2019. The law, drafted in cooperation with Israeli officials and right-wing civil society activists, forced foreign organisations to be subject to the jurisdiction of US courts if they accept certain forms of assistance from the US government. The ATCA obliges the PA to pay compensation to terror victims who have won civil suits against the PLO in US courts, and paves the way to suing it in similar cases. Consequently, the PA declined to receive any further US funding.[76] Abbas also rejected the monthly tax transfer that Israel collects from Palestinians working in Israel, saying 'we shall not accept the [tax] money if it is not paid in full.' This came in February 2019, following Israel's decision to withhold $138 million, of $222 million, citing the PA's payments to families of those killed, wounded or jailed in Israel after attacking Israelis.[77]

The American ideas stand on three pillars. First, imposition: the powerful side wishes to force the weak to accept its terms and conditions and reproduce the present imbalance rather than minimising it. Second, it is based on the American alliance with authoritarian leaders, and their regional interests and power struggles. The plan ignores popular Arab and Muslim rejection of Israeli sovereignty over al-Aqsa, and the Palestinian popular mythos of the 1948 refugees. Third, the Trump administration assumes that money and material benefits can buy national principles and postpone the liberation struggle. Possibly, Trump and Netanyahu have wrongly concluded that only Jews feel attached to the land. Having a fake national identity, the Palestinians ought to be ready to exchange their national goals for a good price.

### Abbas' Worldwide Campaign

The Palestinian Authority views Trump's parameters as offering them eternal limited autonomy and creating one state with two ruling systems. In doing so, Trump actually formalises and legitimises Israeli apartheid.[78] 'We do not want peace at any cost,' Abbas stated in the al-Azhar conference.[79] To oppose these threats, considered very serious by Abbas, he has transformed into a serial policy initiator, a task that he had not taken upon himself for many years. Abbas initiated far-reaching campaigns inside and outside Palestine to limit Trump's damage, regain domestic and international support and unite the nation in its conflict with the US administration.

Already under Arafat, the PLO made its historical compromise and pinned its hopes on American mediation. In 1988, the PLO accepted UN Resolution 181 of 1947, and agreed to establish Palestine alongside the Jewish state of Israel. In 1993, the

PLO unilaterally recognised Israel (although Israel recognised merely the existence of the Palestinian people and the PLO as its representative, rather than the Palestinian right to self-determination) and accepted UN Security Council Resolution 242. Abbas strongly rejects calls to complement the political track through either popular non-violent protests or terror. He has ruled out stepping back from his stated goal of a Palestinian state based on the 1967 borders, with East Jerusalem as its capital, and a return of Palestinian refugees based on UN Resolution 194 and the Arab Peace Initiative. He rejected PLO Executive Committee Secretary General Saeb Erekat's remark that in reaction to Trump's policy the Palestinians will switch toward waging a civil rights struggle and start demanding one state with equal rights for all within. Moreover, in none of Abbas's speeches since Trump's Jerusalem declaration has he said that he intends to dissolve the PA. On the contrary, he has praised the PA as a realisation, however partial, of national aspirations and as the nucleus for an eventual fully sovereign state along the 1967 lines.

The Trump administration has enlisted Saudi Arabian Crown Prince Muhammed bin Salman and Egypt into pressuring Abbas to accept the American diktats. The Saudi crown prince and Egyptian President Abdel Fattah al-Sisi made it clear to Abbas that the 2002 Arab Peace Initiative is now all but dead. It would be better for Abbas to take what Trump is about to offer, with the hopes that one day the regional balance of power would shift and Abbas would be able to realise his dream of establishing a fully sovereign state within the 1967 borders, including East Jerusalem. The Saudi establishment feels threatened by Iran and wants help from Israel and the US to combat that threat—as such, the Palestinians will have to wait.[80] Hearing Muhammed bin Salman's proposal, Abbas went to see the millennial prince's father, the aging King Salman. Abbas succeeded in January 2018 to bring the king to reiterate Saudi commitment to the 2002

Arab Peace Initiative's principles during the Organisation of the Islamic Cooperation conference. The young crown prince had then no choice but to tell Abbas in February 2019 that he follows his father in supporting the Arab consensus.[81]

Unlike the Saudis, Jordan has never spoken with two voices. The 'state minus' plan endangers Jordan's Hashemite identity. Jordan is afraid that this American/Israeli policy will push many West Bank Palestinians to immigrate to Jordan, which has already absorbed many Palestinians and now hosts increasing numbers of Iraqi and Syrian refugees. In June 2018, Abbas coordinated with King Abdullah of Jordan a joint rejection of the initial American ideas. Netanyahu and the American envoys Greenblatt and Kushner met separately with the King, but failed to bring him over to their side and isolate Abbas.

Abbas acknowledged that he must turn to the masses in order to scupper Trump's plan, and Jerusalem is the vehicle to get there. Abbas, therefore, approached both his own constituency and the wider Muslim world. Abbas' office in Ramallah had earlier information on Trump's decision to move the US embassy and recognise Jerusalem as Israel's capital. Twelve hours prior to Trump's statement, Voice of Palestine, the official radio station, broadcasted protest directives on behalf of the government in the run-up to Trump's announcement. Abbas permitted the Fatah apparatus to organise Days of Rage demonstrations against Israel and Trump's Jerusalem declaration. Criticism of Abbas within Fatah and from Hamas was less strident than it had been in the near past, and Hamas permitted Gaza residents to face-off with IDF soldiers along the border fence with Israel. Voice of Palestine broadcasted live on 16 January 2018 from Al-Azhar University in Cairo, recording the whole day of the conference, and not just President Abbas and Sisi's speeches. Fatah demonstrations, however, were poorly organised. They each lasted just a week and remained sporadic, either due to Fatah's lack of organisational skills and experience, or rank and file mistrust of Abbas. In truth, anti-American demonstrations in Turkey, Indonesia, Malaysia, Pakistan, Morocco and Jordan attracted the masses, but much less so in the West Bank. According to UN, twenty Palestinians and one Israeli were killed in the first month following Trump's declaration. Another 500 Palestinians and 17 Israelis were wounded. In addition, Israel arrested many Palestinians in order to prevent further escalation. According to the Palestinian 'Addameer' Prisoners and Liberties Affairs Association, in the first two months of 2018, Israel detained 1,319 people, including 274 children. Jerusalemites represented the highest number of detainees, at 381.[82]

In December 2017, Abbas addressed the conference of Arab foreign ministers where his foreign minister unsuccessfully asked his Arab colleagues to join the PA in suspending their countries, relations with the Trump administration. However, in the same month Abbas succeeded in humiliating the American government. The Palestinian delegation brought to the UN General Assembly a resolution that opposed Trump's policies regarding Jerusalem. 128 countries supported it, 39 abstained and only nine stood with the US and Israel in opposing the Palestinian resolution.

Abbas tried to block Trump's forthcoming 'deal of the century' with his preemptive counter proposal. In February 2018, he presented the Security Council with his peace plan.[83] Based on international law, a broad international conference was to facilitate a new peace process. At the outset, the conference would recognise Palestine on the 4 June 1967 borders and ask the UN to accept it as a full member. After achieving equal international status to that of Israel, Palestine and Israel would exchange recognition. Then the international conference would appoint a multilateral mediation committee to help the two states achieve a final status agreement and implement it within a short period.

No unilateral actions will be taken during the negotiations, including the implementation of the American recognition of Jerusalem as the capital of Israel. In his plan, Abbas presented new elements as alternatives to the forthcoming 'deal of the century' and the failed Oslo process. These included expanding the mediation team instead of relying on an exclusively American one, solving statehood and border disputes first, and narrowing the power imbalance with Israel by internationalising the process and achieving equal international status with the occupier before the negotiations started.

Abbas shopped unsuccessfully around for new mediators instead of, or alongside, the Americans. He asked the presidents of China, France and Russia and the heads of the EU not to leave him alone in the negotiation room with the US and Israel. He suggested to them basing the new negotiation phase on international resolutions and international law, besides fixing a short deadline for its conclusion.[84] Nevertheless, his hopes were dashed. Each of them recommended that Abbas wait until Trump had presented his plan, and not to reject it out of hand. They also made it clear that they did not intend to enter into a spat with the Trump administration on the Palestinian question, and told Abbas that it is politically impossible to continue boycotting the US. With urgent problems to deal with and the schisms inside the European Union between pro-Israeli and pro-Trump right wing centralist regimes and western European democracies, European Union leaders have been prevented from taking unified stands on Trump's decision nor have they accepted Abbas' request to recognise Palestine as an occupied state. Despite failing to bring in world powers to replace the US, he succeeded in deterring Arab leaders from publicly accepting Trump's policy. Facing public anger and de-legitimation due to the US decision to recognise Israel's annexation of Jerusalem, Egypt and Saudi Arabia recommended that the US postpone the publication of the plan.[85] Facing failure and total rejection, the American administration followed suit.

Abbas reclaimed his leadership and expressed his updated worldview in a series of speeches,[86] among which the most detailed was in the PLO's Central Council session on 14 January 2018. The PA built it up as a national event and it was broadcasted live (the quotations below are from this speech unless otherwise stated).[87] Abbas was untypically angry, emotional and bitter, using strong language against Trump. Also untypically, Abbas based the Palestinian claim of sovereignty in Jerusalem upon Islam. It was not just his rivalry with Hamas (see Chapters Three and Four), who refused to participate in the meeting as long as it was held in Ramallah, that had driven him to employ religious arguments. Abbas is a true believer who, in principle, is against mixing politics and religion. Islam, Abbas believes, provides a spiritual safe network but is not a political action plan. His direct confrontation with the US had evoked in him a siege mentality. Approaching his listeners in Arafat's style, liberally quoting the Qur'an, Abbas integrated into his speech a Qur'anic verse promising victory and God's help to steadfast believers: 'God chose you for this mission' and secures you. 'We do not trust anyone, just God.' Abbas also adopted the Qur'anic motto 'Allah is with the patient,' which was used by Hamas at the end of the 1990s to give the Palestinian public hope that Israel would, one day, be vanquished through armed struggle. Now Abbas deploys this motto for the purpose of gradually building Palestine through political means. Abbas acknowledged that a Palestinian state was not likely anytime soon. He recognised that neither is the current Israeli government a partner for an agreement on the establishment of a Palestinian state, nor is the Trump administration an honest broker that will bring about its creation. The Palestinians would have to move slowly toward statehood, preserving what they had, and turn directly to international institutions to accept the State of Palestine as a member. Thus, if not through negotiation or functioning institutions on the ground, Palestinians could achieve state symbols and international recognition.

Abbas further channelled Arafat in defining Trump's decision as a 'dangerous turning point.' 'We are facing a historical moment either to be or not to be... We stand united in one trench to defend our dream... we will remain steadfast on our land,' Abbas said to the PLO Central Committee on 28 October 2018.[88] Interestingly, in his speeches Abbas moves between two poles. On the one hand, he described Trump's policy as a dangerous conspiracy aimed at shattering Palestinians' dreams and their future. 'We made a great concession, we are ready to get only 22 per cent of our land and enjoy the backing of international law, so why is the international community unable to impose its law and give us our rights,' Abbas wondered at Al-Azhar's international conference.[89] On the other hand, based on his international and national achievements, Abbas expressed his confidence that the Palestinian Authority could overcome Trump and Netanyahu.

Abbas warned against repeating the mistake of 1948—leaving the land—pledging that 'we will remain in Palestine.' Abbas' mission as president, so his speech reads, has been to stick to what exists. 'We refuse to remain an authority without authority,' Abbas said, pointing to his international policy achievements. 'We will not accept the deal the US wants to impose on us, and following its crime against our rights in Jerusalem, we reject it remaining the exclusive mediator.' Hinting at the Saudi pressure on him to accept Trump's deal, Abbas said 'leave us, we know and understand what we are doing just as you are. We are educated and learned people as you are... capable of managing our affairs on our own.'

Abbas' principles for achieving national liberation are: first, operate the Palestinian Authority as a responsible and rational state; second, expand international support for its status as a state in the making; and third, impose upon Israel a peace agreement: 'We see ourselves as a state and therefore we must operate like a state.' This includes fighting terror, encouraging popular non-violent struggle (*Muqawima al-Sha'abiya al-Silmiyah*), maintaining dialogue and cooperation with the Israeli peace camp rather than boycotting it, and expanding mediation efforts to include other powers instead of the US.

Following Abbas' request, the Central Council resolved that the Oslo Accord interim period had ended. It authorised the Executive Committee to suspend the PLO's recognition until Israel recognises Palestine within the 1967 borders, cancels East Jerusalem's annexation, and stops settlement expansion.[90] The decision to terminate the Oslo Agreement is a symbolic rather than practical act since Abbas refuses to dissolve the Palestinian Authority and continues security cooperation and civil affairs coordination with Israel. In addition, his commitment to popular non-violent struggle is limited to international diplomacy.

Out of anger, Abbas spontaneously cursed Trump, 'Yekhreb beitak!' (a saying in colloquial Arabic: literally, 'May your house be demolished'). The outburst was excluded from the official text of Abbas' speech. In addition, in March 2018, at a meeting of the Palestinian leadership in Ramallah, Abbas assailed the US ambassador David Friedman. Referring to Friedman's statement that the settlements are part of Israel, Abbas said, 'Son of a bitch, they [the settlers] are building on their land? You are a settler and your family are settlers.' He added, 'I did not agree and would never agree to give up our principles or the rights of the Palestinian people.'[91]

In speeches to the Central Committee, Abbas rarely addressed domestic affairs. He mentioned his three conditions for a successful reconciliation with Hamas: resolving the issue of Hamas' governance in Gaza, allowing the national unity government to operate all Gaza Strip offices and agencies, and putting Hamas' armed entities under government command. 'I acknowledge that Hamas' leadership is interested in reconciliation,' he offered, but emphasised that due to these three conditions it would 'take time.' Unsurprisingly, in his speech Abbas totally ignored the domestic issues that had been at the root of noisy public criticism of his rule, including the extension of his and the Legislative Council's terms without seeking new elections, the general democratic deficit of his PA, and human rights violations by PA agencies. Abbas opted to bring Palestinians in line behind him against Trump and to bypass public concerns. These are the subjects of the next chapter. While Abbas strives to keep his public mainly passive, civil society organisations outside Palestine and in the Gaza Strip, encouraged and helped by Hamas, decided to act. From the end of March 2018 until 15 May, Nakba Day, they initiated the recurring 'Great March of Return'—weekly mass demonstrations next to the Gaza Strip's border with Israel.

3

# IN-HOUSE ORDER

## WEAK AUTHORITARIAN PRESIDENTS

*Narrow Base, Growing Authoritarianism*

In 1974, twenty years before the foundation of the Palestinian Authority, Arafat succeeded in bringing the Palestinian people to accept the Palestinian Liberation Organisation as its sole legitimate representative. He did this by creating and distributing national myths, appealing to his public's emotions, building the PLO as a consensual, umbrella organisation and evoking a permanent state of emergency. Arafat identified the PLO with himself, much beyond his formal position and title. He became the face of the Palestinian struggle for liberation. When he established the PA, he already enjoyed a strong political base.

The pragmatist Abbas, who disliked Arafat's style and has a very different personality, uses none of Arafat's methods in building his own base. Lacking experience in managing big PLO departments, serving just a few months as the PA prime minister and without his own popular base of support, Abbas entered the Muqata'a with the aid of a borrowed mass of support. He was elected due to the Fatah apparatus' backing, the movement's prestigious international standing and the domestic respect of his seniority as one of the last living Fatah founding fathers. Once in office, he could not build his own power base with the few cards he had. Abbas, therefore, capitalised more. Just one month into his presidency, he replaced seventeen out of twenty-four of Arafat's cabinet members with his own allies.[1] Abbas hoped to end the Oslo process successfully and keep the nation behind him by frequently informing the Palestinians of his international political achievements. Nevertheless, the failure of the political track combined with Israel's policy on the ground hollowed Abbas media reports. The discordance between Abbas' expectations and reality, the split between Marwan Barghouti's young guard and Abbas' old guard on the eve of the 2006 parliamentary elections, and the fissures between Fatah and Hamas following the Islamic movement's electoral victory left the disappointed public without any unifying institutions or vision, save for a passionate yet nebulous sense of national identity. The Palestinian society and polity gradually disintegrated. What remained was a forceful isolated power centre with the president at its top. Thus, whereas Arafat was afraid of losing presidential power but not his popular base, Abbas has had to work to gain both of them. As of 2019, Abbas' political base is limited to loyal security commanders and the PA's dependent employees. The general public criticises him heavily and has removed its support from the president it elected in 2005. Public opinion polls by Palestinian Policy and Survey Research conducted between 2015 and 2018 consistently demonstrate that, when surveyed anonymously, two-thirds of the West Bank public express the desire for Abbas to resign.[2]

In 2010 and 2011, Professor Nathan Brown from George Washington University returned to the West Bank to investigate what had changed since the late 1990s, when he followed the genesis of the PA. In the 1990s, Brown observed that Arafat was reluctant to share power with the newly-elected Palestinian Legislative Council. When the Council voted to open its sessions for the media and the public, Arafat blamed the Council for treating him like 'dirt.' 'The first thing the Council does is break my rules,' he complained angrily.[3] Arafat hoped to dictate the Council's direction, but its members demonstrated their independence. The Council issued laws on its own authority, but could not compel Arafat to approve them against his will. Similarly, the Legislative Council could do nothing to force cabinet members to cooperate. Alternatively, the Council, including Fatah members, seized its authority to constitute legislation, reviewed the budget, and criticised and confronted the government, including on the sensitive issue of ministerial corruption. In certain cases, criticism by the Legislative Council's deputies caused the security services to attack them brutally and illegally. Yet the Council continued its activities unabated. 'In most Arab countries,' writes Professor Brown, 'parliaments have never withdrawn confidence from a single minister, much less the entire cabinet; in several countries, mere talk of doing so has led the head of state to close down the parliament.'[4] In 1997–8, unprecedentedly, the Council issued the Corruption Report and demanded that named ministers be investigated, tried, and forced to resign. In 1998, following the formation of a new government that left Legislative Council members unsatisfied, they continued to call for the removal of confidence from ministers or, in some cases, from the entire cabinet. On 11 September 2002, despite heavy clashes during the second intifada and the Israeli siege on the Muqata'a in March and June of that year, the Legislative Council brought down Arafat's cabinet.[5]

These unprecedented events strongly influenced the pervading political discourse within the establishment and in wider civil society. Both entities reached the conclusion that Arafat had failed and the PA needed to reform in order for statehood to be achieved. Full liberation, and the building of a state that would operate better than the PA, could not be achieved without comprehensive reforms. On the other hand, Arafat and his allies argued that liberation and reforms went hand in hand. Reform could not possibly precede the creation of a real state. Achieving an independent state, several nationalist reformists argued, would by definition weaken Hamas by putting state-building issues at the top of the agenda. But, according to the counter-argument, independence could not be attained without reform. Terrorism, militia fighters, and twelve separate and uncoordinated police units and security services had caused huge damage to Palestinian society by undermining the rule of law and social order. A state could not be built up while armed gangs ruled neighbourhoods and armed partisans waged war outside the supervision of the state authorities.

Meanwhile, a parallel debate was being held on the second intifada's tactics and the political process. Abbas and dovish reformists opposed terrorist attacks and advocated a nonviolent intifada combined with political dialogue with Israel and the US. In mid-2002, under political pressure from the Israeli military, the US, and the EU, Arafat agreed to reform his administration. Arafat presented his own reform plan and mobilised public support for it, while reaffirming the legitimacy of his regime against both external and internal pressures. By this stage, debate over reform was no longer limited to the political elite; the public at large had taken it up, and its views were apparent in public opinion polls. The public debate on reform grew lively, despite Israeli curfews and closures that limited the circulation of printed media. In the absence of freely circulating newspapers due to intifada armed clashes, Palestinians became keen consumers of local, privately owned television and radio broadcasts, satellite channels, and the official Palestinian television and radio stations.[6]

The issues at hand were: what institutions required reform—
for example, the PA's agencies or the political process as a
whole—and what the extent of the reform should be; whether
some institutions needed to be replaced entirely, and if so, by
what; and whether the intifada should continue to use violent
methods or remake itself into a nonviolent struggle. On the subject of what institutions required reform and to what extent,
Arafat and some of his colleagues favoured only minimal changes
in the makeup of the cabinet and the top echelon of the security
services. They claimed that, once achieved, full liberation was the
most radical reform. Besides, after the Israeli reoccupation of the
Palestinian areas in spring 2002, Palestinian society disintegrated
as the PA's central authority eroded. The PA would have to be
reconstituted as a central authority that could carry out the
reforms. Nevertheless, both inside and outside the establishment
there was a widespread hope for radical changes in both the PA's
performance and in its personnel. Once Arafat indicated his willingness to reshuffle his cabinet, pressure groups inside the
Palestinian Legislative Council demanded the dismissal of
Ministers Jamil Tarifi (Civil Affairs) and Nabil Sha'ath (Planning
and International Cooperation), on the grounds that they were
corrupt and had exceeded their legal authority. Fatah members
demanded that non-Fatah minister Yasir Abed Rabbo (Information) be replaced with a Fatah representative, and Saeb Erekat
(Local Government) be removed in favour of an individual who
was more in tune with the movement's grassroots. Finally, they
called on Arafat to relieve his economic adviser, Muhammad
Rashid, of his role as manager of his secret bank accounts.
Others made a far-reaching suggestion that Arafat appoint an
entirely new, technocratic cabinet made entirely of professionals.
Depoliticising the cabinet would ensure, they claimed, tighter
ministerial control of public finances; it would rein in Arafat's
political and bureaucratic power and make it possible to imple-

ment structural changes without interference from political inter-est groups. More radical agents called for the dismantling of the PA, thus theoretically goading Israel into re-establishing its military government. The Palestinian Legislative Council would be reconstituted as a popular assembly that would lead the next stage of the independence struggle.[7]

Arafat himself was not immune to criticism from his senior Fatah colleagues. Nabil Amro, who had in April resigned from his post as minister of parliamentary affairs, issued an open letter to Arafat in September. This sharply critical statement was pub-lished in the official PA daily *al-Hayyat al-Jadida*, where Amro had been editor in chief before entering the cabinet. Amro accused Arafat of having a negative attitude to institutions, rule of law, and state-building. Arafat had ignored professional and ethical standards in forming and running the PA, Amro charged. He had allowed corruption to flourish, misled the people, and brought catastrophe after catastrophe upon them by, among other things, rejecting the proposals put forward by the US and Israel at the Camp David summit of 2000.[8] In other words, Arafat was an impediment to independence. Hanan Ashrawi implied the same when she referred to the PA as a semi-legal system that was inflicting damage on its people as Israel reoc-cupied the Authority's areas.[9]

Inside Fatah and the PA establishment there were voices urg-ing Arafat to nominate Abbas (then secretary-general of the PLO's Executive Committee, unofficially number two in the PLO) as a prime minister with broad authority to implement the reform plan and prepare for Palestinian statehood. In the view of these critics, Arafat bore considerable responsibility for the defects of the current system and had no interest in reforming it. At a Fatah Central Committee meeting in mid-August 2002, nine of the thirteen members present demanded that Arafat appoint Abbas to the post of prime minister and disband the armed militias. Arafat removed the item from the agenda.[10] On 21 September 2002, thirteen of Fatah's senior members, including Abbas allies Nabil Amro and Zuheir Manasara (the new head of the West Bank Preventive Security Service), convened in Ramallah while Arafat was besieged in his compound. They sent him, by fax, a request-cum-ultimatum with three sections: the draft of a public statement, a statement of the Fatah Central Committee's concept of reform, and a list of concrete actions he should take. The latter included not only the dissolution of the al-Aqsa Brigades, Tanzim's military wing, but also the appointment of the Fatah Central Committee as the new PA cabinet, with Abbas as its powerful prime minister. Fatah's Revolutionary Council would serve as a mini-parliament. In addition, the General Conference of Fatah would be called for the first time since the fifth Conference in 1989. In other words, they called for nothing less than a Fatah takeover of the PA and the establishment of a one-party government to replace the coalition that had ruled in the PA since 1994 and in the PLO since 1969. Arafat's reaction came several days later when he used the term 'conspirators' in an address to the Palestinian people on the second anniversary of the intifada. This was the climax of a campaign during which *Wafa* (the official Palestinian news agency) had issued myriad statements by various Fatah bodies condemning said 'conspirators' operating behind Arafat's back. Graffiti against Amro and the 'traitors' advocating Arafat's replacement, as well as newspaper advertisements supporting Arafat, were also part of the campaign, as was gunfire on Amro and Manasara's homes near Ramallah.[11] This campaign was built on the patronage Arafat offered to low-level Fatah-Tanzim militants, and their opposition to Abbas and the old guard. The decentralised and localised structure of Tanzim left even the admired Marwan Barghouti (Tanzim's founder and Fatah's general secretary in the West Bank) with actual control over only some parts of the West

Bank. This, and the undefined relationship between each Tanzim cell and its nominal superiors, helped Arafat's new allies bypass intermediate levels of command. This group was united by their shared interest in preventing these intermediate operators from gaining manoeuvrability and influence through the institution of radical reforms. Thus, low-level Tanzim activists helped Arafat resist such reforms. Other factors helped him as well. The explicit calls made by Israel and the US for reforms that included kicking Arafat upstairs or side-lining him as a precondition to any political process had the effect of rallying the Palestinian population around their leader, as did Israel's reoccupation of Palestinian areas and her long and humiliating siege during which most of the presidential compound was destroyed. With a majority behind him that viewed the reform move as an attempt by Israel and the US to impose another leader on them, Arafat could ask Fatah members who opposed him whether they sided with him or with US President George W. Bush and Israeli Prime Minister Ariel Sharon. Ultimately, Arafat succeeded in shoring up his personal position, but he was not able to end the debate on reforms. Below the cabinet level, a new elected Legislative Council was expected to re-legitimise the PA and substantially improve its democratic processes. The rule of law would be secured in a constitution, as would an independent judiciary, separation of powers, and effective parliamentary oversight of the executive branch.

The discourse on reform also included discussion of the relationship between the proposed reforms and the political process with Israel, as well as the armed struggle that typified the intifada. Both inside and outside the establishment, the voices of dove-reformists against Palestinian terror became more powerful and received greater attention.[12] In June 2002, fifty-five intellectuals and public figures published an urgent appeal in *Al-Quds* urging a stop to suicide bombings. The petition gathered more than 400 additional signatures in subsequent days, while a counter-petition supporting all methods of armed struggle gathered only about 150 signatures.[13]

Recalling these sharp debates, Nathan Brown unexpectedly found that in 2010 and 2011 under Abbas and his Prime Minister Salam Fayyad (in office between 2007–13), both highly appreciated in Washington and Jerusalem, the Palestinians did not come closer to establishing a state. Far more institutions were built under Arafat than have been under Abbas, including when the reformist Fayyad was Abbas' prime minister.[14]

Whereas Abbas worked top-down to achieve independence directly through negotiating with Israel or indirectly by mobilising international pressure on it to make concessions, Fayyad established his cabinet in June 2007 with a bottom-up approach. This meant building the administrative basis for a state rather than waiting for international diplomacy to deliver one. While a diplomatic process would be necessary to turn a state from *de facto* to *de jure*, that task would be made much easier if there was a functioning Palestinian state-like apparatus on the ground.[15]

Fayyad started his career as minister of finance under Arafat. As I have discussed, Arafat was compelled, under heavy international pressure, to reshuffle his cabinet and agree to Fayyad's suggested reforms. The US and the European Union empowered Fayyad to bring public finances and the budget under tight control and to place all PA funds into a single bank account. This was meant to put an end to a system of private accounts, controlled solely by Arafat, that made tracking and accounting for PA income and outlays impossible.

Fayyad served as minister of finance when Israel reoccupied the West Bank in 2002. Israel besieged and divided the West Bank and Gaza Strip and imposed lengthy closures on major Palestinian cities. Israel's strategy of collective punishment pushed Palestinian unemployment, already high, over the

50 per cent mark, and put 50–60 per cent of the inhabitants of the West Bank and 70–80 per cent of those in the Gaza Strip under the poverty line, defined as an income of $2 a day or less. Other results included a sharp increase in violence and crime, especially burglary, drug use and prostitution, as well as growing homelessness and large numbers of people reduced to begging on the streets. The PA nearly ceased to be able to provide any police, health, education and social services. Social solidarity and emergency financial support from Arab states and the European Union helped Palestinian society and the PA survive, but both were chronically on the verge of collapse. Despite these constraints, no sweeping changes took place. Arafat did not allow his new interior ministers to reduce the number of security services, nor could they make senior appointments without his approval. Likewise, Arafat tied the hands of his new finance minister by retaining sole personal access to non-Palestinian Authority funds held by Fatah and income from monopoly enterprises managed by his economic adviser Mohammad Rashid. In September 2002 the Legislative Council, critical of Arafat's management of the reforms, forced the new cabinet's resignation.[16]

Furthermore, under Abbas, Fayyad could not implement his plans for both structural and political limits. Fayyad reached the structural limits that the Oslo accords imposed on the PA and the tough security measures Israel had taken following the second intifada. Israeli control over the 60 per cent of the West Bank where all settlements are located, called Area C in the agreement, prevents the PA from expanding services or helping the some 300,000 Palestinians that live there[17] resist settlement encroachments. Besides, army roadblocks that accompanied the boundaries of Area C made the free flow of goods and people impossible. Above all, due to political rivalry and strategic differences with Abbas, Fayyad was forced to resign in 2013, in a repeat of what President Arafat had done to his prime minister,

Abbas, a decade before. 'The leadership was always worried about Fayyad' observes Hussein Agha, 'where he was going, who was behind him, whether he was making deals behind their backs.'[18]

Despite these difficulties, Brown found that Fayyad indeed sparked sustained economic recovery in the West Bank after the second intifada, reducing corruption, regularising institutions and improving institutional efficiency. The financial system became transparent and government expenses monitored; the security forces' use of torture was on the decline; and PA citizens enjoyed much better personal security. Within limits, the legal system had improved its performance. However, the bottom line of Brown's account was not positive. Under Abbas' presidency, the Palestinians have only regressed domestically. They are further away from independence, and democratic structures have weakened since Arafat's tenure.

Under Arafat, the PA ran several democratic institutions. Very little, if anything, remains of this, Brown argues. The modest Palestinian democracy that existed then has simply ended. The Palestinian Legislative Council does not meet. Both the Council and the President have finished their terms and new elections do not seem to be anywhere on the horizon so long as Abbas remains in office. PA agencies do not respect the rule of law, and severely violate basic human rights. Democratic institutions and principles have ceased to exist. The judicial branch is weak and dependent. Court orders have been ignored by the government and judges have declined to rule on some sensitive political issues. The absolute dependency on international donations has a negative impact on the legal system, as each part of it competes against the others in an attempt to secure its share. The aging Abbas stubbornly refuses to appoint a successor or deputy President (on the succession struggle, see Chapter Four). The PA is deeply divided, both geographically and politically, between the Hamas-led Gaza Strip and Abbas' West Bank.

Under Abbas the security services did indeed become more professional. Having been new on the ground, inexperienced, lacking in professional training and working under Arafat's operational patterns, his security forces operated capriciously. 'More than providing security,' write Zilber and Al-Omari, 'the sector appeared to be an elaborate jobs programme run by Arafat for his associates, militia members, gunmen, and youth.'[19] However, 'with blurred chains of command, competing fiefdoms, unclear functions, and a propensity for corruption, Arafat's Palestinian Authority quickly came to resemble a police state.' The security sector was and still is the largest public employer and the President's loyal guard. 'Israel was seemingly willing to live with Arafat's nascent Palestinian "police state" so long as it delivered on the security front vis-à-vis Hamas and the other rejectionist terrorist groups.'[20]

*Abbas: A Responsible Adult and Big Brother*

In the second intifada, 2000–5, under heavy Israeli military pressure, the fragile PA disintegrated, including in its security sector and militia entities. 'During operations to take over the cities, the local Palestinian security installations and equipment were largely destroyed, with damage estimated in the tens of millions of dollars,' and members of the security forces were detained en masse.[21] Fatah-Tanzim—which Marwan Barghouti established in the mid-1990s to challenge Arafat and the Fatah old guard's seniority—and its al-Aqsa Brigades militia, also suffered from localisation and fragmentation. 'Al-Aqsa Brigades, by virtue of design and circumstance, have never formed a coherent, disciplined military organisation led by a unified command implementing guidelines and decisions of a political leadership,' concluded an International Crisis Group report. The report stressed that 'the endemic fragmentation... is commonly misunderstood as a coherent organization subordinate to the Fatah political leadership and ultimately to Arafat himself.' Rather, 'they are led and organized locally, and receive funding, political patronage, and other assistance from a variety of local, national and often foreign sources.'[22]

American (US Security Coordinator, USSC) and European (EU Police Mission to the Palestinian Territories, EUPOL) training and heavy financial investment turned Abbas' security forces more professional and efficient than during Arafat's time. Between 2007 and 2011, donor countries invested some $60 million annually in Palestinian security training.[23] In 2018, the Palestinian security sector employed 83,276 people, around half of all civil servants. The ratio of security personnel to the population is one of the highest worldwide. It accounts for nearly $1 billion of the budget and receives around 30 per cent of total international aid to the Palestinians. It consumes more of PA's budget than education, health and agriculture combined.[24]

Lacking a solid popular base or charisma to build on his political struggle with opponents and facing heavy pressure from his international supporters to break Hamas, Abbas increased the militarisation and authoritarian leanings of Arafat's regime. With behind-the-scenes support from Israel and the CIA, the security services operated as an autonomous power centre without serious constitutional or parliamentarian restraints. The General Intelligence questions Fatah members suspected of remaining loyal to Dahlan (see below on the Abbas–Dahlan struggle). Security services often violate the law, and military courts try civilians using a law issued by the PLO in exile. They move against political opponents, and implement illegal detentions. Opposition supporters, mainly those of Hamas, have been ousted from the civil service and municipal government, and their organisations have been shuttered.[25] By 2011, authoritarianism had increased. In particular, this trend was made evident by the state's interference in judicial decisions, sharper limitations on public protest and growing reliance on issuing decree-laws by the executive.[26] In addition, in late 2014 the Abbas regime reviewed all the 2,800 NGO operations in its territory. Following the review, it issued a new law requiring prior government approval of any funding sources.

In 2015, according to the Arab Organisation for Human Rights, Palestinian security forces arrested, and in some cases detained without charge, 194 persons including lawyers, university students and lecturers, largely on grounds of political affiliation or expressing opposition opinion, or for criticising PA officials on social media.[27] The security forces oppressed Palestinian civil society members, including journalists and young voices critical of the Palestinian government or supportive of Hamas.[28] A subsequent Human Rights Watch report, published in October 2018 after a two-year investigation, documented a long list of Palestinian Authority systematic arbitrary arrests, torture and abuse in custody, and lack of accountability.[29]

Palestinian security forces did not only prevent or contain confrontations with Israeli soldiers next to checkpoints and settlements. In February 2016, Palestinian security forces set up checkpoints outside major West Bank cities to prevent public school teachers from attending a major demonstration in Ramallah. In Nablus, police officers threatened to revoke the licenses of taxi drivers and punish bus companies if they took teachers to Ramallah for the demonstration.[30] In the same month, when Fatah parliamentarian Najat Abu Bakr accused the minister of local governance of corruption, Abbas issued a warrant for her arrest. She began a sit-in protest at the Parliament building which lasted five weeks, until the warrant was deleted due to the public support she received. In the same month, Abbas fired the governor of Nablus who criticised the Palestinian Authority leadership on social media.[31]

Furthermore, in 2006 Abbas radically changed the Basic Law. Since then the Constitutional Court is no longer allowed to supervise the president and the parliament has no say in nominating judges. When Abbas appointed the Constitutional Court's eighteen judges a decade later, in April 2016—all Fatah members or supporters—the court became effective. Six months later, the new court ruled that Abbas has the power to revoke the parliamentary immunity of Palestinian Legislative Council members, thus effectively enabling him to sideline rivals. This ruling upheld Abbas' order to revoke Dahlan's parliamentary immunity and prevent the Hamas-aligned Legislative Council Speaker Aziz Dweik from becoming acting president should Abbas be unable to fulfil his duties, as stipulated in the PA Basic Law. The decision also enables revoking the immunity of any critical parliamentarian, thus creating a chilling effect that could silence criticism. Ironically, the court that was established in 2003, under heavy international pressure, to limit Arafat's power, increases Abbas' authoritarianism.[32]

The widespread propagation of critical websites impelled President Abbas to sign the 'electronic crime law' in July 2017. This vaguely worded decree allows his government to jail for a period between one year and a lifetime anyone charged with harming 'national unity' or the 'social fabric.' Accordingly, in August 2017 he blocked thirty websites alleged to support Hamas or Dahlan. Five journalists working for news outlets linked to Hamas were detained and four others were called for questioning with regard to social media posts critical of government policy. In the same month, *Palestine Today* journalist Jihad Barakat was detained for filming Palestinian Prime Minister Rami Hamdallah being searched by Israeli soldiers at a checkpoint. And in September, Issa Amro, a prominent human rights activist and the founder of Youth Against Settlements, a group that has long documented alleged human rights abuses perpetrated by the Israeli army and settlers in Hebron, was detained for stoking 'sectarian tensions' online through his call for the PA to respect freedom of speech.[33]

Unsurprisingly, a March 2018 public opinion poll by Palestinian Policy and Survey Research found that 'About two thirds think that the Palestinian Authority security services do indeed eavesdrop on phone calls of citizens and officials and more than 60 per cent believe that such eavesdropping is done illegally and without any just cause. A majority believes that such behaviour benefits the occupation first and foremost and that the Palestinian judiciary is incapable of putting an end to it.'[34] This popular belief is based on a social media report distributed by a former surveillance agent that the PA security services, under the supervision of the CIA, had been working to detect Abbas' allies and rivals. ISS World, a company based in Virginia, provided the equipment, and members of the Palestinian surveillance unit were trained on the sidelines of an ISS World conference in Dubai in early 2014. 'The document alleges that three of the Palestinian security services set up a joint electronic surveillance unit in mid-2014 and monitored the phone calls of thousands of Palestinians, from senior figures in militant groups to judges, lawyers, civic leaders and [even] political allies of Abbas.'[35]

The Abbas regime justifies these operations in the name of national security, a concept it defines broadly. These actions have deepened public mistrust and advanced perceptions that the Palestinian Authority is an obstacle to liberty and independence. Political parties have decline as a result, and unions and civil society organisations have lost their independence. The growing despair among Palestinians that a stable political resolution to the conflict is possible, combined with turmoil over political and religious identities in the Arab world, has expanded the audience and attraction of two Islamist movements—Hamas and Hizb al-Tahrir ('the party of liberation'). The fragmented society has moved to rely on the extended family as a provider of income and security. Customary law are often used to replace the disintegrating and widely mistrusted legal system.[36]

British prime minister Winston Churchill once said, 'Democracy means that if the doorbell rings in the early hours, it is likely to be the milkman.' In the Palestinian Authority, it is the security services. But if front doors are broken down earlier, say at 2 am, it means the Israeli army has arrived. This often is facilitated through security cooperation with Israel. This includes intelligence the Palestinian side transfer over to Israel on opposition actors, mainly Hamas, security forces withdrawing to their bases during Israeli raids in PA-ruled areas and defending the Abbas regime against domestic opponents. Thus, protecting Israeli citizens and protecting the Abbas presidency are intertwined. Since 2015, in order to prevent the stabbing of Israeli citizens and soldiers by young lone wolves, Palestinian security forces have entered schools searching for knives in students' bags and urged teachers to deter their students from such activity. Abbas' security officers also urge religious and local community leaders to control their members.[37] These operations have a chilling effect on opposition to Abbas, but have not successfully eliminated criticism (see below). For obvious political reasons, in some cases the Abbas regime prefers that Israel take charge of detentions and interrogations of Hamas activists. Israel cooperates because it does not trust Abbas to keep them in custody for long, if at all. 'Insofar as security cooperation is seen as an auxiliary function to the occupation,' Hussein Agha and Ahmad Khalidi note, 'it has added to a sense of helplessness and loss of agency and has focused popular anger and frustration away from the struggle for freedom and independence.'[38] Since for Abbas it is a fundamental if not existential issue, he insists on continuing the security cooperation regardless of the public criticism and the PLO's Central Council and its Executive Committee's decisions in 2015–19 to cease it.[39]

Expectedly, the two most popular non-violent anti-Israeli protests broke out in areas where Abbas has almost no control: East Jerusalem in July 2017 and the Gaza Strip in March–May 2018 (on the latter see below). In July 2017, following the killing of two police officers at the site, the Israeli government decided to install metal detectors in al-Aqsa compound gates without consulting with the Muslim authority that manages the holy site, the Waqf. Since the intifada of 2000, referred to as the al-Aqsa Intifada in Palestinian discourse, the holy place is where national-religious extremists from both sides clash. Al-Aqsa religious authorities spontaneously called their public to boycott the detectors and refrain from entering. The public demonstrated restraint and respected the call. Without prior preparation or organisation, tens of thousands gathered next to the holy site gates to carry out mass prayers and sit-in protests. The demonstrators varied widely in terms of age, social class and level of religious devotion. Volunteers provided food and drinks and ensured that the younger demonstrators did not resort to violence. The participants instinctively understood the power of prayer in front of armed forces whereas the Israeli police could not use force in the presence of so many TV cameras. It took about two weeks for the government to dismantle the detectors. After many years of disintegration and lack of local leadership, Jerusalemite Palestinians regained their communal identity.[40]

*Incomplete Authoritarianism*

Arafat operated a limited set of democratic institutions in the context of the shining 1990s, which were marked by economic and cultural globalisation, democratisation in the former Soviet Union countries and the European Union expanding eastward. Abbas' authoritarianism is rooted in a different environment. Britain is preparing to exit the European Union and Putin's

Russia has become a key player in a divided Syria. Under Israeli Prime Minister Benjamin Netanyahu, Israel has lost some of its democratic credentials and maintains close relations with the anti-liberal President Trump and his evangelical supporters. Israel has deepened its cooperation with Saudi Arabia and the United Arab Emirates, and continues to develop relations with authoritarian and far-right regimes in central and eastern Europe.

However, the PA's authoritarianism is limited, either because Abbas fears the loss of Western financial and political support, or due to self-imposed restraints based on genuinely subscribing to a few democratic principles.

'All the information on which I base my analysis,' Nathan Brown wrote, 'was freely and openly supplied by West Bank Palestinians who still show a strong diversity in political views. But on top of a general feeling of political alienation, there is clear nervousness that the wrong kind of politics can hurt your career or, in some cases, lead to your arrest.'[41]

Despite this anxiety, approximately 20,000 protesting teachers marched in February 2016 in Ramallah following a big strike that closed classrooms for a month. In refugee camps autonomous armed groups, including Fatah members, often challenge Abbas' authority. Anti-Abbas demonstrations and a three-day-long general strike broke out in Nablus in August 2016 as a reaction to Security Forces beating to death Ahmed Halawa, a popular local Fatah strongman, while in custody. Following this, the Authority faced resistance when it attempted to impose its rule on the Balata refugee camp near Nablus.[42]

In 2017, a group of judges launched a campaign against 'outside' attempts to influence their decisions, cut salaries, and ignore their rulings. Judiciary members also openly criticised a bill that would blur the separation of powers by giving the president the authority to appoint the head of the High Judicial Council, the official responsible for overseeing the courts and protecting their independence. In addition, the bill would allow the president to appoint the head of a committee that oversees judges. Alongside these was a provision for judges' early retirement, thus implyng that judges whose rulings are not to the liking of the executive branch could be surreptitiously removed from office. The High Judicial Council objected the proposed law and, in September 2018, fourteen Supreme Court judges resigned in protest against proposed amendments to that law. Lower court judges, prosecutors, and the Palestinian bar association protested in 2017–18 against other executive branch interventions. Consequently, the government cut salaries of about thirty judges, including senior members of the bench. The district court subsequently ruled, however, that this salary reduction was illegal.[43]

In June 2018, Palestinian riot police forcefully suppressed protests in Ramallah and Nablus. The protestors demanded that Abbas stop collectively punishing residents of the Gaza Strip, and boldly published video footage documenting incidents of police brutality during the protests onto social media sites.[44]

Finally, in January 2019, thousands arriving to Ramallah from different West Bank cities forced the government to stop implementing a new Social Security Law. The law looked to guarantee old-age allowances, worker's compensation and paid maternity leave to private sector employees. Employers complained that the monetary amount they were bound to contribute towards this new scheme would be too costly, while employees, who joined them, mistrusted Abbas' management. 'Thieves, thieves, a gang of thieves,' was the favourite slogan of the demonstrators weaponised against the government and Abbas. The demonstrators also feared that with Israel's regular withholding of Palestinian Authority tax funds and frequent army incursions into Palestinian areas, including Ramallah, their government was not stable or powerful enough to protect their money.[45]

# IN-HOUSE ORDER

## *The Arab 'Spring': The West Bank Version*

Until the Arab Spring in 2011, Arab countries were either monarchies or authoritarian republics where democracy was formal but not substantial. Their periodical general elections did not end in regime change or create real competition over power. Free media that criticised its own ruler also did not exist. Interestingly, Iraq, Syria, Libya, Yemen, Sudan and South Sudan's disintegration and civil wars, and the popularity of Islamic opposition in Egypt, demonstrate the weakness of the authoritarian republics against the relative stability of monarchies (Jordan, Saudi Arabia, Morocco and the Arab Peninsula Emirates). The PA, thus, is not unique in its authoritarian regime nor in its religious and civil society opposition groups.

Compared to the chaos in other Middle East countries, the West Bank remains quiet, due in large part to the efficiency of the Israeli occupation. Security cooperation—a stipulation for independence laid out in the Oslo Accords—has become a necessary condition for maintaining Abbas' rule and repressing the Islamist opposition. Abbas, who in his past was neither a strong man nor the head of a security service, has maintained his presidency through force.

In his 2010 and 2011 visits to the West Bank, Nathan Brown identified 'deepening despair and cynicism' spreading over Palestinian society. The split with Hamas and growing authoritarianism cut deep into government agencies and civil society organisations. Political parties did not function. 'It is not clear if Fatah really remains a political party in any meaningful sense; instead it consists of an aging old guard monopolizing top positions, a middle generation that stands in the wings (and is no more unified than the old guard), and a host of local branches whose links to the center are tenuous.'[46] Similarly, three Norwegian analysts argued in 2012 that the public's concern had turned inward. Considering the current situation and their future, Palestinian youth have become largely disenfranchised from politics, prioritising personal affairs (family and professional careers) and the difficulties of finding a job. West Bank youth express more optimism about the future than young people in the Gaza Strip, but corruption and political favouritism are experienced as a major problem on the personal level in both areas. The PA and Hamas governments are criticised concerning the state of democracy, freedom of expression and human rights, more so in the Gaza Strip than in the West Bank. However, neither government is completely condemned, on account of their success in raising the level of personal security (the Gaza Strip) and economic prosperity (the West Bank). Widespread discontent with their situation among the youth does not translate into increased political interest or engagement. Instead, the majority has abandoned organised politics and what they consider a political class associated mostly with Fatah and Hamas to which few seem to see any alternative.[47] The old guard elite is not open to criticism and demand full compliance. Politics is not a forum for the exchange of ideas and debates but an instrument with which to rule and control. Moreover, weakening political institutions are driven by personalisation and authoritarianism, where loyalty is given to hierarchy and to the person at the top, not to the law, or value system, or to the state. Alienated, the younger generation has lost interest in public affairs. A Sharek Youth Forum 2013 study found that 73 per cent of young people do not belong to any political faction. 'They have expressed their disappointment and loss of confidence in these factions, especially for their inability to end the state of division, put aside their narrow self-interests, and allow sectors of society, especially youth, a priority in their programmes. Also, with the exception of youth organizations (38 per cent membership), there is a decrease in youth membership in various community organizations.'

Furthermore, 'With low rates of involvement in partisan and societal institutions, youth (individuals or groups) have resorted to seeking out other channels to express their political and social views. This has resulted in a number of activities and manifestations organised by youth movements. However, there is still a lack of clear objectives, priorities and strategies for action.'[48] The young activists of the first intifada, 1987, hoped that the Oslo agreement of 1993 would deliver liberty and self-determination, but their hope has been shattered. Bitter, frustrated and tired after 25–30 years of disappointment, that generation, that meanwhile became part of the old guard, left the direct struggle against Israel for dealing with daily life problems under the growing occupation.

The occupation is visible and nearer than ever to every West Bank native. Settlements expand and radical settlers often attack nearby peasants or travellers. The separation wall with its guard towers, cameras and weapons cuts through the West Bank. In many places, peasants and their lands are separated. The Israeli army violently break into houses at night to search for or arrest suspects. Worse, it raids Palestinian homes even without having to provide warrants or notice. The aims of this method vary: to maintain high operational readiness among the deployed army units, to deter by creating insecurity and upholding the element of surprise. Similarly, arrests are made to collect intelligence and to deter those who, according to Israeli intelligence, may sometimes consider becoming terrorists; 'mowing the lawn' as the intelligence services call it. The relevant Israeli army units inform the local Palestinian security forces on the forthcoming raid and instruct it not to go outside its police station or base. According to Israeli estimations, Israeli forces arrest between two and four thousand West Bank Palestinians each year in these operations.[49] During daytime, its checkpoints and patrols increase fear and insecurity. Commuting consumes extra time due to settlements bypassing roads the Palestinians must use. Thus, for the West Bank Palestinians, the occupation is a daily experience, present not in abstract or remote ways but in their private and public spaces, as well as determining their time consumption. To control space and population in the context of potential popular uprisings, Israel deeply penetrates Palestinian society. It collects intelligence by recruiting collaborators and detecting all sorts of electronic and printed communications. Once analysed and classified, political and personal information is ready for the occupation officers' use when a Palestinian subject applies for a permit to travel abroad, receive medical treatment or work in Israel, or to obtain a license to import/export goods. Regulations frequently change, bureaucratic arbitrary and short-term license validity creates constant dependency on the occupation, constant insecurity and uncertainty demonstrates who rules whom.

Young Palestinians connect Abbas' security cooperation with the occupation acclimatisation. Watching the Arab Spring events in Tunisia and Egypt, they discussed its implications for Palestine. In 2011, Nathan Brown met educated Palestinian youth debating whether to prioritise the occupation or the West Bank-Gaza division and what the connection was between the two. They worried about their ability to reach a mass audience, their relationship with existing political movements, whether they could work on a truly national level (reaching out to Gaza or even to meet Palestinian citizens of Israel) and the precise tools to use. They were fully aware of what Palestinians lack: that the events that took place in Egypt in 2011 depended on years of prior work, tremendous tactical innovation and a very clumsy official response. Their thinking, Brown concluded, is sufficiently realistic and sophisticated to know that they do not have answers to the questions that annoy their elders as well. Yet some were seeking to plunge into action anyway, hoping that the tactics they learned from their Egyptian counterparts could lead the way forward. 'I do not know,' Brown forecasts, 'whether they will be successful, but I left with a general—but still strong—feeling that the unsustainable may not continue forever after all.'[50]

Indeed, the Arab uprisings greatly impressed a few young Palestinian civil society activists. In summer 2012, large anti-PA demonstrations broke out in the West Bank. The young demonstrators combined economic and political complaints. They protested against the rising cost of living and unpaid salaries, called on the PLO to withdraw from the Paris Protocol (the economic chapter of the interim Oslo Accords, signed with Israel) and demanded that Prime Minister Fayyad and President Abbas resign. They 'voiced a lack of confidence in Palestinian politics per se. The same is also true of those Palestinians who openly advocate for political change, whose demands include reform of the PLO, new elections for the Palestine National Council (PNC), the PLO's primary legislative body, and even the dismantlement of the Palestinian Authority.'[51]

In July 2013, young Palestinians established the Facebook group 'Tamarud' ('rebellion') named after the Egyptian mass movement that, in June–July 2013, pushed the army to upend the regime of President Mohammad Morsi, head of the Muslim Brotherhood. The PA version of Tamarud, however, called for democratic elections and rejected the use of force.

'We are a youth initiative that aims at making the voice of the youth heard and enabling its political participation,' Tamarud declared. 'Oh Palestinians, revolt against oppression and division, revolt against those impeding the elections. No one is legitimate; the mandate of everyone has ended. The only legitimacy is that of the people. Our movement in the West Bank and Gaza is peaceful with a clear aim—returning legitimacy to the people.'[52] About the same time, Dr Sufian Abu Zayda, a member of Fatah's Revolutionary Council, a former PA minister and present supporter of Muhammad Dahlan, argued in a critical op-ed article:

'honestly, no one dreamed we would ever arrive at the present situation, in which all authorities and all senior positions are in the hands of a single person.' 'We never imagined there would be anyone ... who would hold the authority that even Arafat, with all his greatness and symbolic importance, did not have.'[53]

But the majority of the public remained indifferent to these calls, despairing of the possibility of change. 'We had our own revolution on March 15, 2011,' declared Mahmoud Yahya regarding civil society demonstrations at that date calling for reconciliation between Hamas and Fatah. 'Our defining chant was "The people want to end the division!" They beat us, slandered us, broke our limbs, smeared our reputation and blackmailed us. We believe in our strength,' but we were romantic. When I saw all of the March 15 activists emigrating and traveling away from Gaza, I knew that we had failed to bring about our Palestinian Spring, so I decided to travel as well.'[54] A fellow activist, Ahmed Balousha, was also openly self-critical: 'We settled for raising banners demanding that the political system be reformed, not toppled ... I feel that we only lied to ourselves, saying that we were representing the Arab spring, when really we failed to take any meaningful action.'[55]

Nasser Barghouti, a young Palestinian, published an impressive, and almost desperate, poem on the Arab Spring that never was, in Palestine or elsewhere in the Arab world:

Three years and counting
from Benghazi to Baghdad
have we forgotten how to count?
Or have we laid to rest all
that, which together
we have breathed
and dreamt
and defended stout.
Tell me if you can

was it sane or was it mad
to heed that call
for my Arab spring that never was
to drop all for what was unsheathed
and for that which was just and a cause
tell me if you can.
I was there in every corner
and every turn,
in every broken bone
and every moan.
I was there
I touched and kissed every tear
year after year
one fading smile after the other
one hopeless yearn after another
I was there
street, capital, and
conference
I no longer dare
to speak
to face or stare
at my Arab spring that never was
here or there.[56]

The bloodshed and chaos that resulted from the Arab uprisings in surrounding countries contributed to a profound pessimism among Palestinian youth. According to a 2013 opinion poll, 57 per cent of Palestinian youth believed that future regional events would negatively affect the Palestinian situation, and only 18 per cent believed they would have a positive effect on it. Moreover, West Bank youth did not endorse the Arab Spring model. Just 26 per cent of them believed that an uprising similar to those that occurred in Egypt and Tunisia could occur against the Palestinian Authority in the West Bank, and only 15 per cent would support it.[57]

Activists that do not want to copy the Egyptian model but to utilise the different situation of occupied Palestinians, suggest replacing Abbas's state discourse and calling upon the international community to put pressure on Israel, by challenging it directly with an individual and collective human rights discourse. Occasionally they organise small protests against Abbas and his futile peace process; against Israeli settlers and the IDF; or in favour of national reconciliation between Fatah and Hamas. Palestinian activists conduct intensive discussions on the Internet, but without building their own institutions or transferring the virtual discussion groups into sustained and coordinated action in the real world beyond the limited success of its anti-normalisation campaign (i.e., ending joint activity with Israeli grassroots organisations because it creates the impression of normal relations in a highly abnormal situation). This is the West Bank version of the international Boycott Divestment and Sanctions (BDS) movement.[58] Attempts to boycott Israel by West Bank Palestinians failed because of their deep dependency on Israel, and as such the young generation of activists have not yet achieved much. To be sure, they can potentially serve as agents of change, since they are fully aware of the deadlock the PA has reached. However, this generation lacks political and organisational skills.

Sporadically, PA leaders have helped the younger generation organise anti-Israeli non-violent protests, but in many other cases they have prevented them from challenging Israel or becoming a nationwide mass movement, fearing that non-violent protests would quickly turn violent, anti-Abbas in nature or both. 'I hold on to security cooperation,' Abbas explained, 'because if we give up on it, there will be chaos here. There will be rifles, there will be explosives, there will be gunmen who will pop up everywhere and want to enter Israel. I put my hands on them and deny them...Without security cooperation a blood-drenched intifada would break out.'[59] The president mistrusts his people and wields his cosh not only by sending his security forces to prevent demonstrations. Approximately half of the civil service employees (see above) work in PA institutions, which provide livelihoods to between a million and a million and half dependent Palestinians. Under Abbas, the PA is an income supplier and political compliance institution much more than national liberation agency. The Palestinian society of the twenty-first century is in a legitimacy crisis, without a united polity, clear vision or any real optimism.[60]

Young intellectuals suggest moving from Abbas' state discourse to collective and individual rights discourse, asking the international community to impose Palestinian liberation on Israel, to demand rights from Israel, the power holder. 'For me, as a Palestinian, I must realize that actually, I might not have a state in the near future,' admitted the Palestinian diplomat Husam Zomlot in September 2015, before moving to Abbas' office as his political advisor and to Washington and London as the head of the Palestinian delegation. 'So what do we do?...The right to vote, the right to social security, the right to move, to love, to marry, to choose your spouse—these are rights that have nothing to do with the form of the solution [to the conflict]. They have waited for too long.'[61]

Actually, those intellectuals endorse the settler-colonialism model and native rights discourse that have been popular in progressive Western academic and activist circles since the 1990s. Their rights claims rely upon this framework. Settlement expansion, the decline of the Palestinian state-building project and the disintegration of the polity, in addition to the futile peace process and the demise of the two-state solution, drove them to look for alternative discourses. They feel intellectually liberated and belong to the right side of history by endorsing these discourses. Yet, they do not translate these abstract concepts to a detailed alternative political programme, nor do they provide convincing answers to the heavy cost of giving up the two-state solution. Unilaterally leaving the international legitimacy the two-state solution enjoys means withdrawing to point zero of the political struggle with Israel without securing international legitimacy to the one state. Moreover, it means giving up Palestinian state status in international institutions, first and foremost in the UN, and turning the struggle with Israel to an Israeli intra-state issue, a domestic problem that the international community is reluctant to intervene in. Zionism succeeded, it should be noted, due in large part to gaining international legitimacy and support that enabled the development of small Jewish communities in Palestine into a state in the making. The Palestinian civic rights discourse is, therefore, more a protest movement against problematic dominant discourse than its domestically and internationally legitimate and popular substitute. Still, it has a significant role in shaking the dominant discourse of which Abbas is the main advocate.

Through the years, the PLO has changed its discourse in relation to both the aims and means of the liberation movement. In 1988, the PLO recalibrated its aims from establishing a state over all Palestine to just part of it. Following this, it altered the means from liberation through armed struggle to achieving independence via an internationalised political process. In 1993, the PLO agreed to establish the Palestinian Authority and state-like institutions prior to gaining full sovereignty. It established a new political discourse based on moving from limited autonomy to full sovereignty. Consequently, Palestinian civil society has undergone intensive discussions on human rights, accountability, transparency and democracy. It expects the Authority to meet its expectations although the struggle for full liberation continues. Interestingly, civil rights discourse in the occupied territories corresponds with claims Israeli Palestinians raise on their rights in the Jewish state.

Unlike the discourse on Palestinian sovereignty over territories occupied in 1967, which allocate to the Israeli Palestinians merely a secondary role as advocates, native rights discourse creates a full partnership between the two communities since it is based on the nativity rather than the international legal status of the land. Educated Israeli Palestinians endorse the alternative discourses as the Israeli-Palestinian conflict transformed in the twenty-first century from border conflict to an ethnic struggle over all Palestine. In the new form of the conflict, the hegemonic Jewish Israeli group considers one's Jewish ethnicity to be the primary determinant in Israeli citizenship. In June 2018 the Knesset accepted the Nation-State Basic Law declaring, 'Israel is the historical homeland of the Jewish people and they have an exclusive right to national self-determination in it.' The new law downgrades the status of Arabic from an official language next to Hebrew, to that of 'special status.' It also stresses the importance of the 'development of Jewish settlement[s] as a national value.'[62]

Besides struggling for equal citizenship, Israeli Palestinians situate their demands alongside those of the West Bank and Gaza Strip Palestinians. On the ground, Israeli Palestinians maintain closer commercial, academic and political relations with their West Bank compatriots than ever. Officially, Israelis are prohibited entering Palestinian Authority cities [defined as area A in the Oslo agreement] but since 2005 the IDF no longer enforces the ban on Israeli Palestinians. At weekends, many Israeli Palestinians shop in the West Bank. In Jenin alone, Israeli Palestinians spent $365 million in 2016 and in 2017 around 700 new shops opened in the city. In 2018 about 8,000 students studied in West Bank universities, and 5,294 in Jenin. An organised transportation system takes the Israeli Palestinian students from their homes to West Bank universities.[63] Similarly, the average West Banker's perception of Israeli Palestinians is changing, and their civic institutions in the Zionist state are seen as a model that West

Bank Palestinians should endorse in order to overcome their disintegration.[64] This marks a historic change in the symbolic status of the Israeli Palestinians; '1948 Palestinians' in the intra-Palestinian discourse. From 1949 to the Land Day, March 1976, the Palestinians outside Israel perceived the 1948 Palestinians as collaborators with the Zionist state, enjoying citizenship benefits while they were stateless and refugees. Israeli Palestinians' counter argument was that they were guardians of the land and its national identity. Had they not remained on the soil, the Zionists would have erased all traces of Palestinian belonging on it. On Land Day in 1976, a mass demonstration of Israeli Palestinians demonstrated against the confiscation of land for the purpose of building a Jewish town. The event, in which six demonstrators lost their lives, marked the rise of a new active generation that took over the community leadership from the old, defeated and subordinated guard. The new generation expressed its support for the PLO political programme of building a Palestinian state in the 1967 occupied territories at a time when the Jewish majority considered it subversive. In addition, since the late 1970s, 1948 Palestinians' steadfastness on the land argument became the PLO guiding principle for the West Bank Palestinians resisting settlement expansion. The role the PLO allocated to 1948 Palestinians was to advocate inside Israel for the two-state solution and for recognising the PLO. After Oslo 1993, the relations between the two wings of the Palestinian nation became even closer. The Palestinian Authority endorsed Land Day, that until then was a community commemoration day, and it became an official national commemoration event. The decline of the Palestinian state project in the twenty-first century and the search for alternatives made Israeli Palestinians a model for some West Bankers. Twenty-first-century Israeli Palestinians vocally expect their state authorities to respect their civil rights and implement full equality with the Jews. They are assertive, are integrated in the Israeli market and culture and are proud Palestinians. The Jewish majority sees, hears, fears and rejects them as the conflict returns to its ethnic roots, after the Oslo period had begun to reframe it as a border conflict.

Troubled Abbas has refused to resign despite the unpleasant polls since 2016 according to which about two thirds of the public would like him to take this step. Unlike the adventurous and capricious Arafat, Abbas hates to take irresponsible risks. Abbas refuses to leave the two-state solution behind and dissolve the Palestinian Authority. He refuses to lose the precious entity, be it limited as it is. He sees it as a historical achievement that must be preserved for the future. Abbas strongly believes that the alternative is worse: security and political chaos with Hamas trying to take over the West Bank. This will compel Israel to reoccupy the West Bank and establish a worse order than the present one.

Abbas' regime of repression and the Israeli occupation's heavy hand has driven Palestinians to choose political passivity, up to the point of internalising the occupation. When prompted by pollsters, they express their criticism, but only occasionally voice their grievances publicly by writing critical articles or participating in street demonstrations. Young qualified professionals, not only Christians, immigrate, their dreams of modern state building and liberation in their lifetime shattered from all sides: radical Islam, Abbas' Palestinian Authority, and the occupation. They complain about an inefficient and corrupt public sector and nepotism. Relying on donor countries, they acknowledge, increases dependency on the outside rather than creativity and initiatives, and encourages pessimism. Their complaints are confirmed by Ghada Karmi's first-hand experience. Ghada Karmi, an English Palestinian of 1948 refugee origin and a powerful Palestinian rights campaigner, went to Ramallah in 2005 to work in the Ministry of Media and Communication. Employee self-expression, she found, was coquettish and self-censored, governed by the imperative to keep their job and salaries whatever the quality of job they produced.[65] The ministry administration was dysfunctional, fully dependent on donation funds. It was common for workers to leave their office early, at 13:30 or 14:00. Palestinian Authority officers were unwilling to hear critical voices other than that of their boss. She soon became disillusioned. The Palestinian Authority is like house of cards, she concludes, a show that everyone believes in, a hollow mimic of a state without capacity to move ahead. She found that 'there was no national cause any more, and no unified struggle for return.'[66] Huge political and mental gaps exist between the European diaspora's perception and the real Palestinian Authority, and between imagined or inspired Palestine and the reality on the ground.

### (Un)engaging Hamas

Both Arafat in 1996 and Abbas in 2006 wanted Hamas to run in legislative council elections and thus, the movement that rejected the Oslo agreements and since its foundation in late 1987 wanted to succeed the PLO, would accept them tacitly. The Oslo II agreements of September 1995, under which Israel withdrew from most of the West Bank's cities, and the January 1996 elections for the Palestinian presidency and legislative council, were together a historic juncture for the Palestinian national movement that Hamas had to confront. Instead of replacing the PLO, as Hamas had hoped to do in its first years, it has had to come to terms with being merely an alternative leadership for the Palestinian Authority. Hamas viewed the establishment of the Authority as a sin, yet the very existence of the Palestinian Authority enjoyed public and international legitimacy. These dramatic political developments intensified the debate within Hamas.

Moderate Hamas leaders began considering taking part in the Palestinian Authority's institutions instead of continuing to operate as a counter-leadership. Assuming that the new reality created by the 1993 Oslo agreement was irreversible, the pragmatists within Hamas' political leadership began claiming that the movement should integrate, either partly or indirectly, into the Palestinian Authority without legitimising the agreement with Israel. Negotiations had already opened in 1994 between Arafat and Hamas leaders regarding Arafat's suggestion to ensure four seats in the future Palestinian Authority cabinet to Hamas, the same number of seats held by official Fatah representatives returning from Tunis. Arafat also discussed giving Hamas the ministry of the Awqaf (religious trusts), the institution upon which Hamas has traditionally based its power. But the movement refused to legitimise the 1993 agreement or accept Arafat's offer while remaining a small minority in the upcoming cabinet, compared to the Fatah members and supporters who had a majority of fourteen seats. Hamas achieved a domestic compromise by agreeing with Arafat that the movement would not participate in nor call to boycott the 1996 elections. Consequently, pragmatist leaders left Hamas and ran as independent candidates under the sponsorship of Fatah. Arafat appointed one of them, Imad al-Faluji, to be minister of communications, a role he undertook from 1996 to 2002. He then remained in the legislative council until 2006 when he and most of the Fatah delegates lost their seats to Hamas. Sheikh Talal al-Sidar of Hebron was appointed minister of youth and sport, serving from 1996 to 1998, and then until 2000 as a minister of state without portfolio.[67]

During the run-up to the first elections to Palestinian Authority institutions, moderates in the Gaza Strip commenced preparations to establish an Islamic National Salvation Party (*Hizb al-Khalas al-Watani al-Islami*). But Arafat did not authorise the establishment of the party until March 1996—after the elections. Apparently, he delayed it for two reasons. First, he did not want Khalas candidates to eat into support for his own Fatah and its former Hamas-allied candidates; second, he did not want to undermine the limited understanding that had been reached with mainstream Hamas. Khalas was composed of young Hamas activists from the second perimeter of the movement's leadership. Ten years later, when Hamas won the second PA elections, these figures would assume key positions in the Palestinian cabinet and Legislative Assembly, first and foremost Ismail Hanyieh, Hamas prime minister between 2006–16 and currently head of the movement's political bureau.[68] Unlike Arafat, Abbas has failed to coexist with Hamas.

In 2006, Abbas planned to employ the international support that elevated him to the presidency in order to pressure Israel and achieve peace. In this context, he thought, it was better to have Hamas members in the Legislative Council than outside it, where it would be easier for them to hinder the talks. Abbas promised the Quartet (the US, the European Union, Russia and the UN) that, after the elections, he would bring about the disarmament of Hamas. 'Once the election was over,' reported the American Consul General in Jerusalem, Jake Walles, on what Abbas told him, 'the first thing that the new Palestinian Legislative Council will do is to ban the militias—so there will be one gun, one authority.'[69] Since then, as I will demonstrate below, Abbas stuck to this goal of 'one gun, one authority' under his exclusive executive control. Following its win, Hamas offered to form a unity government with Fatah, an overture that several senior Fatah were inclined to accept, but which Abbas opposed due to strong US opposition. 'The US clearly pushed for a confrontation between Fatah and Hamas,' writes Alvaro de-Soto, the UN Special Coordinator for the Middle East Peace Process from 2005–7.[70] From then on, the US policy did not change. Under its leadership, the Quartet offered three preconditions for Hamas to meet before it could be considered a legitimate political actor: to agree that the Palestinian state will recognise Israel, to abide by the Oslo agreements and to renounce violence.

Fatah's defeat in the 2006 general elections was an unprecedented achievement for the Islamic movement. For the first time in Arab history, an opposition party, and an Islamic one, came to power in democratic elections. But the US and Israel, with the support of the Quartet, did not respect the Palestinian democratic vote. They tried to reverse the results and bring Fatah back to lead the Palestinian Authority cabinet. They also strongly opposed the establishment of a national unity government and identified Dahlan, then Abbas' national-security adviser, as the person that could overthrow Hamas from power. On 4 October 2006, US Secretary of State Condoleezza Rice travelled to Ramallah to hold a discussion with Abbas regarding his talks with Hamas over a unity government. At that time, Abbas considered bringing Hamas to accept the Quartet precondition indirectly:

> At their joint press conference, Rice smiled as she expressed her nation's "great admiration" for Abbas's leadership. Behind closed doors, however, Rice's tone was sharper... Jake Walles, the consul general in Jerusalem, [told Abbas that] "Hamas should be given a clear choice, with a clear deadline: ... they either accept a new government that meets the Quartet principles, or they reject it. The consequences of Hamas' decision should also be clear: If Hamas does not agree [to the Quartet conditions] within the prescribed time, you should make clear your intention to declare a state of emergency and form an emergency government explicitly committed to that platform."

The American representative offered Abbas an explicit carrot and an implicit stick. 'If you act along these lines, we will support you both materially and politically.' He also encouraged Abbas to 'strengthen [his] team' by including 'credible figures of strong standing in the international community' such as Muhammad Dahlan.[71] But Abbas tried to avoid armed conflict. From the January 2006 elections to the June 2007 Fatah-Hamas armed clash in Gaza, Abbas considered dissolving the Palestinian Authority government of Hamas by calling a referendum on the two-state solution along Oslo agreement lines. Thus, Abbas sought to achieve through his presidential power what Fatah failed to get in the elections. De Soto thinks that Abbas wanted to co-opt Hamas into the Oslo process by imposing on it the referendum results that for sure, Abbas believed, would be in his favour. His advisers, most probably Dahlan and his men in the Fatah elite, who favoured fighting Hamas, told the Americans what they wanted to hear: that Abbas was ready to take Hamas on.[72]

'There is no one more hated among Hamas members than Muhammad Dahlan,' concludes Davis Rose. President George W. Bush 'has met Dahlan on at least three occasions.' After talks at the White House in July 2003, Bush publicly praised Dahlan as 'a good, solid leader.' In private, say multiple Israeli and American officials, the US president described him as 'our guy.' Based on original documents, Rose exposes 'a covert initiative, approved by Bush and implemented by Secretary of State Condoleezza Rice and Deputy National Security Adviser Elliott Abrams, to provoke a Palestinian civil war. The plan was for forces led by Dahlan.' The Americans did not stop their pressure when Abbas agreed in February 2007 with Hamas to form a unity government. They called on Abbas to 'collapse the government' if Hamas refused to alter its attitude toward Israel. For as long as the unity government remained in office, it was essential for Abbas to maintain 'independent control of key security forces.' He was to 'avoid Hamas integration with these services, while eliminating the Executive Force [of Hamas] or mitigating the challenges posed by its continued existence.' In other words, the Americans demanded that Abbas stick to their original strategy but change tactics. Instead of using his presidential power to call a referendum, they wanted him to block the unity government. 'Remember,' under-secretary of state David Welch told Abbas in November 2006, 'we need a government we can work with, which means it must endorse the Quartet principles. It has to be clear, no loopholes.'[73] Nevertheless, 'the secret plan backfired' in June 2007. Hamas initiated a preemptive attack that defeated Dahlan's disorganised forces and succeeded in seizing total control of the Gaza Strip.[74] Interestingly, the Dahlan rival militia inside Fatah and Palestinian Authority Security forces refrained completely from entering the fray to rescue Dahlan forces.[75] Since then, the Palestinian Authority has been divided both geographically and politically. If up to mid-2007 Abbas entertained the idea of engaging Hamas, its brutal attack on Fatah men in the Gaza Strip pushed Abbas to cooperate with the Americans, the Quartet and Israel against Hamas government. Together with Egypt, they launched a heavy siege on the Gaza Strip hoping, unrealistically, that it would lead the population to revolt. In response, Hamas initiated smuggling tunnels to Egypt connecting the Gaza Strip to the outside world. The Gaza Strip population rejected the external pressure despite their inhumane living conditions and suffering heavy casualties from successive Israeli army raids.

## Hamas Has Moved

Ironically, Hamas—founded in 1987 in opposition to the moderation of the PLO—has moved in the same direction. One can measure the changes in Hamas' position through comparing its strategic alignments with its public pronouncements. In this case, the yardstick of progress is its proximity to outsiders' standards, be those Israel's or the Quartet's position. Whoever uses this scale as the only metric is trapped in his or her own way of thinking, and misses the changes taking place within Hamas. In reality, what looks like standing water to Abbas and several of his colleagues, or to Israelis and Europeans, is nothing less than a whirlpool. There are many critiques to be raised against Hamas, and the organisation should be subject to criticism. But it is hard to ignore the impressive ideological trajectory the organisation has gone through over the years. Hamas' political journey began with the Islamic Charter in the summer of 1988, passed through the movement's platform for the Palestinian Legislative Council elections in 2006, and in 2017 is contained in the movement's new principal policy document, that has replaced the more militant Islamic Charter for all intents and purposes.[76]

Along the way, the changes and differences of opinion within Hamas did not lead to a fundamental division on ideological or political grounds as happened in each of the PLO organisations. Moreover, whereas the PLO changed its ideology and policy with Arafat the icon at its top, no Hamas leader became a ubiquitously revered political icon, not even Sheikh Ahmad Yassin, the group's founder, or Khaled Mishaal, who survived a failed Israeli assassination operation. Be it due to its Islamic principles that require surrendering only to Allah and putting Prophet Muhammad as its model, or because of its collective leadership and functioning political institutions, the absence of a cult of personality within Hamas enforces the group's reliance on consensus decision making. Maintaining a common framework requires Hamas to compromise and alter its ideological platform. It is easy to discern tensions, contradictions and ambiguities in the latest document—and I will discuss some of these below—but they are the price paid to keep the movement united.

The original Islamic Charter is a fervent and sweeping religious fundamentalist document. It is one-dimensional and relies on numerous quotations from the Quran. This charter does not distinguish between prophecy and reality, or between the present and the future. Everything can be achieved through jihad, and fulfilling the commandments of Islam and jihad is the central mission.

The party platform of 2006, on the other hand, is an action plan that addresses the here and now with no reference to theology. In addition, the 1988 Islamic Charter was addressed to the Islamic and Arabic world, while the party platform deals only with the Palestinian context, addressing Palestinian society as it really exists rather than as an ideal being sought. The platform is a policy document where Islam is not presented as a magic solution that contains all of the answers to practical and spiritual human problems. Unlike the 1988 Islamic Charter, which established Hamas as an alternative to the PLO (which, according to the Charter, had run its course), the new principal policy document of 2017 wants to preserve the PLO as a national framework into which Hamas can integrate and exert its influence. Moreover, the 1988 Charter presents Hamas as related to the international movement of the Muslim Brotherhood, while the new principal document declares that Hamas is 'a Palestinian-Islamic national liberation and resistance movement' that does not want to interfere in other national liberation struggles. In other words, Hamas does not intend on supporting the Muslim Brotherhood in their struggle against the rule of President Abdelfattah El-Sisi in neighbouring Egypt. From a pan-Muslim movement acting in Palestine has become a national-religious liberation party. One should note that Egypt under Sisi would not have changed its position vis-á-vis Hamas had it not disavowed its links to the Muslim Brotherhood and rebranded itself. When Hamas disassociated itself from the Muslim Brotherhood, the road for strategic cooperation with Egypt opened. Egypt and Hamas need each other in order to fight ISIS-linked groups in the Sinai Peninsula, and Egypt wants to make clear to Israel that it is not solely dependent on the Jewish state in its struggle against Islamist extremists.

In order to evaluate the journey made by Hamas since 1988, it is useful to compare it to the PLO. The PLO changed the Palestinian National Charter in 1968 when it became a coalition organisation led by Fatah. Almost 30 years later, in 1996, the

PLO grit its teeth and cancelled most of the Charter articles, but refrained from producing a new document. In addition, unlike Hamas, for many years the PLO has avoided admitting explicitly that its policy made the charter irrelevant. The 1988 Palestinian Declaration of Independence, an undeniable deviation from the National Charter, entirely ignores the founding document of the organisation and does not include it as one of the sources of the Declaration. The PLO preferred to ignore this document; Hamas, on the other hand, responded without hesitation by acknowledging that change was in order. Indeed, the changes made by the PLO since the mid-1970s are in some ways much more radical than those Hamas proposed in May 2017. Nevertheless, one must appreciate the willingness to admit the need to change, coming from a movement that attributes religious and political significance to texts and ideology. As a religious movement based on sacred texts and written tradition, Hamas takes words seriously. The movement seeks to anchor its development in religious texts, and to express in words its current outlook. Unlike pragmatist parties who prioritise action and are not afraid to deviate from a platform, Hamas wants its words to align with its actions as much as possible in political life.

Already in 2006, senior Hamas figures announced that they were in principle ready to change the charter. Hamas made it in 2017 while simultaneously renouncing one of the main tenets of the Islamic Charter: viewing Jews as a religious and national enemy, and condemning them. In the principal policy document, Hamas explicitly distinguishes between Zionism and Judaism. The movement's struggle is not, as it has declared in the past, against Judaism, but against the Zionist project and the occupation. And for Hamas it is a bitter struggle.

Unlike the PLO, which in 1988 had already accepted the UN 1947 partition resolution and implicitly accepted the existence of Israel as a Jewish state, Hamas's new document rejects 'from the beginning' the Balfour Declaration and the legitimacy of the existence of the State of Israel. Yet this statement contradicts another section of the new document, where Hamas indicates a willingness to accept a Palestinian state on all of the 1967 territories. Hamas makes clear in its new document that an acceptance of a state within the 1967 borders does not constitute a recognition of the Zionist entity, nor a relinquishment of any Palestinian national rights, including the return of refugees and the right to liberate Palestine in its entirety. In other words, Hamas is not positioning itself to sign an end-of-claims agreement with Israel or surrender to the Quartet dictates. However, Hamas's present document indicates that a state across all the 1967 territories, including Jerusalem, is a potential framework for the creation of a national agreement with Fatah. How can one reconcile between the Fatah government and its practice of political compromise with Israel, the pursuit of an agreement that ends mutual claims, and the positions of Hamas's new principal document?

There are other contradictions evident in the document. According to the new document, 'resistance,' or armed struggle, is a strategic choice and not a tactic. Yet at the same time Hamas states that armed struggle must be managed in stages, and 'within the management of the struggle'—that is, subject to tactical considerations. The document also fails to clarify how Hamas plans to achieve a state within 1967 borders without a political process. Moreover, the new document states that the liberation of Palestine is a duty of Arab and Islamic nations, and that the movement rejects any state-building effort that relinquishes any one of the rights of the Palestinian people. These are ideological declarations and unrealistic ambitions in light of the Arab world's devotion to the Arab League's 2002 peace plan, and at a time when Israel's two neighbours, Jordan and Egypt, have signed peace treaties with Israel.

In the middle of 2014's Operation Protective Edge, Khaled Meshaal, the head of the Hamas Political Bureau, held two long talks with Mahmoud Abbas on behalf of Hamas, mediated by Qatar's Emir. In these talks, Meshaal gave Abbas a green light to proceed to negotiate a state within the 1967 borders with Israel and to manage non-violent resistance.[77] The implication was that if Abbas presented a permanent status agreement with Israel, that included, in line with the Arab League's plan, a Palestinian state within the 1967 borders, it was likely that Hamas would accommodate to the new reality as it did in 1994. Then, Hamas recognised the jurisdiction of the PA rather than rebelling against the authority that was based on the Oslo agreement. Hamas repeated this type of pragmatism in 2006 when it ran candidates in the PA Legislative Council elections. In both cases, Hamas pragmatism deviated from its fundamental ideology. According to Hamas' original perspective, the Palestinian Authority institutions were founded in sin, on the grounds of the Oslo Accords that Hamas so strongly attacked in 1993.

The new principal document enshrines into a foundational document the political framework that Meshaal has given Fatah, while trying to maintain ideological purity. The new document allows both extremists and moderates in Hamas to adhere to a common framework. Despite the rigidity of some of the clauses in the document, it is important to remember that Hamas is a dynamic movement, which is not averse to shifting its ideology. The dynamism that characterises the movement implies that this document is not the last stop on its ideological journey. Indeed, Yahya Sinwar, the head of the Hamas political bureau, indicated this in May 2018. Briefing the international media on the Return March (see below), he accused Israel of acting 'as a state above the law and [...] ignoring the international law.' The people of Gaza have the right to remove the fence Israel put inside the Gaza Strip because 'This is not an internationally-recognized border. Based on the Armistice Agreement, Gaza has more than 200km square behind the fence.' Thus, implicitly Sinwar committed Hamas to the standards of international law and to the Gaza Strip's internationally recognised border with Israel, which is that of the pre-1967 border. And in July 2018 Musa Abu Marzuq, number two in Hamas, tweeted in Arabic to his followers: 'What does Hamas want? Hamas wants a Palestinian state in the West Bank and Gaza Strip with Jerusalem as its capital.' Hamas also wants:

> inter-Palestinian reconciliation based on unity, political partnership and removal of the occupation, that the siege of Gaza to be lifted and a plan that will solve its problems. What it rejects? Hamas rejects a state in Gaza Strip, the separation of Gaza Strip from the West Bank, as well as what is known as the deal of the century [referring to US President Donald Trump's proposals].[78]

## Hamas Challenges Abbas

A decade into the siege that Israel, Egypt and the Palestinian Authority launched upon the Gaza Strip in 2007 in order to push the Strip citizens to topple their regime, it became clear that the brutal collective punishment had failed to achieve its political target. Gaza did not revolt. Moreover, as Hamas disassociated itself from the Muslim Brotherhood, Egypt and Hamas could cooperate politically.

In June 2017, following Hamas' decision to end the futile national unity talks with Abbas and establish a cabinet style committee to manage the Gaza Strip,[79] Abbas intensified the siege. He decided to stop funding the electricity that the Gaza Strip receives from Israel. Consequently, Israel cut the supply to the point where the Gaza Strip had between two-to-four hours' worth of electricity per day. In addition, Abbas stopped paying salaries to about 40,000 Palestinian Authority employees in the Strip, and cut the number of Gaza Strip citizens that his authority allowed to receive medical treatment in Israel. Severely cutting access to food, running water, light and electricity-dependent vital services, limiting import of goods, and preventing people's exit and entrance, created a humanitarian catastrophe. These extreme measures, international organisations conclude, will make the Gaza Strip's conditions unliveable by 2020, if not already in 2018.[80]

The humanitarian crisis did not push Hamas to depoliticise and go back to armed resistance. On the contrary, based on the new principal document, Hamas further developed its political track during 2017–18. Under the sponsorship of Egypt, in July 2017, Sinwar, on behalf of Hamas, signed with Muhammad Dahlan an agreement titled 'A National Consensus Document for Trust-Building.' The agreement facilitated the compromise between the two bitter enemies and settled the bloody conflict of 2007 between Hamas and Dahlan, then Fatah and the PA's strongman in the Gaza Strip who had since 1994 conducted a brutal crackdown on Hamas. Dahlan agreed to compensate families of those who his forces killed and provide payment to men injured in the 2007 clashes. Dahlan would head a unity government in the Gaza Strip, in which Hamas would control the Ministry of the Interior. The government administration would incorporate thousands of public workers appointed by Hamas to whom Abbas refused to pay salaries, and Fatah-affiliated clerks that had quit en masse in 2007 on orders from Ramallah, and for whom Abbas had then cut their salaries by half or forced them to retire. In other words, Dahlan would represent the Gaza Strip Fatah unrelated to the Abbas regime, and co-opt significant numbers of its members. Abu Dhabi, who hosted Dahlan, agreed to fund the new administration and the building of a new modern power station that would decrease the Gaza Strip's dependency on Israeli electricity. In addition, Egypt decided to supply fuel to the Gaza Strip in order to cover the shortage Abbas and

Israel created. In exchange, Hamas agreed to control the Jihadists operating from the Gaza Strip against Egyptian forces and civilians in Sinai. In September, Dahlan started compensating the bereaved families of Hamas and Islamic Jihad.[81]

In the same month Hamas manoeuvred politically by dissolving the administrative unity it had established for Dahlan. Instead, Hamas invited a Ramallah based technocrat's government to take over all Gaza Strip civil responsibilities.[82] Many Gazans warmly greeted the Ramallah delegation showing that they preferred ending the split between Hamas and Fatah to institutionalising it. Hamas had to follow its public and agreed to promote reconciliation. Thus, Abbas faced the huge challenge of solving the Gaza Strip's humanitarian problems. In March–June 2018 Abbas faced a new challenge.

'Why do I march in Gaza,' Fadi Abu Shammalah asked rhetorically in April 2018,[83] relating to his participation in the Return March, the title given to a weekly series of unarmed mass protests along the Gaza Strip's border with Israel. Started on Land Day, end of March 2018, the demonstrations reached their peak in mid-May, commemorating the 1948 Nakba and protesting against the inauguration of the American Embassy in Jerusalem that day, and in early June, commemorating the 1967 occupation. By 10 June 2018, Israel had killed 135 demonstrators, and wounded 14,518 people. No Israelis died, only four were injured. By 22 March 2019, Israel had killed 195 Palestinians and wounded 28,939 people in these demonstrations, versus two Israelis killed and fifty-six injured. The largest number of casualties were among protestors hit by live ammunition.[84] 'So why am I willing to risk my life by joining the Great Return March?' posed Fadi Abu Shammalah. 'I fully believe in the March's tactics of unarmed, direct, civilian-led mass action. I have also been inspired by how the action has unified the Palestinian people in the politically fractured Gaza Strip. And the march is an effective way to highlight the unbearable living conditions facing residents of the Gaza Strip: four hours of electricity a day, the indignity of having our economy and borders under siege, the fear of having our homes shelled.' Fadi Abu Shammalah, one of the nongovernmental organisers of the protest, described it as inclusive national event. 'At the border, I haven't seen a single Hamas flag, or Fatah banner... we have flown only one flag—the Palestinian flag... True, Hamas members are participating... But the Great Return March is not Hamas's action. It is all of ours.' Beyond demonstrations next to the Israeli border, the Return March, that at its peak attracted tens of thousands, included raising awareness of Palestinian identity through popular dancing and singing, and eating typical Palestinian dishes while hearing refugee memoirs on pre-1948 lives in native villages. The Return March signalled for Abu Shammalah 'that we exist, we will remain, we are humans deserving of dignity, and we have the right to return to our homes.'

Hamas did not initiate the March nor did it order people to join. It started, recalls Ahmed Abu Artema,

> with a Facebook post I wrote on 7 January in which I wondered what would happen if 200,000 protesters gathered near the Israel fence with the Gaza Strip and entered the lands that are ours, which were occupied by Israel in 1948 carrying the Palestinian flags and the keys of their houses in Mandatory Palestine. I ended the post with the hashtag #GreatMarchofReturn. People engaged with the post, and after two weeks everyone was talking about it.

He was motivated mostly by Trump's announcements on relocating the American embassy to Jerusalem and UNRAWA. The Israeli siege and the Palestinians' devastating life conditions empowered his motivation. The Return March 'is a collective effort by young people, civil society organisations, political parties and factions,' not an exclusive Hamas event.[85]

'I thought we would hold the march for a month or two,' said Hasan al-Kurd, one of the twenty Return March organisers. 'That they are still going is nothing short of astonishing.' The organisers believed in non-violent struggle. 'My original plan was to protest a kilometre and a half from the fence and to approach it very slowly. We really wanted to throw a carnival for the whole family,' said al-Kurd. Looking back a year later, he concludes, 'Some of that actually happened toward the beginning. But the other Palestinian factions, including Hamas, ridiculed us—and me personally—and thought that we needed to approach the fence from the beginning. And look at what happened. In retrospect, I should have insisted on that point. If we had done what we wanted, we could have gotten headlines not only about the blockade but also the return of refugees.'[86] Thus, the organisers lost control over their original idea but with Hamas, the ruling power in Gaza leading they gained a facilitator. Hamas provided the needed logistics to make it a mass demonstration and national integration event. In addition, Hamas members, together with civil society volunteers, took care to keep the demonstrations unarmed and nonpartisan.[87] As the March developed, the role of Hamas in leading the protest grew significantly.

Hamas showed that it is a national-inclusive organisation rather than a divisive sectarian organisation as Abbas claims. In the absence of the PLO anti-occupation struggle, Hamas proved its capability to fill the vacuum. Hamas did what Abbas could have done in the West Bank had he trusted his Fatah colleagues and his citizens to adhere to non-violent means, and had he built an integrated and highly motivated polity.

Hamas also proved its readiness to prefer non-violent means over jihad. Like the PLO between 1974 and 1993, Hamas changed its discourse on armed struggle. Up to 1974, armed struggle was the PLO's exclusive strategy. When the PLO decided to enter international politics and accept its norms, the

PLO began to forswear armed struggle. First, the PLO stopped seeing the armed struggle as its exclusive strategy, and frequently switched between violent and non-violent tactics. Later, politics became the group's hegemonic method, though at times, according to the PLO, it would still require the backing of armed struggle to more effectively function. However, when armed struggle obstructed the PLO's political gains, it was eschewed. The mass uprising of the 1987 intifada showed that terror and guerrilla attacks were irrelevant or less aefective. In the Oslo agreement of 1993, therefore, the PLO opted exclusively for political tactics.

In Hamas' 1988 charter, holy war, or jihad, was described as the only legitimate means through which to liberate Palestine. However, in May 2018, relating to the Return March, Sinwar stated that Hamas had chosen the 'wonderful and civilised' method of non-armed clashes 'which is respected by the world, and which is appropriate for the current circumstances.' If needed by circumstances, it would not hesitate to restore the armed struggle. Yet, Sinwar admitted, the non-violent demonstrations achieved more than the armed struggle. Hamas members could have 'rained thousands of missiles down' on Israeli cities, but instead, symbolically speaking, 'chose to take off their military uniforms and put their weapons aside. They have temporarily abandoned the means of armed struggle and turned to this wonderful civilised method.'[88] Thus, Sinwar publically admitted that when the international community is Hamas' target audience the armed struggle is suspended. He also acknowledged that the armed struggle is politically destructive and uncivilised.

Sinwar glorified the Return March's accomplishments. It 'restored the Right of Return to the Palestinian, Arab, and international consciousness as one of the important rights and principles of the Palestinian people.' 'Another goal fulfilled by these marches,' in Sinwar's account, 'is that they have placed the Palestinian national cause on the world's agenda once again.'

Moreover, 'on behalf of the Arab Palestinian people and all the Arab and Islamic peoples, our people in Gaza have rejected that decision' to move the US embassy to Jerusalem, 'by this great activity and by recording its testimony for the sake of history, and by signing this testimony with the blood of the martyrs.' Hamas succeeded using the media to shape international public opinion, Sinwar added. 'Our people have imposed their agenda upon the whole world. There was supposed to be a romantic picture of the opening of the US embassy in Jerusalem on the world's television screens. But our people, in their collective consciousness, forced the whole world to split the television screens between the footage of fraud, deception, falsehood, and oppression, manifest in the attempt to impose Jerusalem as the capital of the occupation state, and between the image of injustice, oppression, heroism, and determination painted by our own people in their sacrifices—the sacrifice of their children as an offering for Jerusalem and the Right of Return.'[89] Sinwar's positive evaluation of Hamas' non-violent and media strategy achievements signals that the movement is ready to continue along this track. 'Who really wants to confront a nuclear superpower with four slingshots?' he asked rhetorically in October 2018. 'I'm saying I don't want any more wars. What I want is an end to the siege. My first commitment is to act in the interest of my people; to protect them and to defend their right for freedom and independence.'[90]

## Sceptical Abbas

Whereas Arafat saw Hamas' struggle with Fatah and PLO in political terms, as a struggle over national leadership, Abbas insists that Hamas was and remains an Islamist-fundamentalist movement that plans to destroy the Palestinian Authority, take over the West Bank and impose its radical religious order there.

In summer 2014, in the middle of another Israeli army operation in the Gaza Strip, Abbas met with Khaled Mishaal, the head of the movement's political bureau, and argued, in a bizarre manner, that Hamas had unmistakably brought about the Israeli attack. Moreover, despite Mishaal's renunciation, Abbas blamed Hamas for organising a secret team in the West Bank for the purpose of preparing an armed revolt against his Palestinian Authority. Abbas based this allegation on a report he received from the head of the Israeli security service Yoram Cohen. This meeting was not an unusual one. Abbas has admitted that he meets regularly with the head of the Israeli Security Service and they agree on 99 per cent of topics.[91] Yet, based on what the Israeli security service published following the interrogation of these cell members, Abbas went too far in his accusation. A military wing member that Israel deported directed the cell from Turkey rather than Hamas political leaders in Gaza. Its members hid just a few weapons and ammunition, definitely insufficient for a revolt, and its mission was to operate only in case of a leadership vacuum and chaos but not against Abbas.[92]

Abbas, like his predecessor Arafat, is a practicing Muslim who prays daily and fasts during Ramadan, but religious radicalism disgusts him. He insists on distinguishing between state and politics, political decisions and religion. Religious belief and practicing Islam, Abbas argue, should remain in the private sphere. Abbas rejects Hamas' religious martyrdom cult that, substantively, is not different from the national martyrdom cult of Fatah where the armed struggle is its preferred strategy. Abbas wants to cultivate optimism in the physical realm rather than despair and the expectation of an afterlife in heaven.

Abbas agreed to from a national unity government with Hamas for the same strategic reasons he insisted on letting it run in the 2006 elections: to bring Hamas under his supervision, including its armed wing, and to accept the Oslo agreements implicitly if not explicitly. At times he had another reason in mind: to show the US and Israel that he had an alternative to their rejection of his peace deal, as he did in June 2014 in reaction to US secretary of state John Kerry's ideas (see above). On other occasions, Abbas hoped to utilise Hamas losing Arab bases. In 2012, Hamas lost its Syrian base when it refused to support Bashar al-Assad in the civil war, and in 2013 Hamas lost Egypt's support when the army dismissed President Mohamad Morsi and his Muslim Brotherhood regime. As mentioned above, Hamas revised its policy in 2017 and, since then, enjoys Egypt's backing.

Encouraging Abbas to hold to his preconditions, Israel cooperates with him regarding the national unity government. In October 2017, Israel allowed Palestinian delegations to travel through its territory to Gaza. In addition, Israel worried that the harsh reality in Gaza would start to spill over. This threat existed in a literal sense, as the Gaza Strip's untreated sewage started polluting Israel's Mediterranean beaches. The Israeli government has rejected proposals to relieve the situation in the Strip through projects that Hamas could take credit for, such as a treatment plant to deal with the sewage, or the construction of a major seaport under international oversight. Israel also learned long ago that the price of re-occupying Gaza would be too high, and that Abbas would never agree to entering the Gaza Strip atop an IDF tank. Israel has no choice—it must agree to allow Abbas into Gaza as part of national reconciliation efforts.

Seeing that Abbas had failed to impose his conditions on Hamas, in the second half of 2018 Israel negotiated with Hamas over UN special envoy to the peace process Nickolay Mladenov's three-stage proposal for a long-term ceasefire. The first phase included an end to confrontations along the border with Israel and the opening of crossings, bringing an end to the siege that Israel and Egypt placed on Hamas in 2007, which they hoped would bring down its regime. In the second phase of Mladenov's proposal, Israel would allow more electricity into the Strip, and the last phase would include the building of a seaport, an airport, and a power station in Egyptian territory that would serve Gaza. Funding for these projects, for the Israeli electricity, as well as for reconstructing the Gaza Strip's infrastructure, would come from Qatar.[93] In summer 2018, only the first stage was implemented. The sides could not go beyond it due to their disagreement on prisoner release. Israel conditioned further steps with the return of the bodies of two soldiers and its citizens that had crossed the border into the Strip. Hamas agreed to do this only if Israel released the movement prisoners it had re-arrested in 2014 contravening the previous exchange of 2011. Thus, Hamas achieved the end of the blockade and opened the door to being internationally recognised. It also proved to its public that standing strong pays off. In exchange, Israel postponed the probability of a military confrontation with Hamas, which Israel knows it cannot win.

Hence, Hamas discussed two different, yet interrelated agreements: one with Israel, the other with Abbas. In the course of the latter, Hamas agreed to dissolve its local government and let the national unity government enjoy full power over civil affairs including the security control along the Strip borders. To get the military wing to agree to these concessions, Hamas insisted upon keeping fighting tunnels under its control and maintaining its armed entities. According to documents leaked to the Arab press, Hamas agreed with the Egyptian mediators that minor questions, such as Hamas employee salaries, would be resolved first. Hamas demanded that the PA pay the salaries of some 20,000 public sector workers whom Hamas hired during its years in power, some of them to replace Fatah affiliated employees whom Abbas ordered to resign in 2007. Ramallah preconditioned paying these salaries with getting full control of government activities, including Hamas' tax collection that financed the Hamas administration.[94] The sides also debated who had to pay for the additional electricity needed to build a sewage treatment plant. The Palestinian Authority claimed that it was spending a significant portion of its budget on Gaza, while Hamas was not sharing its revenues with the Ramallah administration. Gaza responded that a significant amount of these expenditures were covered by the customs duties the PA collects on merchandise imported to Gaza via Israel. This argument was solved with Qatar agreeing to include these items in its Gaza Strip rehabilitation projects. The interesting point in Egypt's proposal was its support for Hamas' positions. Egypt and Hamas rejected Abbas' precondition that his government would also oversee the tunnels and Hamas' armed wing. Egypt suggested heading a trilateral committee that would discuss the issue of security in the Gaza Strip. In other words, in order to make reconciliation easier, Hamas would be obliged not to use its armed wing unilaterally, while the Ramallah government would not decide on peace with Israel unilaterally. Decisions on war and peace, said Hamas spokespeople, demand a national consensus. In short, Egypt supported Hamas' demand for joint control over Gaza with the Ramallah government.[95]

But Abbas refused to compromise on power sharing. 'We are not a foreign power that is called to give up Gaza Strip completely, but partners,' grumbled Ismail Haniyeh, the head of Hamas' political bureau.[96] Although he had caused them great suffering, Abbas saw himself as rescuing Gazans from Hamas' despotic tendencies. Since the 2006 elections, Abbas has wanted to subordinate Hamas under his government's control, not allowing it to keep any autonomous armed unit or authority. 'We want one state, under one regime, one weapon, one security organisation,' Abbas stated to the PLO Central Committee in January 2018.[97] Abbas showed zero willingness to compromise on these principles although in a few West Bank refugee camps semi-autonomous Fatah armed groups exist.[98] 'We did all we can to make the reconciliation a success, but, unfortunately, the result for empowering the government was zero.' The suspicious Abbas insisted on getting all or nothing. 'We have been working hard for six months and got nothing, not the government, not the crossings, not security, nothing,' he said. 'It's all hypocrisy. They don't want reconciliation,' he added. Abbas accused Hamas of being responsible for the assassination attempt against Prime Minister Rami Hamdallah and intelligence chief Majid Faraj in Gaza City, March 2018.[99] Abbas sees Hamas–Egypt cooperation and Hamas' talks with Israel as collaboration with the Trump administration—tantamount to cooperation with the devil. Such a plot, as Abbas sees it, aims to destroy the Palestinian national project by developing a separate state in Gaza.

Consequently, in early 2019, Abbas further widened the schism with Hamas. In January, he ordered his employees to pull out from the Gaza Strip, letting Hamas taking full control of it including the border crossings.[100] He also decided to dissolve the Palestinian parliament, hold elections within half a year and form a new political cabinet instead of the professional caretaker government. Moreover, in February, Abbas stopped paying salaries to 5,000 Palestinian Authority employees in the Gaza Strip.[101]

Simultaneously, Israel changed its strategy after failing to bring down the Hamas regime or impose the Abbas regime upon it. Instead, it wants to de-escalate its southern border by creating a mutual deterrence between it and the Islamic movement and integrate the Gaza Strip administration in Trump's deal. Israel and Egypt agreed to bypass Abbas' objection to transfer aid funding to Gaza by allowing Qatar's envoy to carry cash money to the Gaza Strip. Netanyahu admitted that letting Qatar donate money to Hamas is part of Israel's broader strategy to keep the Palestinians divided. Exacerbating the separation between Hamas and the PA helps to prevent a Palestinian state.[102] Israeli overtures towards Hamas and Egypt has distanced Israel from Abbas. The Israeli security establishment published its conclusion that Abbas is a key obstacle to Gaza's rehabilitation. Abbas, according to the Israeli intelligence report, shows no interest in Gazans' suffering. The eighty-three-year-old president spends only a few hours a day in office and before it is too late, he is working to secure the wealth his two sons made, much of it due to his presidency. The Israeli establishment has concluded that Abbas' perspective on the Gaza Strip is irrational and shaped by conspiracy theories. Abbas is sure that Hamas is behind the West Bank demonstrations calling on him to lift the sanctions he placed on the Strip.[103]

4

# SUCCESSION STRUGGLE

In May 2018 Ramallah was awash with rumours over Abbas' deteriorating health, long before Israeli intelligence, and later the president's office, confirmed. Abbas suffered from pneumonia and his doctors feared a complete system shutdown. Israel learned of his rapidly deteriorating condition and decided to send a specialist to Ramallah to join the team of foreign doctors already treating Abbas. After two days in intensive care and one week in hospital, Abbas returned home.[1]

The rumour mill creates an alternative media in a landscape where Palestinians often consider official spokespeople to be purveyors of fake news regarding Abbas' health. Rumours, thus, are a symptom of the political environment. Rumours and alternative media channels flourish in centralised regimes, especially when they face embarrassment, and a vacuum is created. For years, Abbas has rejected the requests of Fatah members and Arab politicians to appoint a deputy. This is likely borne out of his desire to prevent a struggle between those who deem themselves worthy of replacing him and those who could opt for subversion should they not be selected. Individuals deemed to be threats to Abbas' rule in the past, such as Muhammed Dahlan and Salam Fayyad, were dealt with harshly.

Under Arafat, succession was not an issue. The consensus around Arafat pushed Abu Musa in 1983, who sought to undermine him, out of Fatah and the PLO, and soon his small organisation and the alternative PLO that his Syrian patron established, ceased to be active organisations. Even when Israel subjected Yasser Arafat to a physical siege and when his health was slowly fading, no war of succession took place. This was not because his administration was calcifying. On the contrary, disagreements prevailed, and often his colleagues demanded reforms in his decision-making process. However, everyone accepted his seniority. Abbas ultimately benefited from the leadership vacuum that Arafat left behind. With two individuals, Abu Jihad and Abu Iyad, both alive and wielding greater sway within Fatah and among the public, Abbas looked likely to lose any succession struggle at that time. For the same reason, the weakening Abbas fails to prevent a succession struggle presently.

Arafat's death created a symbolic vacuum that Mahmoud Abbas is unqualified to fill. Abbas did not succeed in achieving liberation and state sovereignty that could have served as new unifying institutions and symbols. Worse, the few institutions that the Palestinian Authority possess have stopped functioning under Abbas. The unhealthy old president is under political siege both externally, by those who want to impose on him a solution to the conflict with Israel that he rejects, and domestically, by the vast majority of his public who see him as a failed leader. Since 2016, almost two thirds of Palestinians have expressed a desire to see Abbas step down according to polls published by Dr Khalil Shikaki.[2] While Abbas insistently clings to power, the rug is being pulled out from under his feet.

The struggle within Fatah over his succession began in 2016 and has rapidly been gaining traction ever since. The political chaos in Ramallah affected the Palestinian Authority's international agenda. West European governments suspended their efforts to resume the Israeli-Palestinian peace process when Abbas was hospitalised or when the succession struggle intensified. Out of this struggle emerged five types of successor: the alternative movement; the Abbas-compatible leader; the security service man; the ousted; and the popular leader in captivity.

*The Alternative Movement*

Hamas turned in 1994–6 from an anti-establishment movement aiming to replace the PLO to an extra-establishment opposition waiting for the public to call upon it to assume the leadership. By running in the 2006 elections, Hamas entered the Palestinian Authority and changed its aim to replace Fatah as the ruler, or at least share power with it. Hamas' win in 2006 vaulted senior Legislative Council member Aziz Dweik to the speakership and, according to the Basic Law, next in line to the presidency until the general elections. Not without Abbas' influence, the Palestinian Constitutional Court ruled on November 2016 that the president has the power to revoke the parliamentary immunity of Palestinian Legislative Council members. Thus in 2017 Abbas was able to revoke Dahlan's parliamentary immunity and prevent Legislative Council Speaker Aziz Dweik, of Hamas, from becoming acting president as stipulated in the Palestinian Authority Basic Law. For the same ends, in summer 2018 Abbas considered replacing the PLO Central Council with the PA Legislative Council.[3]

The struggle between Fatah and Hamas is mainly over the possession of powerful government posts. Since Hamas entered the Palestinian Authority and changed its terms and conditions on settling the conflict with Israel (see above), the differences between the two movements have narrowed. Moreover, since

Fatah has no party doctrine on domestic affairs in general and on state religious relations in particular, and with the West Bank Muslims becoming increasingly orthodox since 2000, secular Fatah members maintain a low profile. The status of Islam in the public sphere is not a site of open contention between Hamas and Fatah. Instead, the fight over high-ranking governmental positions constitutes the primary fissure between the groups.

### The Compatible

In 2017 Abbas nominated his loyal negotiator Saeb Erekat, the PLO Executive Committee's General Secretary, as his number two in the PLO's top institution. Erekat replaced Yasser Abed Rabbo who previously represented FIDA (the Palestinian Democratic Union) and, since 2002, was an independent Executive Committee member. Abed Rabbo was fully loyal to Arafat and, representing FIDA and later as a nonaffiliated Executive Committee member, he could not challenge the Chairman or claim succession. Abbas showed him the exit in July 2015 based on suspicions that he was cooperating with Dahlan.

Saeb Erekat may claim the throne, arguing that according to the Basic Law the Palestinian Authority is subordinated to the PLO. The Executive Committee is the body charged with running the organisation and the secretary-general, therefore, should succeed Abbas. However, Erekat's standing inside Fatah is not strong enough for that. His political power is drawn almost entirely from Abbas's patronage. He has no power base among the security services nor does he exude the aura of an imprisoned resistance fighter. Erekat does not have the electoral assets to enable himself or Fatah to emerge victorious against Hamas.

Abbas also reshuffled the Fatah Central Committee. In November 2016 he worked to scupper Marwan Barghouti's election as his deputy in the Central Committee. Instead, he selected

Mahmoud Al-Aloul, giving him just a modest boost in the race to succeed the Palestinian leader. Abbas' authority is only formal, and he does not have the legitimacy to crown Al-Aloul his successor.

In Abbas' eyes, al-Aloul, aged 68, is an ideal deputy, for the same reasons that Anwar Sadat was chosen by Gamel Abdel Nasser: a member of the old guard, not particularly charismatic, and having sworn loyalty to his superiors. In the eyes of his peers, as well as Israeli intelligence, Sadat was viewed as someone who lacked all leadership qualities—someone to fill the revered Nasser's shoes for a matter of months until the competing power holders in the party, the army and the government decide who will be president. Sadat got rid of those stakeholders rather quickly, and set his own path. Even if al-Aloul is cut from similar cloth to Sadat, he is not the vice president of the Palestinian Authority but just number two in Fatah.

Al-Aloul was arrested by Israeli forces when he was 17, just after the occupation began, and spent three years in prison before being deported to Jordan. He joined Fatah and became a combatant under the command of Abu Jihad. Over the years, he replaced his support for armed struggle as a means of achieving independence with support for peace talks and the Oslo Accords. Israel allowed him to return to the West Bank in 1995, and a year later Yasser Arafat appointed him governor of Nablus. He entered the public consciousness after the IDF killed his son, Jihad, during the second intifada. In 2006 al-Aloul was elected to the Palestinian Legislative Council and was appointed welfare minister by Abbas (a position previously held by Abu Jihad's widow). In 2009 he became a member of the Fatah Central Committee. Al-Aloul lacks diplomatic experience, and like Abbas he is suspicious of Hamas' willingness to compromise with Fatah.

Al-Aloul is first and foremost Abbas' man, as opposed to Dahlan and Jibril Rajoub's (number three in Fatah hierarchy), who claim to be Abbas' successors. Dahlan and Rajub were appointed and groomed by Arafat in 1994 to head the Preventive Security Service in the Gaza Strip and the West Bank, respectively, whereas Marwan Barghouti built his own power base in Fatah and challenged Arafat's policy without ever undermining his leadership.

Should Abbas step down, al-Aloul will have to transform himself from Fatah's number two to president of the Palestinian Authority in three ways. First, he will need to show that his path toward Palestinian independence is different from Abbas' failed one; he will have to ingratiate himself, not without difficulty, among his younger and better known competitors and get the backing of the security establishment; and he will need to gain formal public legitimacy. This can take place either through the formal route of general elections or informally through organised and committed resistance to the Israeli occupation.

*The Security Service Man*

As Abbas' political descent has taken a turn for the worse, he has begun relying on his security forces. Abbas uses them to suppress Hamas and civil society opposition. In a political system where the lines between party loyalty and civil service are blurred, and when job security is predicated on membership in Fatah, the security and intelligence forces are political players. They are the guardians of the present order and their special status within it. The head of the Palestinian Security Services, Majid Faraj, enjoys Abbas' trust. Abbas sends him to political missions as his special envoy. In 2017, when Saeb Erekat, the Palestinian chief negotiator and PLO Executive Committee General Secretary was ill, Abbas nominated Faraj to take Erekat's post in the Palestinian peace negotiating team.

Faraj was born in Daheisha refugee camp near Bethlehem. His father was killed by Israel in the second intifada and his family is active in the Israeli-Palestinian bereaved family forum for peace and reconciliation (Parents Circle Family Forum, founded in 1995). Despite lacking popularity and being labelled as collaborators with the occupier, Faraj and the Palestinian Security Service may be unwilling to lose their political power on the day after Abbas' tenure. Faraj can promise Fatah seniors that he will ensure stability and their position in his administration. Faraj can also build on his appreciation by Israeli and US intelligence officials—due to a joint effort against Hamas—and expect them to pave his way to presidency. He may face opposition from those who stay outside Abbas' tiny, ruling elite—representatives of the people who do not take kindly to the Palestinian Authority's coordination with Israel, and the lasting occupation that impedes Palestinian democracy.

Faraj, Erekat or Rjoub the head of the Palestinian Football Association and number three in Fatah, do not challenge Abbas. They are the backbones of his administration. Abbas pushes them forward to block other competitors, as well as to ensure that one of his trustworthy allies enters the presidency and continues to carry out his policy agenda. 'Palestinian Authority security forces have become the most efficient, visible, and functional arm of Palestinian governance,' Agha and Khalidi presume on the day after Abbas leaves office. 'In the absence of countervailing legal and political institutions, organized popular movements, or capable representative bodies, there will be a strong temptation for the security forces to fill the vacuum of a frail national leadership, if only to avoid a comprehensive institutional collapse.'[4]

### The Ousted

Abbas kicked Mohammed Dahlan out of Fatah in 2011, and since then he has sought political refuge in the United Arab Emirates. In 2016, Dahlan and his Emirates patron wanted to do away with

Abbas, and tried to gain the support of Egypt and Jordan in their plan.[5] Dahlan enjoys strong ties with the Egyptian military brass, and, in 2014, harshly attacked Abbas on Egyptian television.[6] Egypt had other worries apart from the future of Palestinian succession. It was looking for a way to stop the support by Hamas' military wing for Islamic State affiliates in Sinai, and to cut off Hamas from the Muslim Brotherhood. Dahlan, who in 2007 fought against Hamas and lost, promised Egypt in 2016 to take care of the Islamist group with great efficiency when he defeats Abbas. By bringing the Emirates, Egypt, and Jordan to his side, Dahlan hoped to force Abbas to resign, before uniting Fatah under his leadership and initiating elections. Dahlan then believed that Hamas was weak and suffering from internal splits, and thought that Fatah under his leadership would continue to successfully exploit his major rivals' difficulties. Abbas, however, rejected the Egyptian pressure to challenge Hamas with a united Fatah, and refused to reconcile with Dahlan or let him return to the Palestinian Authority's territory. Abbas also publicly criticised Egypt's intervention in Palestinian domestic affairs. The Egyptian media responded by criticising Abbas in turn.[7]

Dahlan also had strong ties to officials in the Israeli security establishment. As the former head of the Palestinian Preventive Security forces in Gaza, he worked with the Israeli internal security and the Israeli army against Hamas, collaborated with retired Israeli officials on lucrative economic initiatives, and negotiated with Israel on temporary arrangements as well as a final-status agreement. He shares former Defence Minister Avigdor Lieberman's desire to see Abbas go. Dahlan has promised Israel that, once elected, he will both continue suppressing Hamas and bring about a regional peace agreement.

The Hashemite Kingdom was uninterested in getting its hands dirty in the succession struggle, while at the same time hoped that it would be able to safeguard its interests at al-Aqsa/Temple

Mount and fight radical Islam alongside Israel, should Dahlan become the new Palestinian leader. Jordan scrutinised Dahlan's status in the occupied territories and whether his ties to Israel and the money he poured into the Gaza Strip—in order to buy support—made him a superior candidate. The Jordanians have good reason to worry. Dahlan is known for being belligerent, corrupt, and hedonistic; he does not hesitate to do everything in his power to promote his status. According to Palestinian media reports, Dahlan is supported by Arafat's nephew and former foreign minister Nasser al-Qudwa, former Palestinian Prime Minister Salam Fayyad and Abed Rabbo. In July 2015, when Abbas suspected that Fayyad received donations from Dahlan and his United Arab Emirates sponsor, Abbas ordered the Security Service to confiscate Fayyad's bank account on the basis that Fayyad received the funds to undermine him. The Palestinian High Court, however, found that Abbas' order was illegal.[8]

Subsequently, Fayyad left the West Bank for the United States. That same month, Abbas dismissed Yasser Abed Rabbo from the PLO's Executive Committee. Since neither Fayyad nor Abed Rabbo were members of Fatah, and their popular support was marginal, Abbas experienced no political fallout from these actions. Al-Qudwa, however, is a member of Fatah's Central Committee.

Egypt, for its part, was looking at other ways than through Dahlan of reaching its strategic goals. In November 2016, three former Egyptian foreign ministers, two of them also former Arab League General Secretaries, and the third still holding this position, visited Ramallah. They asked Abbas to nominate a deputy president to prevent chaos in case he was unable to fulfil his presidential duties, as well as to block Speaker Dweik's path to the presidency as stipulated by Palestinian Basic Law. The Egyptian delegation raised the names of Dahlan, Marwan Barghouti and al-Qudwa as adequate deputy president candidates. If Abbas selected Barghouti, they promised, Egypt would put pressure on Israel to release him. The three senior Egyptians advised Abbas to let Dahlan return to Fatah and end his campaign against political rivals. Abbas rejected their demands, strongly condemning Egypt's intervention in Fatah and the Palestinian Authority's domestic affairs.[9]

In late 2016 Abbas took further steps against Dahlan and his supporters. As Fatah members ran election campaigns for the movement's forthcoming General Conference in November, Abbas enacted a resolute response to Dahlan's attempts to build his base of support inside Fatah. Palestinian security forces dispersed a meeting organised by Legislative Council member Jihad Tummaleh in al-Amari refugee camp near Ramallah. Abbas discharged him from the Fatah movement together with Fatah's spokesperson for the Jerusalem office, Rafat Elayyan, who also participated in that meeting. Fatah parliamentarian Najat Abu Bakr was expelled earlier, in August (see above). Abbas has stopped paying the salaries of about 500 Palestinian Authority officials in Gaza because of their alleged support for Dahlan. West Bank Palestinian Authority employees suspected of supporting Dahlan were summoned to a hearing in the Preventive Security office. These individuals were fired if they could not disprove the allegation, and those categorised as suspects were fined.[10]

*The Popular Leader in Captivity*

Al-Aloul's weak spots are precisely where jailed popular Palestinian leader Marwan Barghouti has an advantage. He enjoys widespread support among both Fatah members and the Palestinian public, and his status as a prisoner only augments his image. As opposed to Dahlan who mostly markets his personality and ties with his foreign sponsors, or Faraj who manages the undignified security cooperation with Israel, Barghouti turns inwardly to the Palestinian public, and offers a fundamentally different liberation strategy.

Barghouti's popularity relies on his imprisonment and being the head of the Fatah Tanzim. At the end of 1997, members of the young leadership of Fatah headed by Barghouti who were left on the periphery of the PA establishment decided to breathe life into the movement and to establish their power base. The opposition that organised itself among the rank and file of Fatah succeeded in establishing itself in refugee camps, villages and towns competing with the national leadership and intelligence agencies to a great extent thanks to the local leadership—'the field leadership'—that joined it. The Tanzim demanded that the national leadership take hawkish positions in negotiations with Israel, and include them in Fatah top leadership. This new opposition from within drew legitimacy from the role its key members played in the first intifada and from the new issues the Oslo Agreements introduced in the public discourse. It made claims in the name of the 'values of the intifada'; called to correct Arafat mismanagement by 'building institutions'; and desired 'democratic legitimacy,' 'transparency and supervision of the activities of the Palestinian regime,' 'the separation of powers,' 'proper working procedures in the executive authority,' and 'struggle against despotism and arbitrariness.'[11] The new opposition discourse combined the first intifada militant ethos with the Palestinian Authority challenges, the need to build clean and functioning institutions; establish an independent judiciary; prevent the intervention of military commanders in politics and create respect for the rule of law; and institute transparency and oversight of Palestinian Authority activities. During the second intifada, the Tanzim chain of command collapsed and Israel handed Barghouti a quintuple life sentence in prison.

From jail, Barghouti criticises Abbas more intensely than he criticised Arafat. Abbas is carrying out a one-man rule with 'a pathetic policy disconnected from the reality on the ground.' It is 'nothing more than self-delusion.' Abbas oppresses the Palestinian people and forestalls their liberation. The corrupt despot uses extreme force against his own people but none against the occupier, Barghouti charges. Abbas' regime prevents the younger generation's advancement within the political hierarchy, and refuses to adjust its course. These obstacles have made political Islam a popular alternative among young people, concludes Barghouti. Present leadership has moved far away from Fatah founders who combined liberation with democracy and justice. Barghouti does not find one single aspect of the Palestinian Authority's rule that continues the path of the founders of the PLO, who were once considered among the 'forces of liberation, democracy, and justice.' In order to return to that path, Barghouti seeks a total revision, 'a revolution in the education system, in the way we think, in culture, and in our legal system.'[12]

As the Palestinian public reels from feelings of crisis, despair, and despondency, as well as a deep suspicion vis-à-vis the interests driving those fighting over Abbas' succession, Barghouti has the ability to win support, as he suggests a comprehensive alternative and believes in the populace's power to take control. Indeed, Barghouti's goal is no different from that of Abbas or even the Arab Peace Initiative: a Palestinian state based on 1967 borders and implementing UN Resolution 194 regarding Palestinian refugee right of return. The difference is in the means Barghouti proposes to use to achieve these goals. As opposed to Abbas and his competitors, Barghouti supporters believe that the key to liberation is not on the international stage but in the Palestinian arena. Abbas' insistence on using exclusively international channels is the problem, not the solution. Abbas' policy is poor and allows Israel to continue its colonial project. Noticeably, Barghouti opposes lone wolf attacks on Israeli soldiers and citizens on the basis that these tactics lack strategy and discipline. The alternative is recruiting the masses to a concerted, sustained and popular nonviolent struggle. Barghouti also suggests changing the Palestinian discourse from one of politics to one of liberation. The change must first come from below, only later will it translate into tangible political manoeuvring. The struggle will end only after independence is achieved, not in exchange for Israel agreeing to negotiate, as was the case in the Oslo process.

As opposed to Abbas' other opponents, as well as Abbas himself, Barghouti was always close to high-ranking Hamas members, and in 2006–7 he formulated, along with senior Hamas members in prison, 'the prisoners document,' a national reconciliation platform. In early 2016, his confidants agreed with senior Hamas leaders on a joint action plan for a popular unarmed struggle to end the Israeli occupation over the 1967 territories and replace it with an independent Palestinian state.[13] The Barghouti–Hamas understanding does not forbid negotiations with Israel, but reframed it in a different context, and outside the Oslo Accords framework.

The immediate step Barghouti proposes for Fatah is achieving sincere national reconciliation with Hamas with the aim of building a fair partnership in power. On this basis, both sides will call elections to the PLO and Palestinian Authority institutions. The new leadership will request a pan-Palestinian—meaning both Palestine and the diaspora—approval for its action plan. It must be thorough and detailed—down to daily and weekly action items—that are to be coordinated with all the wings and factions that implement it, and managed efficiently with PLO oversight. A driven, determined leadership is necessary, as is proper central planning, mobilisation and oversight, in order to manage a successful, popular and sustained nonviolent struggle. The struggle will open with a declaration of the end of the Oslo Accords, an end to security coordination, rescinding the PLO recognition of Israel, and a declaration of its willingness to enter into negotiations based on new principles in line with the international consensus, with a short timetable for the end of negotiations. On the first day of the struggle, Palestinians will burn their IDF-issued identification cards, thus symbolically cutting off ties with Israel. The nonviolent struggle will focus on disrupting the daily lives of Israeli settlers and soldiers in the West Bank by cutting off roads, water and electricity lines, and besieging settlements and Israeli neighbourhoods in East Jerusalem. The crown jewel of the struggle will be a mass march to Jerusalem, which will be led by the new head of the PLO, most likely Barghouti. He will declare that the goal of the march is to realise the right to pray at Al Aqsa Mosque, and demonstrators are not to leave the site until independence is achieved. The marchers will join masses of Palestinian citizens of Israel and citizens of foreign countries who will come to Israel in order to participate in the protest. Those whom Israel refuses to let in will organise actions outside Israeli embassies across the world. At the same time Palestinian refugees will march toward Israel's borders, demanding their right of return, while refugee flotillas will make their way by sea.

Meanwhile Palestinians must build a united community that is determined to struggle and is ready for sacrifice. The Palestinian Authority, Barghouti suggests, will not be dismantled but will retain security cooperation with Israel and turn into a body that aids the Palestinian public in withstanding the daily burden as a result of their uprising through a mutual support system to be developed by the Palestinian Authority. The PLO will take the place of the Palestinian Authority as the central body leading the Palestinian struggle. Media outlets will be instructed to provide reliable, non-exaggerated reports, since trust is a central condition for the success of the struggle. The Barghouti camp is well aware that it is easy to turn the

Palestinian public toward violence, and says that there will be zero tolerance for those who stray from the nonviolent struggle and violate the leadership directives. The Return March (see above) of early 2018 demonstrated that, save for a few exceptions, Palestinians are able to stick to non-armed resistance and Hamas is ready to endorse it. Yet, the Return March did not expand to the West Bank, where Barghouti's primary aspirations lie in his strategic plan.

It is not difficult to identify the obstacles in Barghouti's highly ambitious plan. On the one hand, it is far-reaching, comprehensive and even too ambitious; on the other hand, it sews the seeds of its own failure by announcing that its success depends on width of scope, precision, proper management and enforced compliance. It does not take into account the inefficient operating patterns of both the PLO and Fatah, the lack of compliance with the leadership, as well as general inefficiency within the movement. The plan also ignores Israel's capabilities to drive a stake through the uprising, and does not offer ways to deal with this issue.

It is a mistake, however, to believe that the Barghouti, Hamas or other groups arguing for civil unarmed struggle will ditch this or similar plans entirely. It is more probable that they will make changes and adjustments or prefer to implement a plan in one area, and only partially, and face the aforementioned obstacles. Yet, a popular uprising could erupt as the result of one cell, and spread like wildfire.

The founders of Fatah faced a similar dilemma in 1964. They founded the small group in 1959 in Kuwait and believed that they needed to broaden their ranks and gain support for their revolutionary ideology in Lebanese and Jordanian Palestinian refugee camps before they launched an armed struggle against Israel. The establishment of the PLO under the command of Egypt's popular leader Gamal Abd al-Nasser, who opposed Fatah armed struggle doctrine, threatened to destroy the small organisation's chances of winning the hearts and minds of the masses. Facing the dilemma between methodically preparing and expanding the group or immediately launching an armed struggle in order to compete with the PLO, the majority sided with the latter. Barghouti's suggestions are, in a sense, a rehashing of Fatah's early years. Just as the establishment of an organisational infrastructure was abandoned then, the same thing can happen this time around.

The struggle over Abbas' succession signals a generational change among the Palestinian leadership. The old guard, the 1948 refugees whose families were dispersed across the Arab world, established Fatah and the PLO and spent many years in the diaspora, will be replaced by younger people who have spent the majority of their lives in Palestine among their family members. They acquired the majority of their experience and public status in the intifadas or in Israeli prisons. This is precisely how the new generation is different from the old guard, whose status was built on the legacy of armed struggle. Abbas' generation used this status to convince the public of the necessity of going the political route. The failure of his approach has only hastened the rise of the new generation.

*Israel*

The aging Abbas and his serious pneumonia in May 2018 threatened the status quo, and Israel reaped the benefits from it. Since his election in 2005, Abbas has been a convenient partner for Israel. He has allowed it to control the entire West Bank while expanding settlements, and has never really posed a serious political threat. This is one of the few things that both the Israeli and Palestinian public—which disagree on nearly every other issue—agree on. In response, Israel has allowed Abbas and his supporters to imagine the feeble PA as a kind of 'state in the making,' while enjoying a handful of victories. Palestinians, however, view the PA in a different light. For many Palestinians, it is a mechanism to create employment and generate income in the present—not a promise for a start in the future.

It is precisely at this point that the interest of the Palestinian public meets Abbas' policies. Abbas creates quiet. This is what convinces European states to donate large sums on a yearly basis to prop up the PA, despite its rampant corruption, without ever knowing when the Palestinians will be able to end their dependence on Europe's generosity. This works as long as clashes between Palestinians and Israeli security forces are kept to a minimum, as long as protests do not sweep the capitals of western Europe, and the masses do not flood the streets calling to stop Israel. Moreover, those same western European states enjoy security coordination with Israeli intelligence against jihadist groups with their western European volunteers, and have no reason to cease this relationship. The truth is that Israel is the one chipping away at the status quo. But as long as it does not chip too hard, these problems can be delayed. Thus, the Israeli security establishment and the donor countries have joint interest in Abbas' successor continuing the current president's policy agenda and preventing chaos. If chaos prevails on the ground, Israel is ready to intervene to protect its settlers, army bases, water resources and other infrastructural interests.

Nevertheless, Israeli right-wing politicians and activists wish to change this order, not to preserve or restore it. They discuss how to exploit the expected chaos on the day after Abbas leaves office in order to replace the Palestinian Authority with a set of autonomous municipalities in the West Bank.[14] They aim to do away entirely with Areas A, B and C, and the Oslo Accords. Besides annexation, they envision creating expanded municipalities such as Greater Nablus or Greater Ramallah. Each municipality would operate independently without the umbrella of the Palestinian Authority. This way the Israeli right plans to stop the Palestinian march toward statehood. The move can be justified by security concerns and would be presented as temporary. If the Palestinians rise up against the move, it would only strengthen the Israeli security argument. The occupation, which also began as a temporary step in 1967, has survived for nearly 50 years and, if anything, is only becoming more deeply entrenched. Why wouldn't the new situation last for just as long? Considering the weakness of the Palestinian establishment, the makeup of the current Israeli government, and the diversion of world attention from Palestine to other Middle Eastern problems (Syria first and foremost), the Israeli right has good reason to think its plan could indeed be implemented.

It is an optimistic plan that seeks to roll back time, back to the first decades of the occupation. At the time, Israel ruled the West Bank and Gaza Strip vis-à-vis local mayors and rejected their proposals to create a national leadership that would include representatives from East Jerusalem.[15] Any hopes that situation might last, however, were shot down within a few years. In 1976, the PLO won municipal elections in key cities. The villages association that Israel created at the end of the 1970s in order to erode the municipalities' power had failed, as did efforts to destroy the PLO in the 1982 War. The idea that destroying the Palestinian political system will also destroy aspirations for independence, or that such aspirations can be suppressed with force, is simply delusional. It is a fact that there is near demographic parity of Jews and Arabs between the Jordan River and the sea. It is a fact that Israeli settlements are multiplying and penetrate deep into Palestinian territory. It is a fact that the Israeli government is putting an emphasis on the state's Jewishness and is isolating and disenfranchising its Palestinian citizens. Implementing the right's plan will lead to the Balkanisation of

Israel-Palestine, which could well have similar consequences to the aftermath of the break-up of Yugoslavia.

*Historical Record*

How will history record Arafat and Abbas' presidencies? Will future historians perceive them as preparing the ground to state-hood or will they be judged for missing chances and assisting the occupation? 'Looking back,' Ahmad Samih Khalidi and Hussein Agha observe,[16] 'the 1993 Oslo Accords marked the Palestinian national movement's highest political accomplishment and the beginning of its slow decline. From then onward, the PA has been trapped between its original revolutionary mission as an agent for liberation and its new responsibilities as a proto-state, with its attendant civil, bureaucratic, and security establishments.' Actually, the trap is built in to the Oslo agreements. Without accepting it, the PLO could not have accomplished its pinnacle achievement. Tragically, it failed to release itself from this trap. Nevertheless, as the PA's problems grow, Israel's problems increase as well. It rapidly retrogrades toward apartheid on an ethnic basis.

History always looks backward, and historians' conclusions depend on their individual perspective and the point from where they look back. Thus, the same 1993 Oslo Accords that Ahmad Khalidi and Hussein Agha consider to be PLO's highest political accomplishment, Edward Said declared 'an instrument of Palestinian surrender, a Palestinian Versailles.'[17] At present, views on Arafat's acceptance of the Oslo agreements are divided. Palestinians see Arafat as the peace seeker who became a victim of Israeli aggression if not assassination.[18] Israeli and American conservatives hold the opposite view. They conclude that Arafat never truly relinquished the military option. Some go further and argue that he accepted the two-state solution merely as a departure point to gain all Palestine. When he failed to impose on Israel his terms and conditions in Camp David in 2000, he orchestrated the second bloody intifada.[19] Future opinions, most likely, will be no less divided or mixed.

Leaders are unable to avoid mistakes. Quite commonly, a politician's list of mistakes is longer than that of their achievements. What divides leaders, therefore, is their readiness to admit mistakes and their public inclination to tolerate, forgive or forget them. In democracies, each election is an account of politicians' mistakes, but there have been just two general elections in the occupied PA in its twenty-six years of existence. Accordingly, at this stage it is clear that both presidents failed achieving independence and building a functioning democracy. Future evaluations may view Abbas' PA as the nucleus of independent Palestine.

Yet, we are able to offer few interim conclusions. Neither Arafat nor Abbas admitted mistakes. Arafat did not regret supporting Saddam Hussein in 1991 or promoting corrupted and/or failed seniors. Abbas did not admit his inclination to cede too much credit to Israeli and American negotiators, nor did he regret suppressing civil society opposition. However, the Palestinian public, in general, was easier on Arafat than it is with Abbas. Intellectuals such as Edward Said and Rashid Khalidi heavily criticised Arafat,[20] but the public pardoned him for his mistakes and never stopped iconising him. Critical views of Abbas are widely held across the political spectrum.

Political leaders manoeuvre between creating divisions and building coalitions. During his halcyon days in the PLO, Arafat did not hesitate to push the Popular Front for the Liberation of Palestine out of the PLO Executive Committee, and later reached a compromise with it. He implemented the same method with regard to his Fatah and Palestinian Authority colleagues. Abbas, however, enjoys much less political flexibility and manoeuvrability. He is quick to end relations with those who lose his trust and finds it hard to forgive them.

Arafat and Abbas, like any political leaders, were activists and operators. They motivated people to trust their judgment and even to sacrifice their lives for goals they put ahead of them. Rarely are political leaders also thinkers. Based on their over-estimation of their own abilities and their confidence, common political leaders portend to be outstanding statesmen. Even mistakenly, no one can include Arafat or Abbas among the exceptional.

Both Arafat and Abbas assumed the presidency at a senior age when it is difficult to change old habits, and after living most of their lives out of Palestine. In 1994, they came to a country that had changed dramatically from the place they remembered—respectively, Jerusalem, where young Arafat had visited to meet with his relatives, and Safed, where Abbas spent his early years. Little of their previous careers prepared them for the Palestinian Authority presidency. Several experiences and disqualifications that each of them brought to office were counterproductive or destructive. Heading neither a state nor a national liberation movement, just a limited autonomy over hardly connected West Bank areas that remained separated from the Gaza Strip, they struggled with a powerful and expanding Israel. Each man enjoyed a short moment of glory and international support at the opening of his term. Later, under Israeli and Western physical and political siege, they were ultimately neglected and betrayed.

Both Arafat and Abbas were looking for a breakthrough to independence. However, since Trump has closed ranks with Netanyahu, Abbas digs in to preserve what already exists. He refuses to take any step that may introduce security chaos and political anarchy that might end with the collapse of the Palestinian Authority.

Arafat and Abbas' presidencies were difficult and inglorious. With the routinisation of the Palestinian Authority and presidency's powers, the romantic era of the Palestinian revolution ended. Both Arafat and Abbas put obstacles to democracy in the way of the Palestinian Authority, and international agencies constantly reported on their administrative corruption and dysfunctionality. These issues left many Palestinians and international supporters disappointed. The Palestinian polity disintegrated. However, resisting Trump's 'deal of the century' reenergises the PA's president and the public.

Abbas perceives himself as Palestine's responsible adult; a bulwark against the total collapse of the PA. He sees himself the guardian that rescued the national project from the chaos created by irresponsible actors during the second intifada and from the Israeli reoccupation that followed. According to him, those groups are still active. His mission to prevent them from taking over did not end. Although for different reasons, Abbas' responsible adult mind has much in common with the Trump administration's mind and Israeli colonialism. They aim to educate and restrain the aggressive Oriental native. The Abbas regime's security cooperation with Israel has, therefore, a broad base.

Regional and global circumstances also did not help Abbas. The Third World anti-colonial struggle has ended. Arab states are fighting in civil wars, or struggling with Jihadist groups and Iran's hegemonic aspirations. Europe and the US prefer looking inwards. Chauvinist nationalism and calls to protect old national identities against Middle Eastern and African immigrants have taken over Europe's globalised perspective of the 1990s. Thus, within this discouraging context, Abbas concludes, the Palestinians must stick to what he saved for them.

Arab presidential-authoritarian regimes, demonstrates Roger Owen,[21] are a post-independence reaction to colonialism. The authoritarian state is a security state, without political pluralism, or checks and balances. Instead, power is personified and charisma routinised through the leader's admiration. He has indicated no successor, nor is a democratic change in the presidency possible. Key positions are held by those that the president trusts most: his family and close assistants who emerged from the security establishment or party seniors. The regime runs formal political practices, such as elections and party conferences, to gain legitimacy, but the president closely supervises and orchestrates those operations. Arab authoritarianism aimed to replace the fragile sovereignty that national movements achieved with a strong state that will prevent the return of the colonialist state.

Although the PA has not achieved independence and its autonomy is fragile, it has much in common with Arab presidential-authoritarian regimes. It is a security statelet with limited democratic institutions and procedures. Indeed, Arafat faced problems in personifying his power inside the Legislative Council, yet he preserved his iconic status. Abbas, who never had such a vaunted status, bases his rule on sheer force. Moreover, under Abbas, the colonialist power, Israel, has intensified its expansion into the autonomous areas and in its affairs. This and other weaknesses have increased the fragility of the PA. De-colonisation is harder today than ever, and this may fertilise the ground for a future heroic liberation struggle. Moreover, based on post-colonial Arab states' history, post-colonial Palestine is expected to remain authoritarian and to justify this trait by emphasising the need to prevent the indirect return of Israeli colonialism.

# APPENDIX 1

## MAIN POINTS OF DIFFERENCE BETWEEN OLMERT PROPOSAL SEPTEMBER 2008 AND ABBAS POSITIONS[1]

**Territory and Settlements**—Olmert suggested annexing to Israel 6.3 percent of the West Bank in exchange for territory 5.8 percent of the West Bank's size that Palestine would receive from Israel's pre-1967 land. Abbas agreed only to 1.9 per cent annexation and insisted that the land swap base will be 1:1.

Olmert's map included two big settlements: Ariel (about 20 km into the West Bank), and Maale Edomim (about 10 km into the West Bank), and much of the undeveloped land connecting Maale Edomim and East Jerusalem. Abbas refused to let Israel expand this deep into the West Bank, and opposed letting Israel take the land between Maale Edomim and Jerusalem, which would be the only open area into which East Jerusalem (al-Quds, the future capital) could expand.

**Connecting the Gaza Strip to the West Bank**—Olmert suggested a tunnel, Abbas a bridge. In Olmert's offer, tunnels would have also connected Palestinian areas next to the settlements of Ariel and Maale Edomim.

**Jerusalem**—Olmert suggested that Israel, Palestine, Jordan, Saudi Arabia and the United Sates would become the custodians or trustees of the Holy Basin and manage it jointly once Israel dissolved its annexation. The Holy Basin in his proposal included the Old City and Palestinian neighbourhoods outside it. Abbas raised questions on the logic of expanding the Holy Basin from about 1 square kilometre of the Old City to 2.2 square km, and its negative affect on the everyday life and symbolic status of tens of thousands of Palestinians living there.

Olmert suggested establishing a physical border dividing the two cities, but Abbas wished to keep the two cities open.

According to Olmert, Israel would manage the Holy Basin's security affairs. Abbas did not react, but most probably would have disagreed. He also would have rejected Olmert's concept of forming an Israeli-dominated umbrella municipality for both capitals.

**Refugees**—Olmert agreed to absorb between 10–15,000 Palestinian refugees over five years, not as collective returnees but as individual immigrants, justified as an act that would help resolve a humanitarian problem. He refused to recognise the Palestinian right of return or to accept UN General Assembly Resolution 194 from December 1948 that stipulated that the 'refugees wishing to return to their homes and live at peace with their neighbours should be permitted to do so at the earliest practicable date.'[2] Abbas, however, though rejecting Olmert's proposed number, agreed to compromise on the actual return, but not on the principle. The Palestinian delegation demanded the return of 150,000 refugees over ten years, and that Israel recognise its moral and legal responsibility for the creation of the refugee problem and apologise. Israel refused this. Instead, it suggested recognising the fact of the Palestinian refugees' suffering.

The sides disagreed also on compensation. The Palestinians demanded that all refugees be compensated for both their material losses and non-material suffering, in addition to compensation for the host countries. Israel agreed to compensate just those refugees who would not return or resettle elsewhere, and base this on a lump sum.

**Security**—Abbas refused Israel's demands to control Palestine's airspace and electro-magnetic sphere, to redeploy its army inside Palestine in cases of emergency, to divide the West Bank's water resources between the two states, and to have a say in Palestine's border control. These demands, Abbas argued, would seriously violate Palestine's sovereignty.

# APPENDIX 2

## THE SETTLEMENTS PROJECT—AN OVERVIEW

Since 1967, Israel has constantly expanded into the West Bank. Financially and in terms of human resources, it is the country's largest ever national project.

Rather than halting the Israeli settlement enterprise, the 1993 and 1995 Oslo Accords and the 2008 Annapolis peace conference actually intensified it. Thus, under the aegis of the peace process, the number of settlers increased dramatically from 222,000 in 1992 to 489,000 in 2010 and to about 600,000 in 2018. At the end of 2016, nearly 90,000 settlers were living to the east of the Separation Barrier.[1] The settlements have spliced Palestinian territory into hardly connected pieces, preventing the establishment of a contiguous Palestinian state.

Settler communities are not limited to one segment of Israeli society. They include religious and ultra-orthodox Jews, the secular and the conservative, right-wing, centre and leftist parties' voters, Ashkenazim and oriental Jews, veterans and newcomers, the wealthy upper middle-class and blue collar manual workers. Also, the settlements vary in size. There are small outposts and large cities, both close to Israel and quite remote, communities both like-minded and diverse.

The settlers are neither geographically nor socially disconnected from mainland society. Modern roads, family ties, and economic and welfare interests maintain the enterprise and even push it forward.

Although the Israeli authorities have never published comprehensive reports on their budgetary investment in settlements, the available evidence is sufficient to prove that, over the years, the settlements became the country's largest collective endeavour.[2] By 2004, Meron Benvenisti has estimated, Israeli governments had spent a total of $40 billion on this project,[3] while the Macro Center for Economics estimated in 2010 that private homes in the settlements excluding Jerusalem are worth a total of $9 billion, with apartments worth $4.5 billion, roads worth $1.7 billion, and public institutions, synagogues and bathhouses combined worth $0.5 billion. According to the study, Israeli settlements are home to 868 publicly owned facilities occupying 488,769 square metres. As for residential units, the total number of apartments stands at 32,711 spread over a space of around 3.27 million square metres, as well as 22,997 private homes over 5.74 million square metres.[4] This data does not include the classified security expenses, special grants, or benefits that settlers enjoy including in income and council taxes.

As Israel became more ensconced in the occupied West Bank and broadened its settlement project, the links between the settlements, the army and the state bureaucracy grew tighter, to the point that it has become difficult to make out where one ends and the other begins. The outcome is a military-settlement-bureaucracy complex that stifles the Palestinian inhabitants of the territories.

For further data, see Klein, *The Shift*, Chapter Three.

# ACKNOWLEDGMENTS

It would have been impossible to publish this book without the good will and cooperation of Hillel Schenker and Ziad Abu Zayyad, the editors of *Palestine-Israel Journal*, where parts of Chapter One were published in 2004. No less thankful am I to the editors of *+972 Magazine*, who let me include my articles on Mahmoud Abbas and Hamas in this book. Hillel Schenker of *Palestine-Israel Journal*, and Edo Konrad, Natasha Rowland, Joshua Leifer and Michael Schaeffer Omer-Man of *+972* skilfully and professionally translated my Hebrew texts. *+972* published them in coordination with the online Hebrew-language magazine *Local Call*. After updating, I integrated those articles into this book's chapters.

I thank also the two anonymous readers for their careful comments, which greatly improved the manuscript, and I am grateful to the whole team at Hurst Publishers. Of course, none of those who have helped in the book's creation bear responsibility for any of its mistakes or erroneous conclusions. The analysis, interpretations and errors are all mine.

I wrote this book between February and August 2018 in London, enjoying the warm hospitality of the Department of Middle Eastern Studies at King's College. I am very grateful to the department's academic and administrative staff for their assistance and friendship.

# NOTES

PROLOGUE

1. Ron Pundak, 'Oslo Twenty Years Later, A Personal and Historical Perspective', in Reuven Pedahzur and Efraim Lavi, eds, *Twenty Years of Oslo Agreements* (Tel Aviv: Tel Aviv University, Steinitz Center and Daniel S. Abraham Center for Strategic Dialogue in Netanya College, 2014), p. 7. Interview with Yossi Beilin, *Palestine-Israel Journal*, Vol. 23 No. 2–3, (2018), pp. 137–8.

1. ARAFAT, THE ICON AS PRESIDENT, AND HIS ANTIHERO SUCCESSOR

1. Yezid Sayigh, *Armed Struggle and the Search for State: The Palestinian National Movement 1949—1993* (Oxford: Oxford University Press, 1997), pp. 174–80; Andrew Terrill, 'The Political Mythology of the Battle of Karameh', *Middle East Journal* 55, No. 1 (2001), pp. 91–111.
2. Danny Rubinstein, *The Mystery of Arafat* (Lebanon, NH: Steerforth, 1995).
3. Baruch Kimmerling and Joel S. Migdal, *The Palestinian People: A History* (Cambridge, MA: Harvard University Press, 2003), pp. 1–168; Issa Khalaf, *Politics in Palestine: Arab Factionalism and Social Disintegration 1939–1948* (New York, SUNY Press, 1991), pp. 25–60.
4. Matti Steinberg, *In Search of Modern Palestinian Nationhood* (New York: Syracuse University Press, 2017); Muna Abu Eid, *Mahmoud Darwish: Literature and the Politics of Palestinian Identity* (London: IB Tauris, 2016).

5. Raviv Drucker and Ofer Shelah, *Bumerang*, (Tel Aviv: Keter, 2005), pp. 229–41 (in Hebrew); Ronen Bergman, *Rise and Kill First: The Secret History of Israel's Targeted Assassinations* (New York: Random House, 2018).

6. For instance see Israel Ministry of Foreign Affairs, 'Incitement to Violence Against Israel by Leadership of Palestinian Authority', 27 November 1996, https://mfa.gov.il/MFA/ForeignPolicy/Peace/MFADocuments/Pages/INCITEMENT%20TO%20VIOLENCE%20AGAINST%20ISRAEL%20BY%20LEADERSHI.aspx

7. Ari Shavit, 'The Big Freeze', *Haaretz*, 7 October 2004, https://www.haaretz.com/1.4710587

8. Tim Palmer, 'Report', *ABC*, 13 December 2001, http://www.abc.net.au/pm/stories/s439966.htm

9. Israel Ministry of Foreign Affairs, 'The Involvement of Arafat PA Senior Officials and Apparatus in Terrorism Against Israel Corruption and Crime', 6 May 2002, http://mfa.gov.il/MFA/ForeignPolicy/Terrorism/Palestinian/Pages/The%20Involvement%20of%20Arafat-%20PA%20Senior%20Officials%20and.aspx; Lt. Col. (ret.) Jonathan D. Halevi, 'The Palestinian's Authority Responsibility for the Outbreak of the Second Intifada—Its Own Damning Testimony', Jerusalem Center for Public Affairs, March–April 2013, http://jcpa.org/article/the-palestinian-authoritys-responsibility-for-the-outbreak-of-the-second-intifada-its-own-damning-testimony/

10. International Crisis Group, 'Who Governs the West Bank? Palestinian Administration under Israeli Occupation', 28 September 2004, https://d2071andvip0wj.cloudfront.net/32-who-governs-the-west-bank-palestinian-administration-under-israeli-occupation.pdf

11. Ben Fenton, 'No Peace with Arafat in Power Says Barak', *The Telegraph*, 16 July 2001, https://www.telegraph.co.uk/news/worldnews/middleeast/israel/1334226/No-peace-with-Arafat-in-power-says-Barak.html; Benny Morris and Ehud Barak, 'Camp David and After: An Exchange', *New York Review of Books*, 13 June 2002, http://www.nybooks.com/articles/2002/06/13/camp-david-and-after-an-exchange-1-an-interview-wi/; 'Camp David and After: Continued—Benny Morris and Ehud Barak Reply to Robert Malley and Hussein Agha', *New York*

*Review of Books*, 27 June 2002, http://www.nybooks.com/articles/2002/06/27/camp-david-and-aftercontinued/

12. Meron Benvenisti, *Son of Cypresses: Memories, Reflection and Regrets from a Political Life*, trans. Maxine Kaufman (Berkeley, CA: University of California Press, p. 127).

13. Salah Khalaf, 'Lowering the Sword', *Foreign Affairs*, Spring 1990, pp. 91–112; Abu Iyad with Eric Rouleau, *My Home, My Land: A Narrative of the Palestinian Struggle* (New York: Times Books, 1981).

14. Anis Sayegh, *About Anis Sayegh* (Beirut: Riad El-Rayyes, 2006), pp. 289–336 [in Arabic].

15. *Al-Wasat*, 6 November 1993, 13 December 1993; *Al-Majala*, 25 December 1993; *Al-Sharq Al-Awsat*, 22 November 1993, 25 November 1993; Hanan Ashrawi, *This Side of Peace: A Personal Account* (New York: Simon and Schuster, 1995), pp. 48–278.

16. Aluf Benn, 'Shimon Peres, as Captured in a Confidant's Diary: Suicidal Thoughts, Manipulations and Locker Room Talk', *Haaretz Magazine*, 15 March 2018, https://www.haaretz.com/israel-news/.premium.MAGAZINE-shimon-peres-as-captured-in-a-confidant-s-diary-1.5908124

17. Khalil Shikaki, 'Palestinians Divided: Old Guard, Young Guard', *Foreign Affairs* 81, No. 1 (January–February 2002), pp. 89–105; Yezid Sayigh, 'Arafat and the Anatomy of a Revolt', *Survival* 43, No. 3 (2001), pp. 47–60.

18. Grant Rumley and Amir Tibon, *The Last Palestinian: The Rise and Reign of Mahmoud Abbas* (New York: Prometheus Books, 2017), pp. 17–18, 28, 53–54, 65, 96; Nathan Brown, *Palestinian Politics After the Oslo Accords: Resuming Arab Palestine* (Berkeley: University of California Press: 2003), pp. 94–137. Nigel Parsons, *The Politics of the Palestinian Authority from Oslo to al-Aqsa* (New York: Routledge, 2005), p. 49.

19. Khalil Shikaki, 'Old Guard, Young Guard: The Palestinian Authority and the Peace Process at a Crossroads', http://www.pcpsr.org/en/node/267, originally published in *Foreign Affairs* January/February 2002.

20. Asher Zeiger, 'Abbas Says He Has No Right to Live in Safed and No Territorial Demands on pre-1967 Israel', *The Times of Israel*, 1 November

2012, https://www.timesofisrael.com/abbas-says-he-has-no-right-to-live-in-safed-and-has-no-demands-on-pre-1967-israel/

21. http://english.wafa.ps/page.aspx?id=hWTZzja51779170212ahWTZzj

22. Jacob Hoigilt, 'Fatah from Below: The Clash of Generations in Palestine', *British Journal of Middle Eastern Studies* 43, No. 4 (2016), pp. 456–71.

23. http://www.pcbs.gov.ps/Downloads/book2176.pdf

24. Grant Rumley and Amir Tibon, *The Last Palestinian: The Rise and Reign of Mahmoud Abbas* (New York: Prometheus Books, 2017), pp. 161–4.

25. Hussein Agah and Ahmad Samih Khalidi, 'The End of This Road: The Decline of the Palestinian National Movement', *The New Yorker*, 6 August 2017, http://www.newyorker.com/news/news-desk/the-end-of-this-road-the-decline-of-the-palestinian-national-movement

## 2. FOREIGN POLICY: ABBAS, THE DESERTED PEACE SEEKER

1. Mahmoud Abbas, *Through Secret Channels: The Road to Oslo—Senior PLO Leader Abu Mazen's Revealing Story of the Negotiations with Israel* (Reading: Garnet, 1995), p. 219.

2. Yezid Sayigh, 'Who Killed the Oslo Accords', *Al-Jazeera Opinion*, 1 October 2015, https://www.aljazeera.com/indepth/opinion/2015/10/killed-oslo-accords-151001072411049.html

3. Peace Now data, http://peacenow.org.il/en/settlements-watch/settlements-data/lands

4. See Menachem Klein, 'Acknowledging the (Violent) Elephant in the Room', *Palestine-Israel Journal*, 2019.

5. Nathan Thrall, 'Israel–Palestine: The Real Reason There's Still No Peace', *The Guardian*, 16 May 2017, https://www.theguardian.com/world/2017/may/16/the-real-reason-the-israel-palestine-peace-process-always-fails

6. Jonathan Lis and Yarden Zur, 'Education Council Supports Application of Israeli Law to West Bank Universities', *Haaretz*, 25 January 2018, https://www.haaretz.com/israel-news/.premium-education-panel-backs-applying-israeli-law-to-west-bank-universities-1.5764957

7. Aron Heller and Mohammed Daraghameh, 'Expansion Plan Highlights: Crowded West Bank City's Plight', *Associated Press*, 12 July 2017.

https://www.washingtontimes.com/news/2017/jul/12/expansion-plan-highlights-crowded-west-bank-citys-/

8. Raoul Wootlife, 'Final Text of Jewish Nation State Law Approved by the Knesset Early on July 19', *The Times of Israel*, 19 July 2018, https://www.timesofisrael.com/final-text-of-jewish-nation-state-bill-set-to-become-law/

9. Menachem Klein, *The Shift: Israel–Palestine from Border Struggle to Ethnic Conflict* (London and New York: Hurst/Columbia University Press, 2010).

10. Yael Berda, *Living Emergency: Israel's Permit Regime in the Occupied West Bank* (Palo Alto, CA: Stanford University Press, 2017).

11. Nathan Thrall, 'Our Man in Palestine', *New York Review of Books*, 14 October 2010, http://www.nybooks.com/articles/archives/2010/oct/14/our-man-palestine/

12. Omar Dajani and Hugh Lovatt, 'Rethinking Oslo: How Europe Can Promote Peace in Israel–Palestine', European Council on Foreign Relations, July 2017, http://www.ecfr.eu/publications/summary/rethinking_oslo_how_europe_can_promote_peace_in_israel_palestine_7219

13. Amira Hass, 'The Big Trap of the Palestinian Bureaucracy Under Israel's Watchful Eye', *Haaretz*, 20 January 2018, https://www.haaretz.com/middle-east-news/palestinians/.premium-the-big-trap-of-palestinian-bureaucracy-under-israel-s-watchful-eye-1.5747165

14. 'Despite Everything Abbas Tells Israelis Peace is Attainable', *The Time of Israel*, 1 April 2016, http://www.timesofisrael.com/despite-every-thing-abbas-tells-israelis-he-hasnt-given-up-on-peace/

15. https://www.timesofisrael.com/full-text-of-abbas-speech-to-un/

16. https://www.haaretz.com/middle-east-news/palestinians/full-text-abbas-address-to-un-general-assembly-1.5452564

17. Nathan Thrall, 'BDS: How a Controversial Non-Violent Movement Has Transformed the Israeli–Palestinian Debate', *The Guardian*, 14 August 2018, https://www.theguardian.com/news/2018/aug/14/bds-boycott-divestment-sanctions-movement-transformed-israeli-palestinian-debate

18. 'Abbas Failed to Accept My Peace Offer Because He Is No Hero Said

Olmert', *The Times of Israel*, 24 May 2013, https://www.timesofisrael. com/abbas-failed-to-accept-my-peace-offer-because-hes-no-hero/

19. The following pages are based on my role as an advisor to the Israeli negotiating team, the memoirs published by Israeli, Palestinian and American actors, and the studies included in note 20 below.

20. Menachem Klein, *A Possible Peace between Israel and Palestine: An Insider's Account of the Geneva Initiative* (New York: Columbia University Press, 2007), pp. 145–51; Omar M. Dajani, 'Surviving Opportunities: Palestinian Negotiating Patterns in Peace Talks with Israel', in Tamara Cofman Wittes, ed., *How Israelis and Palestinians Negotiate: A Cross-Cultural Analysis of the Oslo Peace Process*, (Washington DC: United States Institute of Peace Press, 2005), pp. 39–80; Aharon Kleiman, 'Israeli Negotiating Culture', in Cofman Wittes, ed., *How Israelis and Palestinians Negotiate*, pp. 81–132.

21. Ron Pundak, *Secret Channel Oslo* (Tel Aviv: Yediot Ahronoth, 2013), p. 369 [in Hebrew].

22. Hussein Agha and Robert Malley, 'Abu Mazen: Palestine's Last Best Hope', *Le Monde Diplomatique*, (English Edition), 7 February 2005, https://mondediplo.com/2005/02/07mazen

23. Lori Allen, *The Rise and Fall of Human Rights: Cynicism and Politics in Occupied Palestine*, (Palo Alto, CA: Stanford University Press, 2013), pp. 23–28.

24. Omer Zanany, *The Annapolis Process (2007–2008): Oasis or Mirage*, (Tel Aviv: Tel Aviv University Tami Steinmets Center for Peace Studies/ Molad, 2015), [in Hebrew]; 'The Palestinian Papers', *Al-Jazeera Investigations*, http://transparency.aljazeera.net/Services/Search/default. aspx; 'This Week in History: Wye River memorandum Land-for-Peace-Deal', *The Jerusalem Post*, 21 October 2012, http://www.jpost.com/ Features/In-Thespotlight/This-Week-in-History-Wye-River-land-for-peace-deal

25. Itamar Eichner, 'Netanyahu: Abbas Tore Off the Mask, without Change in Position There Will Be No Peace', *Ynet*, 15 January 2018, https:// www.ynetnews.com/articles/0,7340,L-5071419,00.html; see also Joshua Davidovich, 'Netanyahu: Abbas "Helping" Israel with Anti-Semitic, anti-Trump Rant', *The Times of Israel*, 15 January 2018,

https://www.timesofisrael.com/netanyahu-abbas-helping-israel-with-anti-trump-rant/; Noa Landau, 'Netanyahu: Abbas Again Proves Palestinians Are the One Who Don't Want Peace', *Haaretz*, 24 December 2017, https://www.haaretz.com/israel-news/netanyahu-abbas-proves-palestinians-don-t-want-peace-1.5629502

26. 'Abbas' Speech at the Opening of the Palestinian National Council', *Wafa*, 1 May 2018, http://www.wafa.ps/ar_page.aspx?id=GWBxsja81 9376530489aGWBxsj [in Arabic].

27. 'Mahmoud Abbas Blames Jews' "Social Behavior" for the Holocaust', *JTA*, 1 May 2018, https://www.jta.org/2018/05/01/news-opinion/mahmoud-abbas-jews-caused-holocaust-social-behavior; Michael Bachner, 'Netanyahu: Abbas Peddles the "Most Contemptible Anti-Semitic Slogans"', *The Time of Israel*, 2 May 2018, https://www.timesofisrael.com/abbas-drenched-in-anti-semitism-minister-says-after-jew-bashing-speech/; Noa Landau and Reuters, 'EU Slams "Unacceptable" Abbas Remarks About Jews: Harms Two-State Solution', *Haaretz*, 2 May 2018, https://www.haaretz.com/world-news/europe/eu-slams-unacceptable-abbas-remark's-about-jews-1.6051955

28. 'Palestinian Leader's Speech Condemned as Anti-Semitic', *Time Magazine*, http://time.com/5263459/palestinian-leader-speech-anti-semitic/; Tovah Lazaroff and Tamara Zieve, 'World Fumes Over Abbas's Antisemitism', *The Jerusalem Post*, 3 May 2018, https://www.jpost.com/Arab-Israeli-Conflict/World-fumes-over-Abbass-antisemitism-553351; Editorial, 'Let Abbas's Vile Words Be His Last as Palestinian Leader', *The New York Times*, 2 May 2018, https://www.nytimes.com/2018/05/02/opinion/abbas-palestine-israel.html

29. Jack Khoury, 'Abbas Apologizes to "Jewish People" for Offensive Comments Condemning Holocaust and anti-Semitism', *Haaretz*, 4 May 2018, https://www.haaretz.com/middle-east-news/palestinians/abbas-apologizes-to-jewish-people-we-condemn-anti-semitism-in-all-its-forms-1.6054431

30. Elhanan Miller, 'Mahmoud Abbas and Zionism from Struggle to Acceptance', The Forum for Regional Thinking, http://www.regthink.org/en/articles/mahmoud-abbas-and-zionism-from-struggle-to-acceptance

31. 'Abbas' Speech at the Opening of the Palestinian National Council'; 'Abbas' Speech to the PLO Central Council', *Wafa*, 14 January 2018, http://www.wafa.ps/ar_page.aspx?id=ZjYthda809138523468aZjYthd [in Arabic]; 'Abbas Speech in al-Azhar International Conference', *Wafa*, 17 January 2018, http://www.wafa.ps/ar_page.aspx?id=7GdE8Ka8093 84075742a7GdE8K [in Arabic].

32. *Wafa*, 14 January 2018, http://www.wafa.ps/ar_page.aspx?id=ZjYthda 809138523468aZjYthd [in Arabic].

33. 'Abbas' Speech at the Opening of the Palestinian National Council'.

34. Adam Entous, 'Donald Trump's New World Order', *The New Yorker*, 18 June 2018, https://www.newyorker.com/magazine/2018/06/18/donald-trumps-new-world-order

35. David Rose, 'The Gaza Bombshell', *Vanity Fair*, April 2008, http://www.vanityfair.com/news/2008/04/gaza200804

36. Jacob Magid, 'Obama's Peace Envoy: Israel is Carrying Out "Reversed Oslo" in West Bank', *The Times of Israel*, 24 July 2018, https://www.timesofisrael.com/obamas-peace-envoy-israel-carrying-out-reversed-oslo-in-west-bank/; Adam Entous, 'The Maps of Israeli Settlements that Shocked Barack Obama', *The New Yorker*, 9 July 2018, https://www.newyorker.com/news/news-desk/the-map-of-israeli-settlements-that-shocked-barack-obama

37. Entous, 'Donald Trump's New World Order'.

38. 'The Full Text of John Kerry's Remarks at Saban Forum 2016', *The Times of Israel*, https://www.timesofisrael.com/full-text-of-john-kerrys-remarks-at-saban-forum-2016/

39. Aaron David Miller, *The Much Too Promised Land: America's Elusive Search for Arab–Israeli Peace* (New York: Bantam, 2008).

40. Amir Tibon, 'Exclusive: Obama's Detailed Plans for Mideast Peace Revealed and How Everything Fell Apart', *Haaretz*, 8 June 2017, https://www.haaretz.com/israel-news/.premium.MAGAZINE-exclusive-obamas-plans-for-mideast-peace-revealed-1.5481322

41. 'Secretary of State John Kerry's Speech', *The Times of Israel*, 28 December 2016, https://www.timesofisrael.com/full-text-of-john-kerrys-speech-on-middle-east-peace-december-28–2016/

42. The Arab Peace Initiative, http://www.europarl.europa.eu/meet-

docs/2009_2014/documents/empa/dv/1_arab-initiative-beirut_/1_
arab-initiative-beirut_en.pdf

43. Appendix three in Menachem Klein, *The Jerusalem Problem: The
    Struggle for Permanent Status* (Gainesville, FL: University Press of
    Florida, 2003).

44. Agha and Malley, 'Abu Mazen: Palestine's Last Best Hope'.

45. 'The Full Text of the UNSC Resolution', *The Times of Israel*,
    23 December 2016, http://www.timesofisrael.com/full-text-of-unsc-
    resolution-approved-dec-23-demanding-israel-stop-all-settlement-
    activity

46. Entous, 'Donald Trump's New World Order'.

47. Larry Derfner, 'The Fraud that is the Temple Mount Movement', *972
    Magazine*, 31 October 2014, https://972mag.com/the-fraud-that-is-
    the-temple-mount-movement/98250/; 'Dangerous Liaison Dynamics
    of the Temple Movements', Ir Amim, http://www.ir-amim.org.il/en/
    report/dangerous-liaison

48. Menachem Klein, 'Rule and Role in Jerusalem: Israel, Jordan and the
    PLO in a Peace Building Process', in Marshal J. Breger and Ora
    Ahimeir, eds, *Jerusalem: Essays Towards Peacemaking* (Syracuse, NY:
    Syracuse University Press, 2002): pp. 137–74.

49. 'Full Text of the Jordanian–Palestinian Agreement on Holy Places in
    Jerusalem', Latin Patriarchate of Jerusalem, http://en.lpj.org/2013/04/
    04/full-text-of-the-jordanian-palestinian-agreement-on-holy-places-
    in-jerusalem/

50. Rick Gladstone and Jodi Rudoren, 'Mahmoud Abbas at UN Says
    Palestinians Are No Longer Bound by Oslo Accords', *The New York
    Times*, 30 September 2015, https://www.nytimes.com/2015/10/01/
    world/middleeast/mahmoud-abbas-palestinian-authority-un-speech.
    html

51. 'Abbas' Full Speech at the UN General Assembly', *Haaretz*, 22 Sept-
    ember 2016, https://www.haaretz.com/israel-news/abbas-full-speech-
    at-the-un-general-assembly-1.5441471

52. 'Netanyahu Says Palestinians Can Have a "State Minus"', *The Times of
    Israel*, 22 January 2017, http://www.timesofisrael.com/netanyahu-says-
    palestinians-can-have-a-state-minus/

53. Oded Yaron, 'Has Lieberman Killed Hamas' Leader Yet? New Website Keeps You Up to Speed', *Haaretz*, 30 May 2016, https://www.haaretz.com/israel-news/.premium-has-lieberman-killed-haniyeh-yet-check-the-website-1.5388907

54. Ben Sales, 'Netanyahu Says He Supports a Palestinian "State-minus" Controlled by Israeli Security', *Jewish Telegraphic Agency*, 24 October 2018, https://www.jta.org/2018/10/24/top-headlines/netanyahu-suggests-support-state-minus-palestinians

55. 'John Kerry's Full Speech on Israeli Settlements and a Two-State Solution', *Time Magazine*, 28 December 2016, http://time.com/4619064/john-kerrys-speech-israel-transcript/

56. Haggai Matar, 'Israel Land Theft Law Is Just the Tip of the Settlements Iceberg', *972 Magazine*, 7 February 2017, https://972mag.com/israels-land-theft-law-is-just-the-tip-of-the-settlement-iceberg/125071/

57. Associated Press, 'Peace Now: Settlements Grew Under Trump Presidency', *Ynet*, 26 March 2018, https://www.ynetnews.com/articles/0,7340,L-5197826,00.html; 'Annexation Legislation Database', Yesh Din, 1 April 2019, https://www.yesh-din.org/en/about-the-database/

58. 'Netanyahu says "occupation is baloney" if a country is powerful enough—report', *The Times of Israel*, 6 November 2018, https://www.timesofisrael.com/netanyahu-says-occupation-is-baloney-if-a-country-is-powerful-enough-reports/

59. Alaa Tartir, 'The Limits of Securitized Peace: The EU's Sponsorship of Palestinian Authoritarianism', *Middle East Critique*, 2018, https://www.tandfonline.com/doi/full/10.1080/19436149.2018.1516337; Jeremy Wildeman, 'EU Development Aid in the Palestinian Occupied Territory between Aid Effectiveness and World Bank Guidance', *Global Affairs* 4, no. 1, (2018), pp. 115–28.

60. Shlomi Eldar, 'Palestinians Pin Hopes on Pompeo', *Al-Monitor*, 14 March 2018, https://www.al-monitor.com/pulse/originals/2018/03/israel-palestinians-rex-tillerson-mike-pompeo-mahmoud-abbas.html

61. 'Trump Reportedly Considering Pulling Out of Israeli-Palestinian Peace Talks', *Ma'an News Agency*, 25 June 2017, https://www.maannews.com/Content.aspx?id=777794

62. Entous, 'Donald Trump's New World Order'.

63. Ibid.

64. Shmuel Meir, 'The Real Impact of UN Resolution 2334 Has Yet to Come', *972 Magazine*, 10 January 2017, https://972mag.com/the-real-impact-of-un-resolution-2334-has-yet-to-come/124307/

65. Ibid.

66. Roi Maor, 'Trump and Netanyahu Are Allies in a Losing Battle', *972 Magazine*, 9 February 2017, https://972mag.com/trump-and-netan-yahu-are-allies-in-a-losing-battle/125116/

67. Colum Lynch and Robbie Gramer, 'Trump and Allies Seek End to Refugee Status for Millions of Palestinians', *Foreign Policy*, 3 August 2018, https://foreignpolicy.com/2018/08/03/trump-palestinians-israel-refugees-unrwaand-allies-seek-end-to-refugee-status-for-millions-of-palestinians-united-nations-relief-and-works-agency-unrwa-israel-pal-estine-peace-plan-jared-kushner-greenb/; 'Trump Cut Millions from UN Agency for Palestinian Refugees: Officials' *The Guardian*, 14 January 2018, https://www.theguardian.com/world/2018/jan/14/trump-cut-millions-united-nations-agency-palestinian-refugees

68. Barak Ravid, 'Scoop: Netanyahu Asked U.S. to Cut Aid for Palestinian Refugee', *Axios*, 3 September 2018, https://www.axios.com/benjamin-netanyahu-israel-policy-unrwa-palestine-aid-5a92b1ed-babd-42d9-a933–6aec816da717.html

69. 'Donors Increase UNRWA Support and Funding Despite US Cuts', *Al-Jazeera*, 2 September 2018, https://www.aljazeera.com/news/2018/09/donors-increase-palestine-refugee-agency-funding-cuts-180902085540064.html

70. Summary of Trump's plan based on Saeb Erekat's official document at *Ma'an News Agency*, 3 March 2018, http://www.maannews.net/Content.aspx?id=941186 [in Arabic].

71. Yanir Cozin, 'Sources: Trump To Ask Israel To Withdraw From 4 East Jerusalem Neighborhoods', *The Jerusalem Post*, 4 May 2018, https://www.jpost.com/Arab-Israeli-Conflict/Trump-to-tell-Israel-Withdraw-from-four-east-Jerusalem-neighborhoods-553491

72. Amir Tibon, 'Kushner Attacks Abbas in Rare Palestinian Interview Questions His Ability to Reach a Deal', *Haaretz*, 24 June 2018, https://

www.haaretz.com/us-news/jared-kushner-criticizes-abbas-in-rare-palestinian-newspaper-interview-1.6200287

73. Robin Wright, 'Trump Shatters the Palestinian Diplomatic Mission and Middle East Peace', *The New Yorker*, 10 September 2018, https://www.newyorker.com/news/news-desk/trump-shutters-the-palestinian-diplomatic-missionand-middle-east-peace

74. 'US downgrades Jerusalem diplomatic mission to Palestinians', *AP*, 17 October 2018, https://www.apnews.com/d586cb33f7a1461e9ceae0915a101cbc; on the history of the consulate see Jake Walles, 'Requiem for a Consulate', Carnegie Middle East Centre, 23 October 2018, https://carnegie-mec.org/diwan/77553

75. Eylon Aslan-Levy, 'The US Freezes Palestinian Aid Budget', *i24 News*, 24 June 2018, https://www.i24news.tv/en/news/international/international/177909–180624-exclusive-us-freezes-palestinian-aid-budget

76. Barak Ravid, Channel 13 News, https://www.axios.com/government-shutdown-threatens-derail-israeli-palestine-security-a4327e68-6e8b-46ef-ace8-aeb2d69ef7b2.html; 'Palestinians turn down US funding over litigation fears', *JTA*, 1 February 2019, https://www.jta.org/quick-reads/palestinians-turn-down-us-funding-over-litigation-fears; see also Matthew Lee and Zeke Miller, 'Trump Staff Up Mideast Team for Peace Plan Rollout', *AP*, 3 August 2018, https://www.apnews.com/099069cecd5244b8b766fa77e264b58b; Amir Tibon and Jack Khoury, 'US Freeze on Palestinian Aid Threatening Coexistence and Humanitarian Groups Warn Officials', *Haaretz*, 23 July 2018, https://www.haaretz.com/us-news/.premium-u-s-freeze-on-palestinian-aid-threatening-coexistence-groups-1.6310811; 'Trump Axes $25m in Aid for Palestinians in East Jerusalem Hospitals', *The Guardian*, 8 September 2018, https://www.theguardian.com/world/2018/sep/08/trump-palestinian-aid-cut-east-jerusalem-hospitals

77. 'Palestine rejects monthly tax transfer from Israel after deductions', *The National*, 27 February 2019, https://www.thenational.ae/world/mena/palestine-rejects-monthly-tax-transfer-from-israel-after-deductions-1.831143; 'Abbas Rejects All Tax Revenues from Israel over Terror Payment Deduction', *The Times of Israel*, 20 February 2019, https://

www.timesofisrael.com/abbas-rejects-all-tax-revenues-from-israel-over-terror-payment-deduction/

78. Saeb Erekat, 'Official Document', *Ma'an News Agency*, 3 March 2018, http://www.maannews.net/Content.aspx?id=941186 [in Arabic].

79. 'Abbas at al-Azhar Conference: We Will Use All Options But Not Violence', *Wafa*, 17 January 2018, http://english.wafa.ps/page.aspx?id=28Dwtra96091838139a28Dwtr

80. 'Saudi Crown Prince: Palestinians Should Take What the US Offers', Israeli TV Channel 10 in *Axios*, https://www.axios.com/saudi-crown-prince-tells-jewish-leaders-palestinians-should-take-what-they-are-offered-or-stop-complaining-1525025098-e7f0faf8–4f3f-442c-8478–6737ddb5a553.html; Gamal Abd al-Jawad, *Al-Ahram*, 21 December 2017, http://www.memri.org.il/cgi-webaxy/item?4637

81. 'Abu Mazen: Al-Quds is Red Line and We Reject US Mediation', *Ma'an News*, 13 December 2017, http://www.maannews.net/Content.aspx?id=932986 [in Arabic]; 'Abbas at OIC: We Will Seek UNSC to Annul US Recognition of Jerusalem as Israel's Capital', *Wafa*, 13 December 2017, http://ehes nglish.wafa.ps/page.aspx?id=9Levria9 5605492356a9Levri; Adam Rasgon, 'Meeting Abbas, MBS backs Palestinian state with East Jerusalem as its capital', *The Times of Israel*, 13 February 2019, https://www.timesofisrael.com/meeting-abbas-mbs-backs-palestinian-state-with-east-jerusalem-as-its-capital/

82. 'Report: Israel Detains 1319 Palestinians 274 Minors During January and February', *Ma'an News*, 14 March 2018, http://www.maannews.com/Content.aspx?id=779941

83. 'Palestinian President Presents Plan to Relaunch Peace Talks with Israel Says New Multilateral Mechanism Should Guide Process in Briefing to Security Council', United Nations, 20 February 2018, https://www.un.org/press/en/2018/sc13213.doc.htm

84. 'This Is What the Palestinian Delegation Discussed with Russia on Trump's Decision', *Ma'an News Agency*, 21 December 2017, http://www.maannews.net/Content.aspx?id=933846 [in Arabic].

85. Amir Tibon, 'Saudi King Tells US That Peace Plan Must Include Jerusalem as Palestinian Capital', *Haaretz*, 30 July 2018, https://www.haaretz.com/israel-news/saudis-say-u-s-peace-plan-must-include-e-j-l-as-palestinian-capital-1.6319323

86. 'Abbas' Speech at the Opening of the Palestinian National Council'; *Wafa*, January 14, 2018; 'Abbas' Speech to the PLO Central Council'; 'Abbas' Speech at al-Azhar International Conference'; 'Abbas' Speech to the National Council' [all in Arabic].

87. 'The President Calls the Central Committee to Reexamine the Agreements the PLO Signed with Israel', *Wafa*, 14 January 2018, http://www.wafa.ps/ar_page.aspx?id=ZjYthda809138523468aZjYthd [in Arabic]; 'Abbas' Speech at the Opening of the National Council', *Wafa*, 30 April 2018, http://www.wafa.ps/ar_page.aspx?id=GWBxsja 819376530489aGWBxsj [in Arabic].

88. http://www.wafa.ps/ar_page.aspx?id=SQOb1Ja841345844988aSQOb1J

89. 'Abbas' Speech at al-Azhar International Conference' [in Arabic].

90. 'Erekat Document', http://www.maannews.net/Content.aspx?id=9411 86 [in Arabic].

91. Jack Khoury, Dina Kraft and Noa Landau, 'Abbas Assails U.S. Ambassador David Friedman: "Son of a Dog, Settler"', *Haaretz*, 19 March 2018, https://www.haaretz.com/middle-east-news/palestin ians/abbas-assails-u-s-ambassador-david-friedman-son-of-a-bitch-set tler-1.5917897

## 3. IN-HOUSE ORDER: WEAK AUTHORITARIAN PRESIDENTS

1. Grant Rumley and Amir Tibon, 'The Political Education of Mahmoud Abbas', *The Atlantic*, 2 July 2017, https://www.theatlantic.com/inter national/archive/2017/07/abbass-ascension-arafat/531804/

2. Palestinian Policy and Survey Research polls 2015–18, http://www. pcpsr.org/en/node/154

3. Nathan Brown, *Palestinian Politics after the Oslo Accords: Resuming Arab Palestine* (Berkeley, CA: University of California Press, 2003), p. 100.

4. Ibid, p. 111

5. Ibid, pp. 100–17.

6. Menachem Klein, 'By Conviction, Not by Infliction: The Debate over Reforming the Palestinian Authority', *Middle East Journal* Vol. 57, No. 2 (April 2003), pp. 194–212; Yezid Sayigh, 'Arafat and the Anatomy of a Revolt', *Survival* 43, No. 3 (2001), pp. 47–60; Hanan Ashrawi, 'Leadership and Authority: An Assessment of the Palestinian Condition', *Miftah*, 1 August 2002, www.miftah.org

7. Yezid Sayigh, 'The Palestinian Strategic Impasse', *Survival* Volume 44, No. 4 (Winter 2002–3), pp. 8, 12–14. Klein, 'By Conviction, Not by Infliction'.

8. Nabil Amro, 'Legitimacy Demands Leadership: An Open Letter to Yasser Arafat', *Counterpunch Magazine*, 3 September 2002; *Al-Hayyat al-Jadida*, 2 September 2002 (in Arabic).

9. Ashrawi, 'Leadership and Authority'.

10. Arnon Regular, 'Of Treason, Loyalty and a Forest of Guns', *Haaretz*, 29 September 2002 (in Hebrew).

11. Danny Rubinstein, 'The City Streets Were Full of Slogans Describing the Leaders' Heroism', *Haaretz*, 29 November 2002 (in Hebrew).

12. Ashrawi, 'Leadership and Authority'.

13. Human Rights Watch, *Erased In A Moment: Suicide Bombing Attacks Against Israeli Civilians* (New York: Human Rights Watch, 2002), pp. 1, 11–14, 84–5, https://www.hrw.org/reports/2002/isrl-pa/; on Fatah's debate in September–October 2002 on attacking Israeli civilians see Klein, 'By Conviction, Not by Infliction', pp. 194–212; Akiva Eldar, 'The Main Points in the Fatah and Tanzim Declaration on Rejecting Terrorist Attacks against Israelis', *Haaretz*, 12 September 2002 (in Hebrew).

14. Nathan J. Brown, 'Are Palestinians Building A State?', Carnegie Report, June 2010, http://carnegieendowment.org/files/palestinian_state1.pdf; Nathan J. Brown, 'Palestinians: The Unsustainable May No Longer Be Sustainable', *Carnegie Commentary*, 22 February 2011, http://carnegieendowment.org/2011/02/22/palestinians-unsustainable-may-no-longer-be-sustainable/2dt9; Nathan J. Brown, 'Requiem for Fayyadism', *Foreign Policy*, 17 April 2013, http://www.foreignpolicy.com/articles/2013/04/17/requiem_for_fayyadism

15. Brown, *Palestinian Politics after the Oslo Accords*.

16. Yezid Sayigh, 'The Palestinian Strategic Impasse', *Survival* Volume 44, No. 4 (Winter 2002–3), pp. 8, 12–13; Klein, 'By Conviction, Not by Infliction', pp. 194–212.

17. Amira Hass, 'UN Report: 300,000 Palestinians Live in Area C of the West Bank', *Haaretz*, 5 March 2014, https://www.haaretz.com/.premium-un-300k-palestinians-live-in-area-c-1.5329286

18. Hussein Agha, 'We Must Liberate Our Thinking from Oslo Straitjacket', *Fathom*, August 2018, http://fathomjournal.org/oslo25-we-must-liberate-our-thinking-from-the-oslo-straitjacket-an-interview-with-hussein-agha/

19. Neri Zilber and Ghaith Al-Omari, 'State With No Army, Army with No State', The Washington Institute for Near East Policy, Policy Focus 154 (2 April 2018), pp. 1–140, p. 9, https://www.washingtoninstitute.org/uploads/Documents/pubs/PolicyFocus154-ZilberOmari.pdf

20. Ibid, p. 12.

21. Ibid, p. 22.

22. 'Who Governs the West Bank? Palestinian Administration Under Israeli Occupation', International Crisis Group, Report No. 32 (28 September 2004), pp. 29, 31, https://d2071andvip0wj.cloudfront.net/32-who-governs-the-west-bank-palestinian-administration-under-israeli-occupation.pdf; see also 'Al Aqsa Martyrs Brigades', Council on Foreign Relations, 1 November 2005, https://www.cfr.org/backgrounder/al-aqsa-martyrs-brigade

23. Yezid Sayigh, 'Policing the People, Building The State: Authoritarian Transformation in the West Bank and Gaza', Carnegie Papers (February 2011), pp. 5, 12–22, http://carnegieendowment.org/files/gaza_west_bank_security.pdf

24. 'Security Agencies Consume Palestinian Authority Budget', *Middle East Monitor*, 4 May 2014, https://www.middleeastmonitor.com/20140504-security-agencies-consume-palestinian-authority-budget/; Alaa Tartir, 'The Limits of Securitized Peace: The EU's Sponsorship of Palestinian Authoritarianism', *Middle East Critique* (2018), https://www.tandfonline.com/doi/full/10.1080/19436149.2018.1516337

25. Brown, 'Are Palestinians Building A State?'

26. Brown, 'Palestinians: The Unsustainable May No Longer Be Sustainable'.

27. Arab Organisation for Human Rights in the UK, http://aohr.org.uk/index.php/en/all-releases-2/4573-palestinian-authority-security-forces-summon-and-arrest-194-in-august.html; Human Rights Watch, 'PA Arrested Students for Their Political Views', *Middle East*

*Monitor*, 8 May 2015, https://www.middleeastmonitor.com/20150508-hrw-pa-arrests-students-for-their-political-views/

28. 'Group Urges Investigation in the PA Violations Against Journalists', *Ma'an News*, 28 December 2015, https://www.maannews.com/Content.aspx?id=769547

29. Human Rights Watch, 'Two Authorities, One Way, Zero Dissent: Arbitrary Arrest and Torture under the Palestinian Authority and Hamas', October 2018, https://www.hrw.org/report/2018/10/23/two-authorities-one-way-zero-dissent/arbitrary-arrest-and-torture-under; https://www.haaretz.co.il/embeds/pdf_upload/2018/20181023-094745.pdf

30. 'Palestinian security set up checkpoints to stop teachers protest', *Ma'an News*, 23 February 2016, http://www.maannews.com/Content.aspx?id=770405

31. Grant Rumley, 'Barack Obama's West Bank Strongman Mahmoud Abbas', *Newsweek*, 1 May 2016, http://europe.newsweek.com/obamas-west-bank-strongman-mahmoud-abbas-453311?rm=eu; 'Palestinian MP Continues Parliamentary Sit-In Protest Against Arrest', *The New Arab*, 3 March 2016, https://www.alaraby.co.uk/english/news/2016/3/3/palestinian-mp-continues-parliamentary-sit-in-protest-against-arrest; Jonathan Schanzer and Grant Rumley, 'Palestine's Anti-Corruption Crusader', *The Daily Beast*, 14 March 2016, https://www.thedailybeast.com/palestines-anti-corruption-crusader

32. Amira Hass, 'Palestinians Fear Abbas Is Increasingly Becoming a Dictator', *Haaretz*, 11 November 2016, https://www.haaretz.com/israel-news/.premium-palestinians-fear-abbas-is-increasingly-becoming-a-dictator-1.5460252

33. Mohammed Daghaghmeh, 'PA Chief Abbas Issues Decree Curbing Free Speech Online', *The Times of Israel*, 11 August 2017, http://www.timesofisrael.com/pa-chief-abbas-issues-decree-curbing-free-speech-online/; 'Palestinian Authority shows its "authoritarian" face through Cyber Crimes Law', *Ma'an News*, 22 August 2017, https://www.maannews.com/Content.aspx?id=778773; 'Activist on Hunger Strike as Palestinian Authorities Extended His Detention', *Middle East Eye*, 7 September 2017, http://www.middleeasteye.net/news/Palestinian-prosecutor-extend-detention-high-profile-activist-1941657098

34. Palestinian Center for Policy and Survey Research, 'Public Opinion Poll 67', April 2018, http://www.pcpsr.org/en/node/723

35. 'Abbas' government sued over alleged CIA-backed wiretapping', *Associated Press*, 6 February 2018, https://apnews.com/1433ee22ec334 3878be9c78368dfd500

36. Furat Awadallah, 'The Other Occupation', *972 Magazine*, 13 January 2016, www.972mag.com/the-other-occupation/115892/; Jonathan Spyer, 'The Rise and Rise of Hizbut-Tahrir', *The Guardian*, 9 October 2007, https://www.theguardian.com/commentisfree/2007/oct/09/theriseandriseofhizbuttahrir; Jacob Hoigilt, 'Fatah from Below: The Clash of Generations in Palestine', *British Journal of Middle Eastern Studies* Vol. 43, No. 4 (2016), pp. 456–71; Philip Leech, 'Who Owns "The Spring" in Palestine? Rethinking Popular Consent and Resistance in the Context of the "Palestinian State" and the "Arab Spring"', *Democratization* Vol. 22, No. 6 (2015), pp. 1011–29.

37. Zilber and Al-Omari, 'State With No Army, Army with No State', p. 60.

38. Hussein Agha and Ahmad Samih Khalidi, 'The End of This Road: The Decline of the Palestinian National Movement', *The New Yorker*, 6 August 2017, http://www.newyorker.com/news/news-desk/the-end-of-this-road-the-decline-of-the-palestinian-national-movement

39. B. Shanee, 'PLO Executive Committee to End Security Coordination with Israel Sparks Debate Within the Organization', *MEMRI*, 6 June 2016, https://www.memri.org/reports/plo-executive-committees-decision-end-security-coordination-israel-sparks-debate-within; see also Brynjar Lia, *Police Force Without a State: A History of the Palestinian Security Forces in the West Bank and Gaza* (Reading: International Specialized Book, 2006).

40. Edo Konrad, 'Why the World Missed a Week of Palestinian Civil Disobedience', *972 Magazine*, 24 July 2017, https://972mag.com/why-the-world-missed-a-week-of-palestinian-civil-disobedience/128886/; Ir Amim, 'Everything You Need to Know About Tensions in Jerusalem's Holiest Site', *972 Magazine*, 20 July 2017, https://972mag.com/everything-you-need-to-know-about-tensions-at-jerusalems-holiest-site/128799/

41. Brown, 'Are Palestinians Building A State?'

42. 'Palestinian Security Set Up Checkpoints to Stop Teachers Protest', *Ma'an*, 23 February 2016, http://www.maannews.com/Content. aspx?id=770405; Joshua Mitnick, 'Why Refugees In This West Bank Camp Are Rebelling Against the Palestinian Authority', *LA Times*, 18 October 2016, http://www.latimes.com/world/middleeast/la-fg-palestinian-chaos-snap-story.html; Neri Zilber, 'Fatah's Civil War Letter from Nablus', *Foreign Affairs*, 29 September 2016, https://www. foreignaffairs.com/articles/palestinian-authority/2016–09–29/fatahs-civil-war

43. Amira Hass, 'Palestinian Judges launch a campaign against further erosion of their independence', *Haaretz*, 27 August 2017, https://www. haaretz.com/middle-east-news/palestinians/.premium-palestinian-judges-protest-further-erosion-of-their-independence-1.5446122

44. Amira Hass and Jack Khoury, 'Journalist Beaten, Cameras Destroyed: Palestinian Police Break Up Anti-Abbas Protest in Ramallah', *Haaretz*, 14 June 2018, https://www.haaretz.com/middle-east-news/palestinians/.premium-palestinian-forcefully-police-break-up-anti-abbas-protest-in-ramallah-1.6175290; Ahmed el-Komi, 'Palestinian Judges Resign in Protest Against Executive Branch Interference', *Al-Monitor*, 12 September 2018, https://www.al-monitor.com/pulse/originals/ 2018/09/palestinian-judiciary-mass-resignations-amendments-law-abbas.html; Rami Younis, 'The Night The Palestinian Authority Showed Us Whose Side It Is On', *972 Magazine*, 14 June 2018, https://972mag.com/the-night-the-palestinian-authority-showed-us-whose-side-it-is-on/136200/

45. Amira Hass, 'Abbas Will Have a Hard Time Ignoring the Social Protest in the West Bank', *Haaretz*, 18 January 2019, https://www.haaretz. com/middle-east-news/palestinians/.premium-abbas-will-have-a-hard-time-ignoring-the-social-protests-in-the-west-bank-1.6851010; 'Tuesday Strike', *Ma'an News*, 19 January 2019, http://www.maan-news.net/Content.aspx?id=972597 (in Arabic); Adam Ragson, 'Wary of PA "Corruption", Palestinians Launch Protest of New Social Security Law', *The Times of Israel*, 9 January 2019, https://www.timesofisrael. com/wary-of-pa-corruption-palestinians-launch-protest-of-new-so-

cial-security-law/; Akram al-Waara, 'There is no Trust: Palestinian Unrest Continues over Social Security Law', *Middle East Eye*, 24 January 2019, https://www.middleeasteye.net/news/no-trust-palestinians-promise-continued-unrest-over-social-security-law-1023745454

46. Brown, 'Are Palestinians Building A State?'
47. Mona Christophersen, Jacob Høigilt and Åge A. Tiltnes, 'Palestinian Youth and the Arab Spring', NOREF (Norwegian Peace Building Resource Centre) Report, February 2012, http://www.peacebuilding.no/var/ezflow_site/storage/original/application/562d62ccb49d92227b6865a8b2d11e1a.pdf; see also Menachem Klein, 'Sunset at Dawn: The Disintegration of the Palestinian National Project', in Brandon Friedman and Bruce Maddy-Weitzman, eds., *Inglorious Revolutions: State Cohesion in the Middle East after the Arab Spring* (Tel Aviv: Tel Aviv University, 2014), pp. 293–308; Mazin Qumsiyeh, *Popular Resistance in Palestine: A History of Hope and Empowerment* (London: Pluto, 2011).
48. 'The Status of Youth in Palestine', Sharek Youth Forum, 2013, Ramallah, pp. 10–11.
49. Zilber and Al-Omari, *State With No Army, Army with No State*, p. 61.
50. Brown, 'Palestinians: The Unsustainable May No Longer Be Sustainable'; Brown, 'Requiem for Fayyadism'; International Crisis Group, 'Ruling Palestine 2: The West Bank Model', *Middle East Report* No. 79 (July 2008), http://www.crisisgroup.org/en/regions/middle-east-north-africa/israel-palestine/079-ruling-palestine-II-the-west-bank-model.aspx
51. Alexander Kouttab and Mattia Toaldo, 'In Search of Legitimacy: The Palestinian National Movement 20 Years After Oslo', Policy Brief of the European Council on Foreign Relations, p. 2, http://ecfr.eu/page/-/ECFR89_PALESTINE_BRIEF_AW.pdf
52. Asmaa Al-Ghoul, 'Tamarod Comes to Palestine', *Al-Monitor*, 11 July 2013, http://www.al-monitor.com/pulse/originals/2013/07/hamas-tamarod-palestine-gaza-egypt.html#ixzz2YqCsIDSk
53. For additional information, see 'In rare scathing article prominent Fatah member calls Abbas tyrant and dictator', *Haaretz*, 12 July 2013, http://www.haaretz.com/weekend/week-s-end/in-rare-scathing-article-

prominent-fatah-member-calls-abbas-tyrant-and-dictator.pre-mium-1.535449

54. Asmaa al-Ghoul, 'Palestinian Activists Bemoan Their Lost Arab Spring', *Al-Monitor*, 18 January 2013, http://www.al-monitor.com/pulse/originals/2013/01/palestine-failed-arab-spring.html#ixzz2g5UMEc2O

55. Ibid.

56. Nasser Barghouti, 'My Arab Spring that Never Was: A Poem', *The Palestine Chronicle*, 27 September 2013, http://www.palestinechronicle.com/my-arab-spring-that-never-was-a-poem/#.UkVoBYZmidk

57. 'Palestinian Youth on the Arab Spring', Arab World for Research and Development, 2013, http://www.miftah.org/Doc/Polls/PollAWRAD110913.pdf

58. On the BDS movement see https://bdsmovement.net/

59. Zilber and Al-Omari, *State With No Army, Army with No State*, p. 63.

60. Christopherson, Hoigilt and Tiltnes, 'Palestinian Youth and the Arab Spring'; Marwan Darweish and Andrew Rigby, *Popular Protest in Palestine: The Uncertain Future of Unarmed Resistance* (London: Pluto Press, 2015).

61. 'Facts on the Ground, Zomlot: We Are in Limbo', Foundation for Middle East Peace, 30 September 2015, http://fmep.org/blog/2015/09/palestinian-politics-and-strategy-in-challenging-times

62. 'Israel Adopts Divisive Jewish Nation-State Law', *The New York Times*, 19 July 2018, https://www.nytimes.com/reuters/2018/07/19/world/middleeast/19reuters-israel-politics-law.html; 'Jewish Nation State: Israel Approves Controversial Bill', BBC News, 19 July 2018, https://www.bbc.com/news/world-middle-east-44881554

63. Yaser Wakid, 'Israelis Are Now the Majority at This Palestinian University', *Haaretz*, 22 March 2018, https://www.haaretz.com/israel-news/.premium.MAGAZINE-israeli-arabs-flock-to-west-bank-universities-1.5931063; Ahmad Milhem, 'West Bank City Becomes Shopper's Paradise for Palestinians Living in Israel', *Al-Monitor*, 12 June 2018, https://www.al-monitor.com/pulse/originals/2018/06/palestine-green-line-jenin-market-shopping-prices-economy.html

64. Menachem Klein, *The Shift: Israel–Palestine from Border Struggle to*

*Ethnic Conflict* (London/New York: Hurst and Columbia University Press, 2010); Jamil Hilal, 'Palestinian Political Disintegration, Culture and National Identity', *Al-Shabaka*, 15 March 2016, https://al-shabaka.org/commentaries/palestinian-political-disintegration-culture-and-national-identity/

65. Ghada Karmi, *Return: A Palestinian Memoir* (London: Verso, 2006), pp. 29–30

66. Ibid, p. 316.

67. Menachem Klein, 'Competing Brothers: The Web of Hamas-PLO Relations', in *Terrorism and Political Violence* Vol. 8, No. 2 (Summer 1996), pp. 111–32; Menachem Klein, 'Against the Consensus—Oppositionist Voices in Hamas', *Middle Eastern Studies* Volume 45, No. 6 (November 2009), pp. 881–92.

68. Klein, 'Against the Consensus'.

69. Elliot Abrams, *Tested by Zion: The Bush Administration and the Israeli–Palestinian Conflict* (Cambridge: Cambridge University Press, 2013), p. 145.

70. Alvaro de Soto, 'End of Mission Report', May 2007, pp. 15–16, quote from p. 21, http://image.guardian.co.uk/sys-files/Guardian/documents/2007/06/12/DeSotoReport.pdf; Abrams, *Tested by Zion*, pp. 145–6.

71. Davis Rose, 'The Gaza Bombshell', *Vanity Fair*, April 2008, http://www.vanityfair.com/news/2008/04/gaza200804; Abrams, *Tested by Zion*, pp. 208–10.

72. Abrams, *Tested by Zion*, pp. 22, 46.

73. Ibid, p. 208.

74. Rose, 'The Gaza Bombshell', http://www.vanityfair.com/news/2008/04/gaza200804; see also Ian Black, 'The Palestine Papers: Mohammed Dahlan', *The Guardian*, 25 January 2011 http://www.theguardian.com/world/2011/jan/25/palestine-papers-muhammad-dahlan; de Soto, 'End of Mission Report'.

75. Zilber and Al-Omari, *State With No Army, Army with No State*, pp. 29–30.

76. On the 2006 platform and 1988 Charter see Menachem Klein, 'Hamas in Power', *Middle East Journal* Vol. 61, No. 3 (Summer 2007), pp. 442–

59 and Menachem Klein, 'Against the Consensus: Oppositionist Voices in Hamas', *Middle Eastern Studies* Vol. 45, No. 6 (November 2009), pp. 881–92. The 2017 document, in English, is available here: 'Hamas Charter 2017', *Middle East Eye*, 1 May 2017, http://www.middleeasteye.net/news/hamas-charter-1637794876

77. The full official minutes are available from the Lebanese daily *Al-Akhbar*, http://www.al-akhbar.com/sites/default/files/pdfs/20140901/doc20140901.pdf; http://www.al-akhbar.com/sites/default/files/pdfs/20140905/doc20140905.pdf

78. http://hamas.ps/en/post/1311/hamas-palestinian-people-have-been-displaced-oppressed-for-seventh-decade (in Arabic); https://hamas.ps/ar/post/9114/%D8%A7%D9%84%D8%B3%D9%86%D9%88%D8%A7%D8%B1-%D9%85%D8%B3%D9%8A%D8%B1%D8%A7%D8%AA-%D8%A7%D9%84%D8%B9%D9%88%D8%AF%D8%A9-%D9%88%D9%83%D8%B3%D8%B1-%D8%A7%D9%84%D8%AD%D8%B5%D8%A7%D8%B1-%D9%85%D8%B3%D8%AA%D9%85%D8%B1%D8%A9-%D8%AD%D8%AA%D9%89-%D8%AA%D8%AD%D9%82%D9%8A%D9%82-%D8%A3%D9%87%D8%AF%D8%A7%D9%81%D9%87%D8%A7; http://hamas.ps/en/post/1311/hamas-palestinian-people-have-been-displaced-oppressed-for-seventh-decade; Odeh Bisharat, 'A Senior Hamas Official's Scary Tweet', *Ha'aretz*, 9 July 2018, https://www.haaretz.com/opinion/.premium-a-senior-hamas-official-s-scary-tweet-1.6248602; the text translated into Hebrew is in Bisharat's Hebrew article in *Haaretz*, 7 July 2018, https://www.haaretz.co.il/opinions/.premium-1.6248430

79. On the earlier stages of Fatah–Hamas relations see Tareq Baconi, *Hamas Contained: The Rise and Pacification of Palestinian Resistance* (Palo Alto, CA: Stanford University Press, 2018); Dag Tuastad, 'Hamas–PLO Relations Before and After the Arab Spring', Middle East Policy Council, https://www.mepc.org/hamas-plo-relations-and-after-arab-spring

80. Peter Beaumont, 'Gaza Could Soon Become Uninhabitable, UN Report Predicts', *The Guardian*, 2 September 2015, https://www.theguardian.com/world/2015/sep/02/gaza-becoming-uninhabitable-as-society-can-no-longer-support-itself-report

81. 'Leaked Document Says Muhammad Dahlan to Become Leader in Gaza Strip', *Ma'an News*, 26 June 2017, https://www.maannews.com/Content.aspx?id=777807; Elhanan Miller, 'Is Abbas' Arch-rival the Answer to Gaza's Problem?', *972 Magazine*, 29 June 2017, https://972mag.com/is-abbas-arch-rival-the-answer-to-gazas-problems/128432/; Jack Khouri, 'In Boosts to Gaza Reconciliation Efforts, Palestinian Factions Meet to Compensate Bereaved Families of Hamas–Fatah Clashes', *Haaretz*, 14 September 2017, https://www.haaretz.com/middle-east-news/palestinians/.premium-palestinian-factions-meet-to-compensate-victims-of-hamas-fatah-clashes-1.5450968

82. 'Hamas pledges to dissolve administrative committee, hold elections', *Ma'an News*, 17 September 2017 in https://www.maannews.com/Content.aspx?id=779126

83. Fadi Abu Shammalah, 'Why I March in Gaza', *The New York Times*, 27 April 2018, https://www.nytimes.com/2018/04/27/opinion/march-gaza-friday-palestinian.html

84. 'Report', UN Office for the Coordination of Humanitarian Affairs (OCHA), 8 June 2018, https://www.ochaopt.org/content/humanitarian-snapshot-casualties-context-demonstrations-and-hostilities-gaza-30-march-7-june; https://www.ochaopt.org/content/four-palestinians-killed-and-over-600-injured-gaza-during-continuing-demonstrations-along; https://www.ochaopt.org/content/humanitarian-snapshot-casualties-gaza-strip-30-mar-2018–22-mar-2019

85. Mustafa Abu Sneineh, 'Interview: The Palestinian Who Sparked March of Return with a Facebook Post', *Middle East Eye*, 8 June 2018, http://www.middleeasteye.net/news/Gaza-great-march-return-Israel-Ahmed-Abu-Artema

86. Rami Younis, 'Everywhere You Go in Gaza You See People Wounded in the Return March', *972 Magazine*, 28 March 2019, https://972mag.com/everywhere-go-gaza-see-people-wounded-return-march/140726/; see also Tareq Baconi, 'One Year of Gaza Protest, A New Era of Palestinian Struggle?', *New York Review of Books*, 29 March 2019, https://www.nybooks.com/daily/2019/03/29/one-year-of-gaza-protests-a-new-era-of-palestinian-struggle/

87. Amira Hass, 'It's Not a "Hamas March" in Gaza, Its Tens of Thousands

Willing to Die', *Haaretz*, 15 May 2018, https://www.haaretz.com/middle-east-news/palestinians/.premium-to-call-gaza-protests-hamas-march-understates-their-significance-1.6091833

88. Sinwar on *Al-Jazeera* in 'MEMRI Special Dispatch', *MEMRI*, 18 May 2018, https://www.memri.org/reports/hamas-leader-gaza-yahya-sinwar-our-people-took-their-military-uniforms-and-joined-marches

89. Ibid.

90. Francesca Borri, 'Hamas Leader Sinwar: "I Don't Want Any More Wars"', *Ynet*, 4 October 2018, https://www.ynetnews.com/articles/0,7340,L-5363595,00.html

91. 'Shin Bet Head Reportedly Met with Abbas on Hamas Coup', *The Times of Israel*, 1 September 2014, https://www.timesofisrael.com/shin-bet-head-reportedly-met-with-abbas-on-hamas-coup/; Raphael Ahren, 'Abbas Voices Support for Tripartite "Confederation" with Israel and Jordan', *The Times of Israel*, 2 September 2018, https://www.timesofisrael.com/abbas-voices-support-for-tripartite-confederation-with-israel-and-jordan/

92. 'Abbas–Mishaal meeting full protocol', *Al-Akhbar* (Lebanon), http://www.al-akhbar.com/sites/default/files/pdfs/20140901/doc20140901.pdf; http://www.al-akhbar.com/sites/default/files/pdfs/20140905/doc20140905.pdf; the cell's plans were published by Haim Levinson, *Haaretz*, 2 September 2014, http://www.haaretz.co.il/news/politics/.premium-1.2422139 (in Hebrew).

93. 'Hamas Leaders Enters Gaza', *Al-Akhbar*, 3 August 2018, https://al-akhbar.com/Palestine/255462 (in Arabic).

94. Amira Hass, 'Who's behind the attempted assassination of a top Palestinian leader?', *Haaretz*, 14 March 2018.

95. Nour Abu Aisha, 'Hamas Agrees to Egypt-Proposed Reconciliation Bid', *AA*, 19 July 2018, https://www.aa.com.tr/en/middle-east/hamas-agrees-to-egypt-proposed-reconciliation-bid/1208860; 'Egypt's Compromise Document for Palestinian Reconciliation', *Al-Hayat*, 5 August 2018, http://www.alhayat.com/article/4596526 (in Arabic); 'The Cairo Agreement', *Wafa*, 12 December 2011, http://info.wafa.ps/atemplate.aspx?id=7650 (in Arabic).

96. 'Haniyeh, The President Is Not Serious on Compromise and Wish to

Get Rid of Gaza', *Ma'an*, 11 June 2018, http://www.maannews.net/Content.aspx?id=952029

97. 'The President Calls the Central Committee to Reexamine the Agreements the PLO Signed with Israel', *Wafa*, 14 January 2018, http://www.wafa.ps/ar_page.aspx?id=ZjYthda809138523468aZjYthd (in Arabic).

98. Zilber and Al-Omari, *State With No Army, Army with No State*, pp. 55–8.

99. *Wafa*, 19 March 2018, http://english.wafa.ps/page.aspx?id=0G9Qnq a96957933369a0G9Qnq (in English); http://www.wafa.ps/ar_page. aspx?id=M2BgOja814300831740aM2BgOj (in Arabic); 'Abbas Assails US Ambassador David Freidman as a Son of a Bitch Settler', *Haaretz*, 19 March 2018, https://www.haaretz.com/middle-east-news/palestinians/abbas-assails-u-s-ambassador-david-friedman-son-of-a-bitch-settler-1.5917897

100. 'Palestinian Authority pulls employees from Egypt–Gaza crossing', *Al-Arabiya*, 7 January 2019, https://english.alarabiya.net/en/News/middle-east/2019/01/07/Palestinian-Authority-pulls-employees-from-Egypt-Gaza-crossing.html; 'Hamas reclaims Egypt–Gaza border crossing as PA withdraws', *The Times of Israel*, 7 January 2019, https://www.timesofisrael.com/hamas-reclaims-egypt-gaza-border-crossing-as-pa-withdraws/

101. For these and other expressions of Hamas and Fatah's struggle see S. Schneidmann, 'Fatah-Hamas Schism Widens Further Following Ruling By Palestinian Authority Constitutional Court—Established By Palestinian Authority President Abbas—To Disband Palestinian Legislative Council', MEMRI Report, 22 January 2019, https://www.memri.org/reports/fatah-hamas-schism-widens-further-following-ruling-palestinian-authority-constitutional

102. Lahav Harkov, 'Netanyahu: Money to Hamas Part of Strategy to Keep Palestinians Divided', *The Jerusalem Post*, 12 March 2019, https://www.jpost.com/Arab-Israeli-Conflict/Netanyahu-Money-to-Hamas-part-of-strategy-to-keep-Palestinians-divided-583082

103. Amos Harel, 'Abbas Is Key Obstacle To Gaza Rehabilitation Top Israeli Security Brass Warns', *Haaretz*, 3 July 2018, https://www.haaretz.

com/israel-news/.premium-abbas-is-key-obstacle-to-gaza-rehabilitation-israeli-defense-thinks-1.6240501

4. SUCCESSION STRUGGLE

1. Elior Levy, 'Israeli doctor helped save Palestinian leader Abbas's life', *Ynet*, 23 January 2019, https://www.ynetnews.com/articles/0,7340,L-5451457,00.html

2. Palestinian Center for Policy and Survey Research, http://www.pcpsr.org/

3. Ahmad Abu Amer, 'Hamas–Fatah Feud Heats Up As Talks of Abbas Successor Intensifies', *Al-Monitor*, 1 July 2018, https://www.al-monitor.com/pulse/originals/2018/06/palestine-plo-plc-hamas-fatah-abbas-successor.html

4. Hussein Agha and Ahmad Samih Khalidi, 'The End of This Road: The Decline of the Palestinian National Movement', *The New Yorker*, 6 August 2017, http://www.newyorker.com/news/news-desk/the-end-of-this-road-the-decline-of-the-palestinian-national-movement

5. David Hearst, 'The Secret Arab Plan to Oust Palestinian Leader Abbas', *Middle East Eye*, 28 May 2016, http://www.middleeasteye.net/news/exclusive-secret-arab-plan-oust-palestinian-leader-abbas-1419477268; see also, 'Egypt Intelligence Chief Mocks Abbas in Leaked Phone Call with Dahlan', *Middle East Eye*, 25 September 2016, http://www.middleeasteye.net/news/senior-egypt-intelligence-chief-mocks-abbas-leaked-phone-call-dahlan-1357084931

6. Amira Hass, 'Muhammad Dahlan: Abbas is catastrophic for the Palestinian People', *Haaretz*, 3 March 2014, http://www.haaretz.co.il/news/politics/1.2272199 (in Hebrew); Sara Leibovitch-Dar, 'Now It Is My Turn—Muhammad Dahlan, Abbas' Potential Successor', *Maariv*, 2 May 2015, http://www.maariv.co.il/news/world/Article-473600 (in Hebrew).

7. C. Jacob and B. Shanee, 'Tension Between Mahmoud Abbas Arab Quartet Over Initiative for Internal Reconciliation in Fatah', *MEMRI*, 27 September 2016, https://www.memri.org/reports/tension-between-mahmoud-abbas-arab-quartet-over-initiative-internal-reconciliation-fatah-0; 'Supporters of Dismissed Fatah Leader Mohammed Dahlan

Burn Pictures of Abbas in Gaza', *Ma'an News Agency*, 7 October 2016, http://www.maannews.com/Content.aspx?id=773457

8. *Ma'an News*, 8 July 2015, https://www.maannews.com/Content.aspx?id=766386

9. 'Abbas Rejected Arab League pressure to Nominate A Deputy Despite Sanction Threats', *MEMRI Report*, 20 November 2016, http://www.memri.org.il/cgi-webaxy/sal/sal.pl?lang=he&ID=875141_memri&act=show&dbid=articles&dataid=4292 (in Hebrew).

10. 'Abbas Approves Discharge of Fatah Leader', *Ma'an News*, 22 October 2016; 'Jerusalem Spokesman 2nd Fatah Official To Be Discharged After Attending Meeting', *Ma'an News*, 23 October 2016; Shlomi Eldar, 'Is Abbas Persecuting Supporters of his Rival?', *Al Monitor*, 16 November 2016, http://www.al-monitor.com/pulse/originals/2016/11/mahmoud-abbas-mohammed-dahlan-prison-wiretapping-court.html#ixzz4 QE7PG1qv; Avi Issacharoff, 'Abbas Cuts Salaries to Dozens Backing Rival Dahlan', *The Times of Israel*, 15 November 2016, http://www.timesofisrael.com/abbas-cuts-salaries-to-dozens-backing-rival-dahlan/; Grant Rumley, 'The Purge of Abbas' Adversaries Looms Over Ramallah', *The Weekly Standard*, 29 November 2016, http://www.weeklystandard.com/the-purge-of-abbass-adversaries-looms-over-ramallah/article/2005588; B. Shanee, 'The Abbas Dahlan Power Struggle Over the Palestinian Presidential Succession', *MEMRI*, 28 November 2016, https://www.memri.org/reports/abbas-dahlan-power-struggle-over-palestinian-presidential-succession

11. Menachem Klein, *The Jerusalem Problem: The Struggle for Permanent Status* (Gainesville, FL: University Press of Florida, 2003), pp. 154–8.

12. Document published in 2016 by one of Barghouti's camp seniors, which I obtained.

13. Avi Issascharoff, 'Meet the Next Palestinian President', *The Times of Israel*, 15 April 2016, http://www.timesofisrael.com/meet-the-next-palestinian-president/

14. Carolina Landsmann, 'How the Israeli Right-Wing Thinkers Envision the Annexation of the West Bank', *Haaretz*, 18 August 2018, https://www.haaretz.com/israel-news/.premium.MAGAZINE-how-israeli-right-wing-thinkers-envision-the-west-bank-s-annexation-1.6387108

15. Klein, *Lives in Common*, pp. 157–70; Moshe Maoz, *Palestinian Leadership in the West Bank: The Changing Role of the Arab Mayors under Jordan and Israel* (Abingdon: Routledge, 2015).

16. Agha and Khalidi, 'The End of This Road'.

17. Edward Said, 'The Morning After', *London Review of Books* Vol. 15, No. 20 (21 October 1993), https://www.lrb.co.uk/v15/n20/edward-said/the-morning-after

18. Bassam Abu Sharif, *Arafat and the Dream of Palestine: An Insider's Account* (London: Palgrave Macmillan, 2009).

19. Zilber and Al-Omari, *State with No Army, Army with No State*, p. viii; Harvey Sicherman, 'Arafat—the Man Who Wanted Too Much', *Orbis* Vol. 55, No. 3 (Summer 2011), pp. 472–80.

20. Said, 'The Morning After'; Rashid Khalidi, *The Iron Cage: The Story of the Palestinian Struggle for Statehood* (Boston, MA: Beacon Press, 2006).

21. Roger Owen, *The Rise and Fall of Arab Presidents for Life* (Cambridge, MA: Harvard University Press, 2012).

APPENDIX 1: MAIN POINTS OF DIFFERENCE BETWEEN OLMERT PROPOSAL SEPTEMBER 2008 AND ABBAS POSITIONS

1. Based on Omer Zanany, *Annapolis Process (2007–2008): Oasis or Mirage?*, (Tel Aviv: Tel Aviv University Tami Steinmets Center for Peace Studies and Molad, 2015).

2. '194—Progress Report of the United Nations Mediator', UN General Assembly, https://unispal.un.org/DPA/DPR/unispal.nsf/0/C758572B 78D1CD0085256BCF0077E51A

APPENDIX 2: THE SETTLEMENTS PROJECT—AN OVERVIEW

1. *Shaul Arieli*, 'Natural Growth or Immigration?!', http://www.shaularieli.com/image/users/77951/ftp/my_files/Netunim/translated.doc; 'Secretary of State John Kerry's speech', *The Times of Israel*, 29 December 2016, https://www.timesofisrael.com/full-text-of-john-kerrys-speech-on-middle-east-peace-december-28-2016/

2. Gershom Gorenberg, *The Accidental Empire: Israel and the Birth of the Settlements, 1967–1977* (New York: Holt, 2006); Idith Zertal and Akiva

Eldar, *Lords of the Land: The War for Israel's Settlements in the Occupied Territories, 1967–2007* (New York: Nation Books, 2007); 'Settler and settlement statistics', Foundation for Middle East Peace, http://www.fmep.org/settlement_info/

3. Meron Benvenisti, *Son of the Cypresses: Memories, Reflections and Regrets from a Political Life* (Berkeley, CA: University of California Press, 2007), p. 200.

4. Chaim Levinson, 'Settlements Have Cost Israel $17 Billion, Study Says', *Haaretz*, 23 March 2010, http://www.haaretz.com/hasen/pages/ShArtStEng.jhtml

# BIBLIOGRAPHY

Abbas, Mahmoud (Abu Mazen), *Through Secret Channels—The Road to Oslo: Senior PLO Leader Abu Mazen's Revealing Story of the Negotiations with Israel* (Reading: Grant, 1995).

Abrams, Elliot, *Tested by Zion: The Bush Administration and the Israeli–Palestinian Conflict* (Cambridge: Cambridge University Press, 2013).

Abu Eid, Muna, *Mahmoud Darwish: Literature and the Politics of Palestinian Identity* (London: IB Tauris, 2016).

Abu Sharif, Bassam, *Arafat and the Dream of Palestine: An Insider's Account* (London: Palgrave, 2009).

Allen, Lori, *The Rise and Fall of Human Rights: Cynicism and Politics in Occupied Palestine* (Palo Alto: Stanford University Press, 2013).

Ashrawi, Hanan, *This Side of Peace: A Personal Account* (New York: Simon and Schuster, 1995).

Benvenisti, Meron, *Son of Cypresses: Memories, Reflection and Regrets from a Political Life*, trans. Maxine Kaufman-Lacusta (Berkeley, CA: University of California Press, 2000).

Berda, Yael, *Living Emergency: Israel's Permit Regime in the Occupied West Bank* (Palo Alto, CA: Stanford University Press, 2017).

Bergman, Ronen, *Rise and Kill First: The Secret History of Israel's Targeted Assassinations* (New York: Random House, 2018).

Brown, Nathan J., *Palestinian Politics After the Oslo Accords: Resuming Arab Palestine* (Berkeley, CA: University of California Press: 2003).

Lia, Brynjar, *Police Force Without a State: A History of the Palestinian*

*Security Forces in the West Bank and Gaza* (Reading: International Specialized Book, 2006).

Dajani, Omar M., 'Surviving Opportunities: Palestinian Negotiating Patterns in Peace Talks with Israel', in Tamara Cofman Wittes, ed., *How Israelis and Palestinian Negotiate: A Cross-Cultural Analysis of the Oslo Peace Process* (Washington, DC: United States Institute of Peace Press, 2005), pp. 39–80.

Darweish, Marwan and Andrew Rigby, *Popular Protest in Palestine: The Uncertain Future of Unarmed Resistance* (London: Pluto Press, 2015).

Drucker, Raviv and Ofer Shelah, *Bumerang* (Tel Aviv: Keter, 2005), pp. 229–41 (in Hebrew).

Gorenberg, Gershom, *The Accidental Empire: Israel and the Birth of the Settlements 1967–1977* (New York: Holt, 2006).

Hoigilt Jacob, 'Fatah from Below: The Clash of Generatrions in Palestine', *British Journal of Middle Eastern Studies*, Vol. 43, No. 4 (2016), pp. 456–71.

Human Rights Watch, *Erased In A Moment: Suicide Bombing Attacks Against Israeli Civilians* (New York; Human Rights Watch, 2002), https://www.hrw.org/reports/2002/isrl-pa/

International Crisis Group, 'Ruling Palestine 2: The West Bank Model', Middle East Report No. 79 (July 2008), http://www.crisisgroup.org/en/regions/middle-east-north-africa/israel-palestine/079-ruling-palestine-II-the-west-bank-model.aspx

———, 'Who Governs the West Bank? Palestinian Administration under Israeli Occupation', 28 September 2004, https://d2071andvip0wj.cloudfront.net/32-who-governs-the-west-bank-palestinian-administration-under-israeli-occupation.pdf

'Interview with Yossi Beilin', *Palestine–Israel Journal*, Vol. 23, No. 2–3 (2018), pp. 137–8.

Israel Ministry of Foreign Affairs, 'The Involvement of Arafat's PA Senior Officials and Apparatus in Terrorism Against Israel Corruption and Crime', 6 May 2002, http://mfa.gov.il/MFA/ForeignPolicy/Terrorism/Palestinian/Pages/The%20Involvement%20of%20Arafat-%20PA%20Senior%20Officials%20and.aspx

Karmi, Ghada, *Return: A Palestinian Memoir* (London: Verso, 2006).

# BIBLIOGRAPHY

Khalaf, Issa, *Politics in Palestine: Arab Factionalism and Social Disintegration 1939–1948* (New York: SUNY Press, 1991), pp. 25–60.

Khalaf, Salah, 'Lowering the Sword', *Foreign Affairs*, Spring 1990, pp. 91–112.

Khalaf, Salah (Abu Iyad) with Eric Rouleau, *My Home, My Land: A Narrative of the Palestinian Struggle* (New York: Times Books, 1981).

Khalidi, Rashid, *The Iron Cage: The Story of the Palestinian Struggle for Statehood* (Boston, MA: Beacon Press 2006).

Kimmerling, Baruch and Joel S. Migdal, *Palestinians: A History* (Cambridge, MA: Harvard University Press 2003), pp. 1–168.

Kleiman, Aharon, 'Israeli Negotiating Culture', in Tamara Cofman Wittes, ed., *How Israelis and Palestinians Negotiate: A Cross-Cultural Analysis of the Oslo Peace Process* (Washington, DC: United States Institute of Peace Press, 2005).

Klein, Menachem, *A Possible Peace between Israel and Palestine: An Insider's Account of the Geneva Initiative* (New York: Columbia University Press, 2007).

———, *The Jerusalem Problem: The Struggle for Permanent Status* (Gainesville, FL: The University Press of Florida, 2003).

———, *The Shift: Israel–Palestine from Border Struggle to Ethnic Conflict* (London/New York: Hurst and Columbia University Press, 2010).

———, 'Against the Consensus: Oppositionist Voices in Hamas', *Middle Eastern Studies*, Vol. 45, No. 6 (November 2009) pp. 881–92.

———, 'By Conviction, Not by Infliction: The Debate over Reforming the Palestinian Authority', *Middle East Journal*, Vol. 57, No. 2 (April 2003), pp. 194–212.

———, 'Competing Brothers: The Web of Hamas-PLO Relations', *Terrorism and Political Violence* Vol. 8, No. 2 (Summer 1996), pp. 111–32.

———, 'Hamas in Power', *Middle East Journal*, Vol. 61, No. 3 (Summer 2007), pp. 442–59.

———, 'Rule and Role in Jerusalem: Israel, Jordan and the PLO in a Peace Building Process', in Marshal J. Breger and Ora Ahimeir, eds, *Jerusalem: Essays Towards Peacemaking* (Syracuse, NY: Syracuse University Press, 2002), pp. 137–74.

# BIBLIOGRAPHY

———, 'Sunset at Dawn: The Disintegration of the Palestinian National Project', in Brandon Freidman and Bruce Maddy-Weitzman, eds, *Inglorious Revolutions: State Cohesion in the Middle East after the Arab Spring* (Tel Aviv: Tel Aviv University Press, 2014), pp. 293–308.

Kouttab, Alexander and Mattia Toaldo, 'In Search of Legitimacy: The Palestinian National Movement 20 Years After Oslo', Policy Brief of the European Council on Foreign Relations, p. 2, http://ecfr.eu/page/-/ECFR89_PALESTINE_BRIEF_AW.pdf

Latin Patriarchate of Jerusalem, 'Full Text of the Jordanian–Palestinian Agreement on Holy Places in Jerusalem', http://en.lpj.org/2013/04/04/full-text-of-the-jordanian-palestinian-agreement-on-holy-places-in-jerusalem/

Leech, Philip, 'Who Owns "The Spring" in Palestine? Rethinking Popular Consent and Resistance in the Context of the "Palestinian State" and the "Arab Spring"', *Democratization*, Vol. 22, No. 6 (2015), pp. 1011–29.

Maoz, Moshe, *Palestinian Leadership in the West Bank: The Changing Role of the Arab Mayors under Jordan and Israel* (Abingdon: Routledge, 2015).

Miller, Aaron David, *The Much Too Promised Land: America's Elusive Search for Arab–Israeli Peace* (New York: Bantam, 2008).

Owen, Roger, *The Rise and Fall of Arab Presidents for Life* (Cambridge, MA: Harvard University Press, 2012).

Parsons, Nigel, *The Politics of the Palestinian Authority: From Oslo to al-Aqsa* (New York: Routledge, 2005).

Pundak, Ron, *Secret Channel Oslo* (Tel Aviv: Yediot Ahronoth, 2013) (in Hebrew).

———, 'Oslo Twenty Years Later, A Personal and Historical Perspective', in Reuven Pedahzur and Efraim Lavi, eds, *Twenty Years of Oslo Agreements* (Tel Aviv: Tel Aviv University, Steinitz Center and Daniel S. Abraham Center for Strategic Dialogue in Netanya College, 2014).

Qumsiyeh, Mazin, *Popular Resistance in Palestine: A History of Hope and Empowerment* (London: Pluto, 2011).

Rubinstein, Danny, *The Mystery of Arafat* (Lebanon, NH: Steerforth, 1995).

Rumley, Grant and Amir Tibon, *The Last Palestinian: The Rise and Reign of Mahmoud Abbas* (New York: Prometheus Books, 2017).

# BIBLIOGRAPHY

Sayegh, Anis, *About Anis Sayegh* (Beirut: Riad El-Rayyes, 2006), pp. 289–336 (in Arabic).

Sayigh, Yezid, *Armed Struggle and the Search for State: The Palestinian National Movement 1949–1993* (Oxford: Oxford University Press, 1997), pp. 174–80.

Schneidmann, S., 'Fatah-Hamas Schism Widens Further Following Ruling By Palestinian Authority Constitutional Court—Established By Palestinian Authority President Abbas—To Disband Palestinian Legislative Council', *MEMRI Report*, 22 January 2019, https://www.memri.org/reports/fatah-hamas-schism-widens-further-following-ruling-palestinian-authority-constitutional

Sharek Youth Forum, 'The Status of Youth in Palestine', 2013, pp. 10–11.

Sicherman, Harvey, 'Arafat: The Man Who Wanted Too Much', *Orbis*, Vol. 55, No. 3 (Summer 2011), pp. 472–480.

Steinberg, Matti, *In Search of Modern Palestinian Nationhood* (New York: Syracuse University Press, 2017).

United Nations, 'Palestinian President Presents Plan to Relaunch Peace Talks with Israel Says New Multilateral Mechanism Should Guide Process in Briefing to Security Council', 20 February 2018, https://www.un.org/press/en/2018/sc13213.doc.htm

UN General Assembly, '194—Progress Report of the United Nations Mediator', https://unispal.un.org/DPA/DPR/unispal.nsf/0/C758572B78D1CD0085256BCF0077E51A

UN Office for the Coordination of Humanitarian Affairs (OCHA), 'Report', 8 June 2018, https://www.ochaopt.org/content/humanitarian-snapshot-casualties-context-demonstrations-and-hostilities-gaza-30-march-7-juneandhttps://www.ochaopt.org/content/four-palestinians-killed-and-over-600-injured-gaza-during-continuing-demonstrations-along

Wildeman, Jeremy, 'EU Development Aid in the Palestinian Occupied Territory between Aid Effectiveness and World Bank Guidance', *Global Affairs*, Vol. 4, No. 1 (2018), pp. 115–28.

Zanany, Omer, *The Annapolis Process (2007–8): Oasis or Mirage* (Tel Aviv: Tel Aviv University Tami Steinmets Center for Peace Studies and Molad, 2015) (in Hebrew).

# BIBLIOGRAPHY

Zertal, Idith and Akiva Eldar, *Lords of the Land: The War for Israel's Settlements in the Occupied Territories, 1967–2007* (New York: Nation Books, 2007).

Zilber, Neri and Ghaith Al-Omari, *State With No Army, Army with No State* (Washington, DC: The Washington Institute for Near East Policy, 2018).

# INDEX

# INDEX

# INDEX

# INDEX

# INDEX

# INDEX

# INDEX